THE MIDDLE EAST CRISIS

THE MIDDLE EAST CRISIS:

TEST OF
INTERNATIONAL LAW

JOHN W. HALDERMAN

Editor

OCEANA PUBLICATIONS, INC.

Dobbs Ferry, New York

1969

Originally published in Winter 1968

by

LAW AND CONTEMPORARY PROBLEMS

DUKE UNIVERSITY SCHOOL OF LAW

PRINTED IN THE UNITED STATES OF AMERICA

Titles Published in
The Library of Law and Contemporary Problems

POPULATION CONTROL, The Imminent World Crisis
MELVIN G. SHIMM, *Editor*

EUROPEAN REGIONAL COMMUNITIES,
A New Era on the Old Continent
MELVIN G. SHIMM, *Editor*

AFRICAN LAW, New Law for New Nations
HANS W. BAADE, *Editor*

ACADEMIC FREEDOM, The Scholar's Place
in Modern Society
HANS W. BAADE, *Editor*

THE SOVIET IMPACT ON INTERNATIONAL LAW
HANS W. BAADE, *Editor*

URBAN PROBLEMS AND PROSPECTS
ROBINSON O. EVERETT and RICHARD H. LEACH, *Editors*

ANTIPOVERTY PROGRAMS
ROBINSON O. EVERETT, *Editor*

INTERNATIONAL CONTROL OF PROPAGANDA
CLARK C. HAVIGHURST, *Editor*

HOUSING
ROBINSON O. EVERETT and JOHN D. JOHNSTON, JR., *Editors*

MEDICAL PROGRESS AND THE LAW
CLARK C. HAVIGHURST, *Editor*

THE MIDDLE EAST CRISIS: TEST OF INTERNATIONAL LAW
JOHN W. HALDERMAN, *Editor*

CONTENTS

FOREWORD

This symposium consists of papers prepared in connection with a regional meeting of the American Society of International Law which was held at the Duke University School of Law on March 8 and 9, 1968. The meeting was arranged by the Duke International Law Society, to whose student officers and members the symposium's special editor wishes to express his appreciation, both for their work on the conference itself and for making the papers available for publication here.

The title of the conference and symposium, "The Middle East Crisis: Test of International Law," is perhaps provocative in embracing two subjects—law and the Israeli-Arab conflict—which are no doubt regarded by many informed people as having little in common. Discussions of legal aspects of the case therefore inevitably involve divergencies of approach on the part of different authorities, as is reflected in the papers which follow. Any attempt briefly to assess the import of these papers, as in this editorial Foreword, would seem to necessitate an explanation of the view of law against which the assessments are to be made. In the editor's view the general conception of international law may be divided, for present purposes, into two categories.

First, international law may be, and has traditionally been, viewed as consisting of an existing network of legal relationships among states. As stated in the Statute of the International Court of Justice, these relationships are based on treaty, customary international law, the general principles of law recognized by civilized nations, and the writings of qualified authorities. The Statute and the United Nations Charter, of which the Statute forms a part, recognize the legal nature of these relationships and the legally binding nature of judicial decisions in determining questions of the interpretation and application of the Statute and the Charter in particular situations. Thus, peoples and governments, in subscribing to the Charter— the most important treaty in existence—have given their endorsement to this conception of international law. In addition to the decisions and opinions of the International Court of Justice and of other competent international tribunals, the writing of legal authorities also contributes to the jurisprudence of this legal system.

Editor's note: In the footnotes in the symposium, the symbols "U.N. GAOR" and "U.N. SCOR" refer respectively to the official permanent, printed records of the General Assembly and Security Council, including debates of those organs. The symbols "A/PV" and "S/PV" refer to records of General Assembly and Security Council debates which appear in mimeographed, and usually provisional, form prior to the appearance of the printed "Official Records."

The other conception of international law herein postulated has its roots in the observable fact, perhaps best exemplified by the Middle East situation itself, that the area of international relations concerned with the handling of important disputes and situations has little in the way of a legal system capable of bringing about solutions conforming to the goal of peace and security. This approach to law has as its center the problem of how to develop a system, in the nature of a working constitutional system, capable of achieving this goal. The real test of law in this conception is that relevant pronouncements of competent authorities (such as the International Court and the Security Council and General Assembly of the United Nations) should receive at least that degree of compliance that preserves peace and security. The basic prerequisite of such a system must evidently be a minimal consensus among peoples and governments as to the meaning of justice in matters of international concern and as to means of achieving it. The goal must be pursued through channels by no means restricted to law as such—for example, through efforts to diminish social and economic inequality among peoples—but it must also, it is believed, be pursued by legal means in the broad constitutional sense.

Many if not all of the papers in this symposium contain aspects bearing on both of the two concepts mentioned above. Among those which appear predominantly concerned with the first-mentioned concept is that of Professor Quincy Wright, which defines thirteen legal issues arising out of the Middle East situation and undertakes to suggest how relevant rules have been complied with or violated by parties to the conflict. Likewise, Professors Leo Gross and Majid Khadduri follow the general approach in analyzing the relations of states in regard to use of the Gulf of Aqaba and the Suez Canal, respectively.

The papers prepared by official representatives of three of the four states mainly concerned in the controversy also follow the traditional approach. Ambassador El-Farra of Jordan argues that the Charter of the United Nations has been violated in the international handling of the Palestine case. Ambassador Tomeh of Syria discusses various aspects of the refugee question, while Mr. Elaraby, First Secretary of the Permanent Mission of the United Arab Republic to the United Nations, concentrates attention upon the early Partition Plan and armistice agreements.

Ambassador Rosenne of Israel defends the legality of Israel's actions and positions not only as to the rights and obligations of the parties under existing, or allegedly existing, rules but also, of course, in reference to the change of relationships involved in the very establishment of the State of Israel.

The question of change falls within the second broad conception of law under discussion. However, this area of legal inquiry is concerned not only with questions arising from demands for change in existing situations but also with most of the important questions arising from alleged breaches of existing, or allegedly existing, legal relationships. While this latter category of disputes is precisely that which would be appropriate for judicial determination, the practical impossibility of obtaining the necessary submission of the parties to this procedure is one of the better known facts of international life. Disputes of this kind, which one or more parties refuse to submit for adjudication, join the other main category—disputes arising from demands for change—to form the area of disputes and situations which must be handled politically. There are frequent indications that this "political" area is outside all law. One way of describing the conception of law under discussion is as embracing the task of transforming this political area into one governed by the rule of law in the broad, or constitutional, sense.

A matter of great importance, in this latter respect, would appear to be the building up, in the minds of governments and peoples, of a set of substantive principles which may be drawn upon as the basis for solutions of disputes. Several of the papers in this symposium are concerned with the discussion of substantive principles which might contribute to the solution of the Middle East situation and which can readily be argued to constitute constructive contributions to a broader development such as just mentioned. Professor Don Peretz defines the suggestion of a binational Palestine in light of recent developments; his approach is realistic, fully recognizing that this idea seems to have more compelling logic to the outside world than it does to the parties to conflicts involving clashes of rival nationalisms. Professor Shepard Jones surveys religious, historical and other relevant factors in the problem of Jerusalem, and concludes by endorsing some degree of internationalization as having advantages not only for the city itself but for the broader problem of which it is a focal point. Dr. Luke Lee brings arguments to bear in favor of the internationalization of major international canals; centered on the problem as it arises in connection with Suez, this paper also considers the advantages of such a course applied to other strategic canals.

The building and functioning of international institutions is perhaps as important as the development of substantive principles to the goal embraced by the second concept of law under discussion. However, being different in kind, the two aspects of the problem are difficult to compare. One such procedural or functional aspect, namely that of fact-finding by bodies such as truce observation corps, is discussed by Professor Thomas Franck and his colleague. Based on recent studies of human physiological and psychological factors, his paper questions the ability of such bodies to make truly objective findings and suggests a consequent modification in the nature of the function itself.

Finally, the paper prepared by this editor is based on a view which finds it difficult to foresee that the Middle East crisis can be settled in a secure manner except as part of a broader development of law capable of establishing peace and security on a worldwide basis. Even if, by some seeming miracle, peace and security should descend on the Middle East in the absence of such a broader development, it is only to be expected that other intractable disputes will continue and that new ones will arise from time to time in a gradually descending spiral of insecurity leading to ultimate world war. Such would seem, on the basis of history, to be the nature of the world without a minimally adequate rule of law or constitutional system. The question of the relationship of law to a given major dispute becomes, in this view, not how law can be used to resolve the dispute but rather how the dispute can be handled to advance the rule of law. The paper considers that such handling has an inescapable effect on world opinion, which may, however, be either progressive or retrogressive. It employs the Palestine case as a model for discussing the proposition that effective law might be advanced through endeavors, governmental and private, to evolve a sound theory of the Charter and to seize such opportunities as might arise in the handling of concrete cases to transform that theory into reality in the minds of governments and peoples.

John W. Halderman.

LEGAL ASPECTS OF THE MIDDLE EAST SITUATION

QUINCY WRIGHT*

I

BACKGROUND

The Middle Eastern problem which led to the six-day war in June, 1968, began in 1915 when Turkey entered World War I as an ally of Germany, and the Allies in order to gain Arab support decided to end Turkish rule in the Arab countries. By the MacMahon agreement of 1915 with Sharif Husayn of Mecca,[1] the British promised to recognize the independence of the Arab states in the Middle East; but by the Sykes-Picot agreement with France[2] in the same year, they promised to recognize a French sphere in Syria and Lebanon along with a British sphere in Iraq and Palestine (including Trans-Jordan), and by the Balfour Declaration of November 2, 1917,[3] they promised a "national home for the Jewish people" in Palestine.

The Treaty of Versailles included the League of Nations Covenant, which provided in the article dealing with mandates (article 22), that "Certain communities formerly belonging to the Turkish Empire" should be "provisionally recognized [as independent nations] subject to the rendering of administrative advice and assistance by a Mandatory until such time as they are able to stand alone." It further provided that "the wishes of these communities must be a principal consideration in the selection of the Mandatory." Even before peace was finally made with Turkey by the Treaty of Lausanne in 1924, the League of Nations Council confirmed the Middle Eastern mandates[4] which the Allied powers had assigned in the San Remo Conference of April, 1920, in accord with the Sykes-Picot agreement, without regard to the wishes of the inhabitants. These wishes had been indicated in the suppressed report of the King-Crane Mission sent to the area by President Wilson.[5]

The Arab countries accepted the mandatories without enthusiasm. In Palestine

* A.B. 1912, Lombard College; A.M. 1913, Ph.D. 1915, University of Illinois. Professor of International Law Emeritus, University of Chicago. Author, ENFORCEMENT OF INTERNATIONAL LAW THROUGH MUNICIPAL LAW IN THE UNITED STATES (1916); CONTROL OF AMERICAN FOREIGN RELATIONS (1922); MANDATES UNDER THE LEAGUE OF NATIONS (1930); THE CAUSES OF WAR AND THE CONDITIONS OF PEACE (1935); LEGAL PROBLEMS IN FAR EASTERN CONFLICT (1941); PROBLEMS OF STABILITY AND PROGRESS IN INTERNATIONAL RELATIONS (1954); THE STUDY OF INTERNATIONAL RELATIONS (1955); CONTEMPORARY INTERNATIONAL LAW, A BALANCE SHEET (1955); INTERNATIONAL LAW AND THE UNITED NATIONS (1956); THE STRENGTHENING OF INTERNATIONAL LAW (1959); THE ROLE OF INTERNATIONAL LAW IN THE ELIMINATION OF WAR (1961); A STUDY OF WAR (1965).

[1] CMD. No. 5957 (1939).
[2] See DOCUMENTS ON BRITISH FOREIGN POLICY 1919-1939, 1st Ser., vol. IV, at 241-51 (E. Woodward & R. Butler, eds. 1952).
[3] The text is officially quoted in CMD. No. 5479, at 22 (1937).
[4] For text of the Palestine Mandate, see, e.g., CMD. No. 1785 (1923).
[5] [1919] 12 FOREIGN REL. U.S. 745, 772-73 (1947).

the relations of some 900,000 Arabs with 100,000 Jews[6] were moderately good during most of the 1920s after the British had interpreted the provision in their Mandate, which incorporated the Balfour Declaration, as not applying to Trans-Jordan, originally a part of the Palestine mandate, and as not intending a Jewish state but a Jewish community in Palestine with free access to Jewish religious sites, and assuring full protection for the rights of the Arab population. Jewish and Arab villages adjacent to each other cooperated, Jews instructed the Arabs on industrial technology and the Arabs instructed the Jews on agriculture under local conditions.

In the 1930s as Jewish immigration increased, especially after Hitler began his persecution of Jews and as the Jews acquired more land, Arab anxieties increased. Disputes arose over immigration regulations, religious sites (the Wailing Wall, 1929), land ownership, and the position of the Zionist organization in Palestine, leading to a violent Arab revolt in 1936. A British Commission in 1937 (Peel)[7] proposed partition of Palestine between a Jewish state and an Arab area to become part of Trans-Jordan, but this was not implemented because of Arab objections.

After World War II, conflict between Arabs and Jews in Palestine became more intense. The Zionists, both within and outside Palestine, demanded a Jewish state as proposed by the Peel Commission. The British Government made several efforts at conciliation including a promise, in the Chamberlain White Paper of 1939,[8] that immigration would be restricted so as never to permit more than one-third of the Palestine population to be Jewish, and a provisional promise of independence in ten years. This was unacceptable to the Zionists and on April 2, 1947, Britain indicated its intent to resign the mandate and turn the problem over to the United Nations General Assembly.[9] That body recommended on November 29, 1947, over Arab protests, a division of Palestine into a Jewish state of Israel and an Arab state, linked by economic institutions for customs union, common currency, and common regulation of irrigation, transport, and communication.[10] A division of revenues to elevate the lower economic level of the Arabs and internationalization of Jerusalem and surrounding territories including most of the holy sites were also proposed.

This recommendation accorded with the majority report of the United Nations Special Committee on Palestine (UNSCOP)[11] earlier established by the General Assembly to study the problem. A minority report had recommended a federation but the majority thought this would require more cooperation between Jews and

---

[6] This is the average for the decade. Both Arab and Jewish populations increased, the latter at a more rapid rate by immigration of some 10,000 a year. The Jews constituted about 10% of a total population of 800,000 in 1920, 19% of a total population of 1,000,000 in 1930, and 30% of a total population of 1,530,000 in 1940. 17 ENCYCLOPEDIA BRITANNICA 134 (1965). STATEMENT OF BRITISH FOREIGN POLICY (CHURCHILL MEMORANDUM) ON PALESTINE, CMD. No. 1700 (1922). See Wright, *The Palestine Problem*, 41 POL. SCI. Q. 384 (1926), for conditions in 1925.

[7] CMD. No. 5479 (1937).

[8] CMD. No. 6019 (1939).

[9] U.N. GAOR 1st Spec. Sess. 183, U.N. Doc. 286 (1947).

[10] G.A. Res. 181, 2 *id.*, Resolutions 131, 132 (1947).

[11] *Id.*, Supp. 11, U.N. Doc. 364 and Adds. 1-4.

Arabs in Palestine than was available, because of radical disagreement on the issue of immigration. The Zionists accepted the Partition Plan but the Arabs prepared for armed resistance. Hostilities occurred within Palestine in the winter of 1947. Israel declared its independence on May 14, 1948,[12] and was promptly recognized by the United States, the Soviet Union, and other states. Neighboring Arab states opened hostilities against it, were defeated, and half a million Arabs fled from Israel. Count Folke Bernadotte, president of the Swedish Red Cross, was sent by the United Nations as mediator. He concluded temporary truces but was assassinated in the summer of 1948 by Jewish terrorists. Further hostilities took place in the fall of 1948 and Israel's representative in the United Nations, while insisting in the General Assembly that the territory awarded it by the United Nations resolution of November 29, 1947, was the minimum to which Israel was entitled, declared that, in view of the Arab refusal to accept the award and invasion across the boundary, Israel was free to continue its occupations resulting from the war until such time as a permanent boundary was negotiated, and in any case it would not withdraw from the parts of Jerusalem it had occupied nor accept the internationalization of that city proposed in the United Nations resolution of 1947 and reaffirmed in several resolutions.[13] Ralph Bunche of the United Nations Secretariat, who had succeeded Count Bernadotte as mediator, concluded armistice agreements in 1949 between Israel and each of its Arab neighbors, the last on July 20, 1949,[14] all at approximately the line of the Israeli occupation. These lines embraced fifty per cent more territory than had been accorded to Israel by the United Nations resolution of 1947.[15] The United Nations Truce Supervision Organization (UNTSO), already in existence, was continued to supervise the observance of the armistice agreements.[16]

Frequent violations of these agreements came before the Security Council during the next years, culminating in a large-scale invasion of the Sinai Peninsula by Israel in 1956, followed by Anglo-French operations against Egypt because of its nationalization of the Suez Canal. An American-proposed resolution, implying that Israel was the aggressor, was vetoed in the Security Council by Great Britain and France.[17] The problem was then turned over to the General Assembly under the Uniting for Peace Resolution of 1950 and, with vigorous support from the United States and the Soviet Union, the General Assembly succeeded in bringing about a cease-fire, withdrawal of Israeli, British and French forces to their positions before hostilities, and the establishment of a United Nations Emergency Force (UNEF) in Egyptian

---

[12] FUNDAMENTAL LAWS OF THE STATE OF ISRAEL 8 (J. Badi ed. 1961); N.Y. Times, May 15, 1948, at 2, col. 3.

[13] 3 U.N. GAOR, Pt. 1, 1st Comm. 640-43, 644-45, 832, 840-42 (1948). As to subsequent resolutions on Jerusalem see notes 55 and 56 *infra* and accompanying text.

[14] Armistice agreements are cited in Elaraby, in this symposium, p. 104, nn.19-22.

[15] Maps of the boundaries proposed by the United Nations Plan of Partition with Economic Union and the Armistice agreements are included in N. LORCH, THE EDGE OF THE SWORD: ISRAEL'S WAR OF INDEPENDENCE 1947-1948, at 27 (1961).

[16] S.C. Res. 73 (1949).

[17] 11 U.N. SCOR, 749th meeting 31 (1956).

territory south of the cease-fire line.[18] Egypt agreed to the opening of the Straits of Tiran to Israeli shipping to its port of Elath on the Gulf of Aqaba.[19] After 1957, breaches of the cease-fire line on the Egyptian, Jordanian, and Syrian frontiers continued to come before the Security Council which usually passed a resolution criticizing the excessive Israeli retaliation against minor Arab raids.

Against this background a new crisis arose in 1967, with increased border raids in April, President Nasser's demand on May 16 for withdrawal of the United Nations Emergency Force from Egyptian territory, and his declaration on May 23 closing the Straits of Tiran to Israeli shipping.[20] According to David G. Nes, deputy chief of the American Embassay in Cairo, Nasser took these actions because he had intelligence reports from Syria and the Soviet Union warning of intensive Israeli build-ups on the Syrian frontier. The American Embassy on the basis of its own intelligence reports advised the Egyptian foreign ministry that there was no truth in these reports as, indeed, Nasser later recognized, but Egypt, at the time, believed that the United States was covering up for Israel and proceeded with defensive measures. It strengthened its alliances with Jordan and Syria and moved forces into the Aqaba area, the Israeli frontiers in Sinai, and the Gaza strip, although it declared that it would not attack unless Israel launched an armed attack against its Arab neighbors. According to Mr. Nes, if the United States had paid more attention to Egypt's requests for economic aid during the preceding eleven months and had attempted to demonstrate to Nasser "that we were not hostile" to him, we might have been able to dissuade him from the action which led to war. "Nobody in Washington," he said, "was willing to take the political risk involved in doing anything for Egypt."[21]

President Johnson characterized Nes's view as "parochial"[22] but on June 19 he expressed a broad view of the situation suggesting that a blocking of the Gulf of Aqaba was illegal and that it was traditional American policy to support the independence and territorial integrity of all Middle Eastern states, that peace in the Middle East required opening the Suez Canal to Israeli shipping, a solution of the refugee problem, and an end of Arab belligerency against Israel.[23]

II

THE POSITIONS OF THE BELLIGERENTS

According to Israel, as indicated in the United Nations debate, the 1967 crisis began in April with increased Arab violations of Israeli territory, Syrian pressure

---

[18] Developments of 1956-1957 summarized in EVERYMAN'S UNITED NATIONS: A BASIC HISTORY OF THE ORGANIZATION 1945 TO 1963, at 81-89 (United Nations, New York, N.Y., 7th ed. n.d.)

[19] Further on the international waterways, see Sec. IV, H and I, *infra.*

[20] See, *e.g.*, reports by Secretary-General to the Security Council, U.N. Docs. S/7896, May 19, 1967, and S/7906, May 26, 1967.

[21] N.Y. Times, Feb. 9, 1968, at 3, col. 4. See also notes 110, 115, 116 *infra.*

[22] *Id.*

[23] 57 DEP'T STATE BULL. 31, 33-34 (1967).

with Egyptian support, and Nasser's defensive alliance with Jordan, manifesting a policy of encirclement of Israel by Egypt, Jordan, and Syria. Mobilizations and movements of forces to the area from Algeria, Iraq, and Kuwait; Nasser's continuous affirmation that a state of war existed with Israel and had existed since 1948; his continued declaration of a policy to restore Palestine to the Arabs and to terminate the existence of Israel—all added to the latter's anxiety. Nasser's demand on May 16 that the United Nations Emergency Force which had kept moderate peace on the Egyptian frontier since 1957 be withdrawn, Secretary-General U Thant's compliance with this demand on May 18, Nasser's declaration closing the Straits of Tiran and the Gulf of Aqaba to Israeli shipping on May 22, and Nasser's movement of forces into the Aqaba and Sinai areas constituted, in Israel's opinion, clear evidence of aggression. Israel, however, asserted that it withheld its attack on Egyptian forces in Sinai on June 5 until its territory had been attacked on the ground and in the air.[24]

According to Egypt and other Arab countries, in the United Nations debate, the basic problem was the planting of Zionism in Palestine by colonialism to serve colonial interests, and Israel's constant aggressive policy of territorial expansion, together with the expulsion of the indigenous population. Recent provocations had induced the Arab states to cooperate to defend the Arab nation by all measures. The Egyptian request for the removal of UNEF and its closure of the Gulf of Aqaba were said to be within the domestic jurisdiction of Egypt and designed to restore the situation to what it had been before 1956. In any case, they were considered permissible acts in view of the state of war which existed between Israel and the three legitimate littoral states on the Gulf, a situation not affected by the armistice. In fact, the very use of the term "armistice" was said to imply a state of war. Egypt asserted that peace required "a total respect for the Palestine Arab people." It declared, however, that it did not contemplate any offensive action and insisted that it had not taken any such action until attacked by Israel assisted by the United States and Great Britain on June 5, 1967.[25]

III

UNITED NATIONS ACTION

The United Nations Security Council met on request of Canada and Denmark continuously from May 24 to June 14, 1967, and put the Middle Eastern situation on its agenda over the opposition of the Soviet Union, Bulgarian and Mali delegates. It invited the United Arab Republic (Egypt) and Israel to attend, and later Jordan,

---

[24] U.N. Docs. S/PV.1342, May 24, 1967, at 41-45; S/PV.1343, May 29, 1967, at 62-72; S/PV.1348, June 6, 1967, at 71-91. Israel later in effect admitted that its air forces had invaded Egyptian territory before the Egyptian attack. See note 112 *infra*.

[25] U.N. Docs. S/PV.1343, May 29, 1967, at 21-47 (UAR); S/PV.1344, May 20, 1968, at 17-46 (Syria); S/PV.1345, May 31, 1968, at 27-50 (Jordan). In an interview in March 1968, Nasser said that his charge that Israel was assisted by the United States was due to a misunderstanding based on suspicion and faulty information. Attwood, *Nasser Talks*, LOOK, March 19, 1968, at 63; N.Y. Times, March 5, 1968, at 1, col. 3.

Syria, Lebanon, Iraq, Saudi Arabia, Libya, Morocco, Pakistan, and Tunisia.[26] It also discussed the problem on July 8 and 9 and October 25, on request of Israel and the United Arab Republic, to consider violations of the cease-fire, and on November 9-22, on request of the U.A.R., to examine principles and procedures for settlement of the conflict.

The General Assembly met in emergency session on June 17, after Israel had declared the annexation of Jordanian Jerusalem, and continued discussion of the situation through July. On July 4 it passed a resolution (116-0-2) declaring Israel's attempt to change the status of Jerusalem was invalid and calling on it to renounce its action.[27] It also passed a resolution on the same day (99-20-0) calling on the parties to observe humanitarian principles and human rights.[28] On July 21 it requested the Secretary-General to report its debates to the Security Council, which should resume consideration of the situation as a matter of urgency (63-26-27).[29]

The discussions in the Security Council indicated wide differences of opinion about responsibility for the crisis and the hostilities. The Soviet Union, Bulgaria, France and Mali, as well as the Arab states, Lebanon, Syria and Jordan, supported the United Arab Republic's position urging that Israel be found guilty of aggression and that no other aspects of the problem be considered until Israel had withdrawn from the territory that it had occupied as the result of the hostilities. India, Nigeria, and Ethiopia agreed on the latter position but the United States, Great Britain, Brazil, Canada, and Denmark thought that a cease-fire should be established first without consideration of responsibility for initiation of the crisis and that withdrawal from the occupied territories should be contingent on settlement of other aspects of the conflict. They suggested that restoration of the situation which had led to three instances of serious hostility since 1948 was not a proper solution. They did not, however, support the Israeli contention that the U.A.R. was responsible, nor Israel's suggestion that bi-lateral negotiations between Israel and each of its Arab neighbors was the only way to establish peace in the area. The United States representative, Arthur Goldberg, supported a suggestion in Secretary-General U Thant's report of May 26, 1967,[30] that the first step was agreement on a "breathing spell to allow tension to subside from its present explosive level." After that, he thought efforts should be made to deal in longer-range terms with detailed points of tension which the Secretary-General had identified in his report.[31]

The Council was unable to pass any resolutions before hostilities broke out on June 5, but passed several after that date providing for and implementing a cease-

[26] For record of the proceedings see U.N. Docs. S/PV.1341-1361, May 24-June 14, 1967. Summaries in 21 INT'L ORG. 837-861 (1967); 4 U.N. MONTHLY CHRON., No. 6, at 5-26, and No. 7, at 4-32 (1967).

[27] G.A. Res. 2253, 5th Emer. Spec. Sess., Supp. 1, at 4, U.N. Doc. A/6798 (1967).

[28] G.A. Res. 2252, id. at 3.

[29] G.A. Res. 2256, id. at 4.

[30] See note 20 supra.

[31] U.N. Doc. S/PV.1343, May 29, 1967, at 7-21.

fire,[32] and calling for the protection of civilians in occupied territory.[33] These resolutions were all passed unanimously. During the debate, the Soviet representative intimated that the Socialist countries would take measures to effect the withdrawal of Israeli occupation if the United Nations failed to act.[34] It seems to have been somewhat placated by the unanimous passage on November 22 of a resolution[35] introduced by Great Britain providing for the presence of a United Nations mediator in the area to seek conciliation on the basis of principles resembling those stated by President Johnson in an address of June 19, 1967,[36] and recognizing that, eventually, territory occupied by Israel should be evacuated and claims of a state of belligerency by the Arabs terminated.

IV
LEGAL ISSUES

Among thirteen legal problems involved in the Middle Eastern situation, one, (1) the validity of the Balfour Declaration, arose in World War I. Eight arose in the Arab-Israeli war of 1948-49; they include (2) the partition of Palestine, (3) the status of Jerusalem, (4) the legality of Arab belligerency, (5) the boundaries of Israel, (6) the use of Jordan waters, (7) the rights of Palestinian refugees, (8) Israel's rights of navigation in the Suez Canal, and (9) freedom of navigation through the Straits of Tiran and in the Gulf of Aqaba. Four additional problems arose in the crisis of 1967: (10) the status of the United Nations Emergency Force, (11) the obligation of Israel to evacuate occupied territory, (12) the responsibilities of the United Nations and the Great Powers, and (13) the responsibility for initiation of the six-day war. This large and unlucky number of problems means that each can be dealt with only briefly and somewhat categorically.

A. Balfour Declaration

The Arabs claimed that the Balfour Declaration, which provided a national home for the Jewish people in Palestine, and its incorporation in the British Mandate for Palestine, confirmed by the League of Nations in 1922, constituted an imperialistic *demarche* designed to infiltrate a country which had been Arab for centuries with a European population and to assure British dominance in the area adjacent to the Suez Canal, which would be strategically important to Britain if its occupation and protectorate of Egypt should come to an end. Furthermore, the Arabs claimed that the Declaration was contrary to agreements made with the Arabs to gain their support in the war against Turkey during the First World War. Also, the wishes of the inhabitants were not consulted in awarding the Mandate for Palestine to Great

[32] S.C. Res. 233 (1967); S.C. Res. 234 (1967); S.C. Res. 235 (1967); S.C. Res. 236 (1967).
[33] S.C. Res. 237 (1967).
[34] U.N. Doc. S/PV.1353, June 9, 1967, at 27-31.
[35] S.C. Res. 242 (1967). For text, see Rosenne, in this symposium, pp. 44, 56.
[36] 57 DEP'T STATE BULL. 31, 33-34 (1967).

Britain as was required by the League of Nations Covenant. The latter points were supported by some British in the Middle East, such as Colonel T. E. Lawrence and Miss Gertrude Bell, who believed that the Arabs had been double-crossed.

The motives for the Balfour Declaration[37] appear to have been mixed. Gratitude for Jewish support in the war, especially for the chemical experiments of Chaim Weizmann, the head of the Zionist organization, and belief in the legitimacy of the cultural interests of the Jews in Palestine, as well as strategic consideration for British interests in the Middle East, especially to counteract French interests in Lebanon and Syria, were involved. The meaning of the MacMahon agreements of 1915[38] has been controversial. The British contend that in promising to support independent Arab states, Palestine was excluded.[39] The Allies, including the United States, recognized the Balfour Declaration and the British Mandate. Furthermore, the Arab leaders accepted them after Trans-Jordan had been excluded from the national home provision and after the Churchill White Paper of 1922[40] had interpreted the meaning of the "national home," not as a Jewish state of Palestine but as a cultural community in Palestine, and had emphasized the British intention to assure protection for the Arab inhabitants and for the three religions interested in Palestine, as required by both the Balfour Declaration and the Mandate. British policy observed these commitments during the 1920s and the relations between the Arab majority and the Jewish minority were on the whole friendly.[41] However justified the Arab protest against the Balfour Declaration and the British Mandate may have been in 1919, the issue had become moot before 1947 because the legality of the conditions they established had been recognized by most states, including the Arab states, for many years and had been confirmed in the United Nations Charter (article 80).[42]

Only after the large immigration of Jews into Palestine, especially as the result of Hitler's persecutions, was there serious conflict between Jews and Arabs in Palestine and serious anxieties among surrounding states. The Jewish demand for partition and creation of a Jewish state increased Arab alarm and revived objections to the Balfour Declaration.

B. Partition of Palestine

The legality of the General Assembly's recommendation for partition of Palestine was doubtful. Many Zionists had always wanted a Jewish state of Palestine in spite

---

[37] See note 3 *supra.*

[38] See note 1 *supra.*

[39] *See, e.g.,* C. SYKES, CROSSROADS TO ISRAEL 63-65 (1965).

[40] See note 6 *supra.*

[41] Wright, *supra* note 6.

[42] All systems of law provide means such as prescription, general recognition, statutes of limitation, agreements by the interested parties, and legislation, by which situations which originated in illegality become moot or acquire a legal status. The principle *jus ex injuria non oritur* (rights do not arise from wrongs) must be balanced by the principle *ex factis jus oritur* (rights arise from facts), especially in the society of nations which is often unable to rectify wrongs and is faced by a general interest that disputes be terminated. See H. LAUTERPACHT, RECOGNITION IN INTERNATIONAL LAW 427 (1947); Wright, *Recognition, Intervention, and Ideologies,* 7 INDIAN Y.B. INT'L AFF. 89, 95 (1958).

of the acceptance by Chaim Weizmann, Judah Magnes, and other Zionist leaders, of the British concept of a cultural rather than a political Jewish home in Palestine. A Jewish state was, however, increasingly demanded by the Zionists, as the need for a haven from Hitler's persecutions developed in the 1930s, and as the antagonism between Arabs and Jews in Palestine increased with the flood of immigration.

The United Nations Charter provided that mandated territories might be placed under trusteeship (article 77) by agreement of the states directly concerned including the mandatory power (article 79). But the following article added:

> [N]othing in this Chapter shall be construed in or of itself to alter in any manner the rights whatsoever of any states or any peoples or the terms of existing international instruments to which Members of the United Nations may respectively be parties.

The reference to "peoples" in the article seems to have been primarily designed to protect the rights of the Jewish people to a national home in Palestine under the Mandate, but the term also applied to the Arabs in Palestine. The Mandate provided for "safeguarding the civil and religious rights of all the inhabitants of Palestine, irrespective of race and religion" (article 2).

When Britain, despairing of any settlement of the Palestine problem, declared in February 1967 that it would give up the Mandate and withdraw from Palestine by August 1, 1948 (later changed to May 14) and placed the problem before the United Nations General Assembly, the Arabs at once claimed that no change in the Mandate was permissible without the consent of the Arab people of Palestine. The General Assembly's committee,[43] however, recommended the partition of the territory with economic union, and permanent internationalization of Jerusalem and surrounding territory containing most of the religious sites. The Arabs objected and demanded an Advisory Opinion of the International Court of Justice on the compatibility of this action with the Charter (article 80).[44] This demand was rejected by the committee by a vote of 20 to 21 with 13 abstentions.[45] France favored submission to the Court, the United States and the Soviet Union opposed it, and the United Kingdom and China abstained. The General Assembly then accepted the committee's recommendation on November 29, 1947, by a vote of 33 to 13 with 10 abstentions.[46] The United States, the Soviet Union and France voted "aye" and the United Kingdom and China abstained. It was argued that the General Assembly had full power to deal with Palestine because Great Britain, as Mandatory, had under the Mandate (article 1) "full powers of legislation and administration, save as they may be limited by the terms of the mandate" and had transferred these broad powers to the General

---

[43] See text accompanying note 11 *supra*.

[44] 2 U.N. GAOR, Ad Hoc Comm. on the Palestinian Question 299-301, U.N. Doc. A/AC.14/32 (1947).

[45] *Id*. at 203.

[46] 2 U.N. GAOR 1424-425 (1947).

Assembly, which had succeeded to the League of Nations Council in ultimate sovereignty of mandated territories.[47]   Furthermore, article 80 of the Charter, in declaring
that the Chapter on Trusteeship could not "in or of itself" alter the rights of "peoples"
under the Mandate, did not preclude modifications of these rights by permissible
action.[48]

Recognizing that there might be difficulties in implementing its resolution, the
General Assembly "requested" the Security Council to "determine, as a threat to the
peace, breach of the peace or act of aggression in accordance with article 39 of the
Charter, any attempt to alter by force the settlement envisaged by the resolution."
The Security Council, however, refused to authorize enforcement measures. The
principal proponent of this course, the United States Representative (Austin), maintained that the Charter authorized the Council to take such measures only to preserve
international peace, not to enforce a political settlement in the mandated territory.
He considered the Plan of Partition to be a recommendation of the Council.[49]

In view of the terms of the Mandate and the apparent intent of article 80 of
the Charter to protect the rights of all the peoples of Palestine, the Palestinian Arabs
seem to have had a good legal case, though it is unfortunate that an Advisory Opinion
was not obtained on the issue. If the General Assembly's resolution could not be
regarded as authoritative, but as a recommendation ignoring its responsibility under
article 80 of the Charter, and if Great Britain was unable, as it said it was, to meet
its responsibility as Mandatory to protect the rights of the Arab peoples, forcible
resistance to partition by the Arabs of Palestine should be regarded as civil strife
within the domestic jurisdiction of Palestine in which outside states should not intervene, and in which the United Nations should intervene only if the situation
threatened international peace and security.[50] Under this interpretation, however, the
Arab states outside of Palestine acted contrary to their obligations under the Charter
in intervening in Palestine as they did.[51] In view, however, of the obvious threat,
indeed breach of international peace, the Security Council should have acted before

---

[47] T. Lie, In the Cause of Peace 167 (1954); Q. Wright, Mandates Under the League of
Nations 528-30 (1930). On the question of sovereignty of mandated territories, see more generally
id. at 313-537.

[48] See also on the partition of Palestine, Everyman's United Nations, supra note 18, at 70-71; Wright,
Interventions, 1956, 51 Am. J. Int'l L. 257, 264-66 (1957).

[49] 3 U.N. SCOR 253d meeting 265-67 (1948).

[50] In accordance with articles 2(7) and 39 of the Charter. See Wright, International Law and Civil
Strife, 1959 Proceedings, Am. Soc'y Int'l L. 145, 149-51; The Legality of Intervention Under the
United Nations Charter, 1957 id. at 79, 83-85; United States Intervention in the Lebanon, 53 Am. J.
Int'l L. 112, 119-25 (1959); Legal Aspects of the Vietnam Situation, 60 id. at 750, 754-55 (1966).

[51] On May 15, 1948, the Arab states declared that they "were compelled to intervene for the sole purpose of restoring peace and security and establishing law and order in Palestine" because "peace and order
have been completely upset" there, constituting "a serious and direct threat to peace and security within
the territories of the Arab states themselves." Furthermore, "the security of Palestine is a sacred trust
for them," "the spread of disorder and lawlessness to neighboring Arab lands" must be prevented and
"the vacuum created by the termination of the mandate and the failure to replace it by any legally
constituted authority" must be filled. 3 U.N. SCOR, Supp. May 1948, at 83, 87, U.N. Doc. S/745
(1948).

the Israeli Declaration of Independence, not to enforce partition, but to maintain international peace and security. Its efforts to do so were not effective.[52]

After the defeat of the Arabs and the occupation by Israel of large areas of Palestine including parts of Jerusalem, beyond those allotted to it by the General Assembly resolution, the Arab states expressed their willingness to accept, as a basis for peace, the original partition proposal including the internationalization of Jerusalem, to all of which they had at first objected. Israel had at first accepted this proposal but now rejected it, insisting that the territory defined by the armistice belonged to it.[53] In view of the Arab acceptance of the original partition proposal, of the general recognition of Israel as a state, and of its membership in the United Nations since May 1949, an objection to partition as such is probably not legally valid in 1968.[54]

C. Jerusalem

Israel's annexation of Jerusalem appears to be illegal. The original Partition Plan of the United Nations provided for the internationalization of Jerusalem and this internationalization was confirmed by an Assembly resolution of December 11, 1948,[55] and again by a resolution of December 9, 1949,[56] which entrusted the administration of the area to the Trusteeship Council. The president of the Council reported to the General Assembly in June 1950 that Israel and Jordan had refused to cooperate in the matter, but the Assembly took no action.[57] Israel continued to occupy portions of Jerusalem outside of the wall included within the armistice line of 1949, made large investments of capital, and established educational and medical institutions in the area, thus providing a *de facto* but not a *de jure* claim. The annexation by Jordan of old Jerusalem east of the 1949 armistice line was equally contrary to the United Nations resolutions but has also established a *de facto* claim. The Arabs at first

---

[52] S.C. Res. 46 of April 17, 1948, affirmed the responsibility of the United Kingdom, so long as it was the Mandatory Power, to maintain peace and order in Palestine, but called on the Arabs and Jews to cease all acts of a military or paramilitary nature, all acts of violence or terrorism, and all importation of arms or armed bands, and to cooperate with the Mandatory Powers. S.C. Res. 48 of April 23, 1948, established a Truce Commission and the General Assembly on May 14, 1948 authorized the appointment of a mediator to promote peaceful adjustment of the Palestine situation, and to cooperate with the Truce Commission. U.N. GAOR, 2d Spec. Sess., Supp. 2, Resolutions, at 5 (1948).

[53] The Arab states and Israel accepted, at Lausanne on May 12, 1949, a proposal of the U.N. Conciliation Commission which had been established by G.A. Res. 194 of December 11, 1948 (3 U.N. GAOR, Resolutions 21, 22, U.N. Doc. A/810), and composed of representatives of France, Turkey, and the United States. The proposal provided for a territorial settlement substantially in accord with the Plan of Partition with Economic Union. Third Progress Report of the Palestine Conciliation Commission, 4 U.N. GAOR, Ad Hoc Pol. Comm., Annex, vol. II, at 5, 8-9, U.N. Doc. A/927 (1949). A few days later Israel made territorial proposals which the Arab delegations considered to be in flagrant violation of the Protocol. On September 12, 1949, the Commission expressed the opinion that proposals of both sides exceeded the terms of the Protocol. See General Progress Report . . . of the U.N. Conciliation Commission for Palestine . . . , 5 U.N. GAOR, Supp. 18, at 3-4, 19-21, U.N. Doc. A/1367/Rev. 1 (1950).

[54] See note 42 *supra*.

[55] G.A. Res. 194, 3 U.N. GAOR, Resolutions 21, 23, U.N. Doc. A/810 (1948).

[56] G.A. Res. 303, 4 *id.*, Resolutions 25, U.N. Doc. A/1251 (1949).

[57] Special Report of Trusteeship Council, 5 *id.*, Supp. 9, at 1, U.N. Doc. A/1286 (1950); *id.*, Plenary 684 (1950).

rejected but later accepted partition as provided in the original United Nations resolution[58] and continued to insist on the internationalization of Jerusalem. The United States, the United Kingdom, and the Soviet Union voted against subsequent resolutions in the General Assembly affirming the internationalization of Jerusalem, but these resolutions were approved by a two-thirds majority, partly because the Latin American states voted on this issue with other Catholic states, as desired by the Vatican, rather than with the United States.[59] No state seems to have recognized Israel's annexation of old Jerusalem since June 1967, and the General Assembly has declared the annexation invalid.[60] The status of Jerusalem remains controversial. The interest of the Christian and Moslem communities of the world, as well as that of the Jewish community, for full protection of their holy sites in the area, will have to be satisfied before the issue can be settled.

D. State of War Alleged by Arabs

The claim of the Arab states that they have been in a "state of war" with Israel since 1948 and that, therefore, they exercise belligerent rights which are not contrary to the terms of the armistices, including closure of the Suez Canal and the Straits of Tiran to Israeli shipping, is certainly contrary to the obligation of these states under the United Nations Charter by which both they and Israel are bound.

A state of war in the legal sense, as understood in the 19th century, implied a situation in which two or more political entities are equally entitled to settle a conflict by the use of armed force.[61] It implied a continuing threat by each belligerent to use force against the other, actual use of force when deemed expedient, and impartial neutrality by other states. Nineteenth century international law did not limit the right of a sovereign state to initiate a "state of war" in this sense, although the law of war imposed limitations upon the methods permissible during the war. The Hague Conventions of 1907 imposed minor substantive and procedural limitations upon the initiation of war, and the League of Nations Covenant imposed further restrictions. The Kellogg-Briand Pact of 1929, as interpreted by the Nuremberg Tribunal in 1945, and the United Nations Charter, however, put major limitations upon the use of force in international relations and "outlawed" a legal "state of war" altogether.[62] The members of the United Nations are obliged "to settle their international disputes by

---

[58] See note 53 *supra.*

[59] *See, e.g.,* vote of December 9, 1949, 4 U.N. GAOR 607 (1949).

[60] Note 27 *supra.*

[61] Q. WRIGHT, A STUDY OF WAR 8, 685, 698 (1942). See also Wright, *Changes in the Conception of War,* 18 AM. J. INT'L L. 755, 761-67 (1926). F. GROB, THE RELATIVITY OF WAR AND PEACE: A STUDY IN LAW, HISTORY, AND POLITICS (1949) presents numerous instances in which force was used in international relations in various quantities and under various names including "war." He does not distinguish the factual from the legal conception of war and suggests that the latter conception is so lacking in clarity that it is useless.

[62] Q. WRIGHT, A STUDY OF WAR 891-92 (1942); *The Meaning of the Pact of Paris,* 27 AM. J. INT'L L. 39 (1933); *The Law of the Nuremberg Trial,* 41 *id.* 38 (1947); *The Outlawry of War and the Law of War,* 47 *id.* 365 (1953).

peaceful means" and to "refrain in their international relations from the threat or use of force against the territorial integrity or political independence of any state, or in any other manner inconsistent with the purposes of the United Nations."[63]

States may, it is true, use force, in "individual or collective self-defense against armed attack,"[64] or under authority of the United Nations,[65] but in such circumstances the belligerents are not equal; one is in principle the aggressor and the other the defender, and other states may not, according to the Charter, be neutral.[66] A "state of war" is, therefore, "outlawed." Israel, as a state and a member of the United Nations, is recognized under the Charter as the "sovereign equal" of all other members.[67] The Arab states as fellow members of the United Nations cannot, therefore, be in a "state of war" with it. Israel clearly has the right, under the Charter, to demand that the Arab states abandon their claim of belligerency against it and their claim that it has no right to exist.

E. Boundaries

The boundaries of Israel remain undetermined. The United Nations Conciliation Commission at the Lausanne meeting on May 12, 1949, reached agreement with Arab and Israeli delegations in regard to territorial adjustments and related refugee rights, but this was later rejected by Israel[68] and no agreement has since been reached. Cease-fire or armistice lines establish possessory rights, so long as they remain valid, but they do not in principle establish international boundaries.[69] They may do so in the absence of a boundary treaty or adjudication, by the principles of "prescription" and of "general recognition." The first of these principles would establish the title of the occupant up to the cease-fire line if its occupation were not contested by the state adversely affected for a considerable period of time. Fifty years was accepted in the British Guiana-Venezuela arbitration of 1899.[70] The continuous insistence by

---

[63] U.N. CHARTER art. 2, paras. 3 and 4.

[64] Id., art. 51.

[65] Id., arts. 39, 42.

[66] Id., art. 2, para. 5.

[67] Id., para. 1.

[68] Cf. note 53 supra.

[69] Possession of unclaimed territory (territorium nullius) may give good title by the principle of discovery and occupation, but a possessory right to claimed territory established by a cease fire line, while protecting against invasion so long as the cease fire agreement remains valid, does not give title and implies, as did the possessory assizes of Henry II, in 12th century England, that a procedure to determine title should be available. See Williams, Sovereignty, Seisin and the League, 7 BRIT. YB. INT'L L. 24, 36–39 (1926); Q. WRIGHT, THE ROLE OF INTERNATIONAL LAW IN THE ELIMINATION OF WAR 13 (1961). The distinction between a cease fire line and an international boundary was explicitly stated in the 1954 agreement between the French Military Command and Ho Chi Minh which established the cease fire line in Vietnam as a "provisional military demarcation line" and not an "international boundary." The continuing validity of this line was doubtful after withdrawal of one party, France, from the responsibilities it had accepted and violation of the agreement by its successor, Diem. Wright, Legal Aspects of the Vietnam Situation, supra note 50, at 756-57.

[70] See 1 J. B. MOORE, INTERNATIONAL LAW DIGEST 297 (1906). The William Spader claim (United States v. Venezuela, RALSTON'S REPORT 161 (1904)) was not allowed, the Commissioner saying that "a right unasserted for over forty-three years can hardly in justice be called a 'claim' " (id. at 161-62), and thirty-two years' prescription was held to bar the Gentini claim (Italy v. Venezuela, id. at 720). Justice

the Arab states, since the occupation of 1949, that they do not accept the armistice lines
as Israel's boundaries, at least beyond the original United Nations resolution of 1947,
precludes any Israeli title by "prescription" to the enlarged area of Israeli occupation
resulting from the armistices of 1949 or of 1967.

Israel has been "generally recognized" as a state with title to the territory awarded
to it by the United Nations resolution of 1947, which the Arab states were prepared to
accept as a basis for peace in 1949. There seems to be no such "general recognition" of
the additional territory occupied during the hostilities of 1948 or of 1967. Israel's title
to occupied territory beyond that of the United Nations resolution of 1947, therefore,
remains to be determined by agreement with its neighbors or, perhaps, by "general
recognition," manifested by acceptance or acquiescence by most states including the
Arab states, in a resolution of the United Nations General Assembly.[71]

F. Jordan Waters

The Jordan River has tributaries rising in Syria and Lebanon above the Sea of
Galilee, and in Jordan between that Sea and its terminus in the Dead Sea. The lower
part of the river was within Jordan's territory before the June war; it now forms
the boundary between Jordan and the territory occupied by Israel. Proposals by
Israel to divert water from the Sea of Galilee to irrigate the Negev, thus depleting the
water available for irrigation in Jordan, and proposals by Syria, Lebanon and Jordan
to divert or utilize the tributaries of the Jordan in their territories, thus depleting the
water available to Israel, have caused continuous controversy and occasional hostilities.[72]

Apart from rights in respect to navigation, international law recognizes the right
of all states in a river basin to an equitable share of the river waters for purposes of
irrigation, domestic uses, and power; to prohibit diversion or pollution by an upper
riparian in violation of equitable claims by lower riparians (on the principle of *sic
utere tuum*); and to urge agreement among the riparians to determine equitable
shares.[73] No such agreement has been reached among the states of the Jordan basin
and the above noted proposals for unilateral diversion by Israel and the Arab states
seem to violate the principles of international law on the subject. An international

Field, in the U.S. Supreme Court, denied a boundary claim of Virginia against Tennessee on the ground
that "a boundary line between States . . . which has been run out, located and marked upon the earth,
and afterwards recognized and acquiesced in by the parties for a long course of years, is conclusive, even
if it be ascertained that it varies somewhat from the courses given in the original grant. . . ." Virginia
v. Tennessee, 148 U.S. 503, 522 (1893); quoted portion in W. BISHOP, INTERNATIONAL LAW: CASES AND
MATERIALS 363 (2d ed. 1962).

[71] See Wright, *Custom as a Basis of International Law in the Post-War World*, 2 TEXAS INT'L LAW
FORUM 147 (1966); 7 INDIAN J. INT'L L. 1 (1967).

[72] See EVERYMAN'S UNITED NATIONS, *supra* note 18, at 75-76.

[73] Resolution of the Institut de Droit International, Salzburg, Sept. 11, 1961, 49 ANNUAIRE DE L'IN-
STITUT DE DROIT INTERNATIONAL 370 (1961-II). See also Kansas v. Colorado, 206 U.S. 46 (1907);
Wyoming v. Colorado, 259 U.S. 419 (1922); New Jersey v. New York, 283 U.S. 336 (1931); 1 G.
HACKWORTH, DIGEST OF INTERNATIONAL LAW 580-96 (1940).

administration with authority, similar to that of the Tennessee Valley Authority in the United States, to maximize the use and to assure equitable distribution of Jordan waters for irrigation, power, and other purposes has often been advocated, was recommended in the United Nations partition resolution of 1947, and would be beneficial to all the states in the area. Agreement on such an administration is not likely, however, until the political problems have been solved and tension and hostility between Israel and its Arab neighbors have been reduced.

G. Refugees

The Arab states have a good claim under international law to repatriation and compensation for the Arab refugees from Palestine resulting from the hostilities of 1949 and 1967. It is controversial whether the refugees were compelled by Israel to leave or fled from fear aroused by the Israeli destruction of some villages. The law of war, applicable to all *de facto* hostilities, requires the occupant to spare the civil population, and refusal to allow repatriation or compensation would violate that law. Numerous efforts to negotiate a settlement for the million refugees resulting from the war of 1948-49 have been made, and Israel has made some gesture toward compensation. These refugees have, in fact, been living for nearly twenty years in Jordanian, Egyptian, and Syrian territory with support from the United Nations and with little effort made by the Arab states to resettle them in other parts of the Arab world, doubtless because the situation is regarded as an asset in keeping world opinion alive to Arab grievances against Israel. Agreement to solve this problem is of great importance from humanitarian, legal, and political points of view. The problem is magnified by new refugees from the areas occupied by Israel in the six-day war.

Under general international law, a state may protest against, and demand reparation for, injury to its nationals by act or negligence of another state in violation of an obligation under international law. Egypt, Jordan, and Syria may, in accord with this principle, protest to Israel for injuries to their nationals who fled or were expelled from territories which belonged to them before the Israel occupations of 1949 and 1967. Refugees from territory within Palestine, as a result of the 1949 war, were Palestinian nationals and would not be regarded as nationals of neighboring Arab states even though the nationality laws of those states may have granted special privileges to "Arabs."[74] These states may, however, properly protest on humanitarian[75] and human rights[76] grounds, and, in so far as the refugees fled or

---

[74] Q. WRIGHT, MANDATES UNDER THE LEAGUE OF NATIONS 327, 462, 468, 528 (1930); Re *Ezra Goralshvih* (Palestine Supreme Court, 1925), unreported, but summarized by the writer in Wright, *Some Recent Cases on the Status of Mandated Territories*, 20 AM. J. INT'L L. 768, 771 (1926).

[75] Protests have been made in the past against gross inhumanities which "shock the conscience of mankind" as did the Leopoldian persecutions in the Congo, and Russian and Hitlerian persecution of Jews even when the injured individuals were subjects of the persecuting state and within its territory. The Nuremberg trials prosecuted individuals for "crimes against humanity," though only when the crimes were in pursuance of illegal war or in violation of the war. See Wright, *The Law of the Nuremberg Trial, supra* note 62; E. STOWELL, INTERVENTION IN INTERNATIONAL LAW 51-277 (1922).

[76] "The Universal Declaration of Human Rights," approved by the General Assembly on December 10,

were expelled from Palestine and are not permitted to return to their homes, on the ground that they constitute a burden on the state of refuge.[77]   The United Nations has a responsibility for refugees on the general basis of denial of human rights and its support of the Palestinian refugees is an acknowledgment of this responsibility.

H. Suez Canal

Egypt's closure of the Suez Canal to innocent passage by Israeli shipping since 1949 is probably illegal.   It has sought to justify this action on the assertion of a state of war and a duty to protect the Canal.   The claim that a "state of war" exists, as noted above in part IV D, is not valid.   The Constantinople Convention of 1888,[78] among eight major European states and Turkey, declared that the Canal "shall always be free and open in time of war as in time of peace to every vessel of commerce or of war without distinction of flag" (article 1).   This seems to require that the Canal be open to Israeli vessels even if there were a "state of war," but Egypt claims that the further provision in the Convention reserving the "rights and immunities" of the Khedive "not affected by the obligations of the treaty" (article 13) authorized Egypt to take "measures which it might find necessary to take for securing by their own forces the defense of Egypt and the maintenance of public order" (article 11). Egypt can properly inspect vessels using the Canal to assure their innocence but cannot prevent innocent passage of vessels protected by the Convention.

The terms of the Convention, therefore, give no support to Egypt's claims, but there is also the question whether Israel, not a party to the Convention, can share in its benefits.   The terms of the treaty and practice under it, however, indicate that freedom to use the Canal was intended to apply to all states.   The United Nations Security Council on September 1, 1951, denied the Egyptian claim that a state of war or defense necessities justified closing the Canal to Israeli shipping and called upon Egypt to "terminate the restrictions on the passage of international commercial

---

1948 (G.A. Res. 217, 3 U.N. GAOR, pt. 1, Resolutions 71, U.N. Doc. A/810 (1948)), provides in article 13: "1. Everyone has the right to freedom of movement and residence within the borders of each State. 2. Everyone has the right to leave any country, including his own, and to return to his country." "The International Covenant on Civil and Political Rights," approved by the General Assembly on Dec. 16, 1966 (G.A. Res. 2200, 21 U.N. GAOR, Supp. 16, at 49, U.N. Doc. A/6316 (1966)), provides in article 12 (p. 54):

"1. Everyone lawfully within the territory of a State shall, within that territory, have the right to liberty of movement and freedom to choose his residence. 2. Everyone shall be free to leave any country, including his own. 3. The above-mentioned rights shall not be subject to any restrictions except those which are provided by law, are necessary to protect national security, public order (*ordre public*), public health or morals, or the rights and freedoms of others, and are consistent with the other rights recognized in the present Covenant. 4. No one shall be arbitrarily deprived of the right to enter his own country."

[77] The German Federal Republic paid reparations to Israel after the Second World War for the destruction and exile of Jews during the Hitler period, some of whom had fled to Palestine. In an interview in March 1968, Nasser said he considered the refugees the most serious Middle Eastern problem. Attwood, *supra* note 25, at 61, 64.

[78] 79 BRIT. & FOR. STATE PAPERS 18 (1887-88); 3 AM. J. INT'L L. SUPP. 123 (1909).

shipping and goods through the Suez Canal wherever bound."[79] On October 13, 1956, the Council reaffirmed this position declaring "there should be free and open transit through the Canal without discrimination overt or covert."[80] President Eisenhower expressed support for this position on February 20, 1957, and said:

> We should not assume that, if Israel withdraws [from the Sharm el Sheikh area on the Straits of Tiran], Egypt will prevent Israel's shipping from using the Suez Canal or the Gulf of Aqaba. If, unhappily, Egypt does hereafter violate the Armistice Agreement or other international obligations, then they should be dealt with firmly by the society of nations.[81]

Israel's foreign minister said in March 1957 that this statement had weighed heavily in reaching the decision that Israel would withdraw its forces behind the 1949 armistice lines.[82]

On April 24, 1957, Egypt declared that it was "particularly determined . . . to afford and maintain free and uninterrupted navigation for all nations within the limits of and in accordance with the provisions of the Constantinople Convention of 1888" and agreed to submit to the International Court of Justice any dispute on this issue.[83] Egypt, however, did not permit Israel to use the Canal and Israel has not invoked the jurisdiction of the Court probably because it does not wish to raise the issue of the applicability of the Constantinople Convention to non-signatories. Egypt, however, is probably violating international law in closing the Canal to Israeli shipping.

Israel occupied the east bank of the Canal as a result of the June war but it has refused to cooperate in measures which might lead to clearing the Canal of the

---

[79] S.C. Res. 95 (1951); Wright, *Interventions, 1956, supra* note 48, at 261-72.

[80] S.C. Res. 118 (1956).

[81] 36 DEP'T STATE BULL. 387, 390 (1957). Secretary of State Dulles declared in an aide memoire to the Israeli Ambassador on February 11, 1957 that

"[T]he United States believes that the Gulf comprehends international waters and that no nation has the right to prevent free and innocent passage in the Gulf and through the Straits giving access thereto . . . .

. . . .

"In the absence of some overriding decision to the contrary, as by the International Court of Justice, the United States, on behalf of vessels of United States registry, is prepared to exercise the right of free and innocent passage and to join with others to secure general recognition of this right."

Id. at 393.

[82] 11 U.N. GAOR 1275-76 (1957). See also the position enunciated by Secretary of State Dulles in the General Assembly (U.N. GAOR, 1st Emer. Spec. Sess. 10-12 (1956)) introducing the resolution adopted as G.A. Res. 997, *id.* Supp. 1, at 2, U.N. Doc. A/3354 (1956). It called for a cease fire and "urged that upon the cease fire being effective, steps be taken to reopen the Suez Canal and restore secure freedom of navigation." Egypt accepted it "on the condition, of course, that it could not implement the resolution in case attacking armies continued their aggression." *Id.*, Annexes, Agenda Item no. 5, at 3, U.N. Doc. A/3266 (1956). The resolution was adopted against the opposition of Australia, France, Israel, New Zealand, and Great Britain, with abstentions by Belgium, Canada, Laos, Netherlands, Portugal, and South Africa. U.N. GAOR, 1st Emer. Spec. Sess. 34-35 (1956).

[83] 12 U.N. SCOR, Supp. April-June 1957, at 8, 9, 11, U.N. Doc. S/3818 (1957); [1956-1957] I.C.J.Y.B. 212.

vessels sunk during the war until Egypt makes a new pledge to open the Canal to its ships and cargoes.[84]

In December 1967 an agreement was reached through United Nations Ambassador Jarring permitting survey and clearing of the southern part of the Canal to permit fifteen foreign vessels, stranded in the center of the Canal, to get out, but Israel claimed that Egypt began to survey the northern sector of the Canal, contrary to the agreement. Hostilities ensued, as a result of which Egypt suspended the entire operation.[85] Israel insisted that Egyptian compliance or non-compliance with this agreement, the first between the two countries since the armistice, was important because it would indicate Egypt's general readiness to honor future agreements with Israel.[86] The incident indicated the mutual suspicions that made progress toward opening the Canal or settlement of other problems difficult.

I. Gulf of Aqaba and Straits of Tiran

The legal situation in regard to the Straits of Tiran and the Gulf of Aqaba is similar to that of the Suez Canal. Under international law, and the Convention of 1958 on the territorial sea, which, however, Egypt has not ratified, international straits connecting portions of the high seas are open to "innocent passage" by vessels of all states.[87] The high seas include seas like the Baltic and the Black Sea with ports of a number of states, in the absence of agreements by all to make it a *mare clausum*. Egypt, Saudi Arabia, Jordan, and Israel all have ports on the Gulf of Aqaba. The Israeli port of Elath is on the territory within the boundaries of Israel as provided in the United Nations resolution of 1947. It is, therefore, within Israel's jurisdiction and makes the Gulf of Aqaba an international sea. Even if the three Arab states on the Gulf attempted to deny Israel's title to Elath and, by agreement, attempted to make it a closed sea (*mare clausum*), it would still be open under the Convention of 1958 which provides for "innocent passage" through straits used for international navigation not only between parts of the high seas but also between the high seas and the territorial sea of a foreign state.

The freedom of the Straits and the Sea of Aqaba was assumed after the hostilities of 1949 and 1956, particularly by the United States, and the withdrawal of Israel from the Sinai area was to some extent contingent on this assumption.[88] Egypt's closure of the Straits in May 1967 was a violation of the rights of Israel as well as of other states.

[84] This purpose was indicated in a letter of January 31, 1968 from the Israeli Government to the Secretary-General reiterating its previous refusal to allow the UAR to survey the Canal north of ships stranded there, and justifying the use of force on the previous day which is referred to in the ensuing principal text. U.N. Doc. S/7930/Add.63, Jan. 31, 1968, at 14-17.

[85] N.Y. Times, Jan. 31, 1968, at 1, col. 5.

[86] Letter of Jan. 31, 1968, *supra* note 84.

[87] Corfu Channel Case, [1949] I.C.J. 4, 28-30. Convention on the Territorial Sea, art. 16(4), [1958] 15 U.S.T. 1606, T.I.A.S. No. 5639; 52 AM. J. INT'L L. 834 (1958).

[88] See text accompanying notes 81 and 82 *supra*.

J. United Nations Emergency Force

The status of the United Nations Emergency Force, which had kept moderate peace on the Israel-Egyptian frontier for nearly ten years, has been controversial, but elaborate exposition by Secretary-General U Thant on June 26, 1967, of the correspondence between Secretary-General Dag Hammarskjöld and Egypt in 1956 makes it clear that the Force could remain in Egyptian territory only with the latter's permission. Consequently, the Secretary-General was obliged to withdraw it when Egypt so demanded in May 1967.[89] This position was supported by two states which had contingents in UNEF and prepared to withdraw them at Egypt's demand.[90] The refusal of Israel to allow the United Nations Force to operate on its side of the cease-fire line in 1956, or in 1967 when the Secretary-General suggested that it be moved across the line from Egypt,[91] also indicates the need for consent of the state where such a force is stationed on the basis of a "recommendation" of the General Assembly. The Security Council seems to have power to make a "decision" binding on all the members of the United Nations to maintain a force in the territory of a state when it deems such action necessary as a provisional or an enforcement measure to maintain international peace and security.[92] That power was exercised in the Congo in 1960, although the original sending of the force to that country was at the request of the Congo Government.[93]

In any case, the sending of the United Nations Emergency Force to the Middle East was based on a recommendation by the General Assembly, which has no power to make decisions binding on the members.[94] The problem of the United Nations forces is complicated by the refusal of France, the Soviet Union and other members to consider the cost of such forces as a charge on the regular budget of the United Nations to be apportioned among the members of the General Assembly, although the International Court of Justice held in an Advisory Opinion that it can be so apportioned.[95] This "financial veto" by important countries has, however, made the maintenance of such forces subject to voluntary contributions.

---

[89] See Report of the Secretary-General on the withdrawal of the United Nations Emergency Force, U.N. Doc. A/6730/Add. 3, June 26, 1967; 4 U.N. MONTHLY CHRON. No. 7, at 135 (1967).

[90] Memorandum cited note 89 *supra,* at paras. 23 and 50.

[91] *Id.,* paras. 21, 87-93.

[92] Such a power of the Security Council may be inferred in respect to both investigating commissions and peace-keeping forces from articles 25, 29, 34, 40, 104, and 105 of the Charter. 2 REPERTORY OF PRACTICE OF UNITED NATIONS ORGANS art. 29, paras. 17-28; art. 34, paras. 2-14 (1955). See also Q. WRIGHT, INTERNATIONAL LAW AND THE UNITED NATIONS 122 (1960); COMMISSION TO STUDY THE ORGANIZATION OF PEACE, U.N. GUARDS 9 (Spec. Report 1948); CHARTER REVIEW CONFERENCE 32 (9th Report 1948); STRENGTHENING THE UNITED NATIONS 36-38 (10th Report 1957); ORGANIZING PEACE IN THE NUCLEAR AGE 42 (11th Report 1959); NEW DIMENSIONS OF THE UNITED NATIONS 27-28 (17th Report 1966).

[93] Wright, *Legal Aspects of the Congo Situation,* 4 INT'L STUDIES: JOURNAL OF THE INDIAN SCHOOL OF INTERNATIONAL STUDIES 1, 16-22 (1962).

[94] 1 REPERTORY OF PRACTICE OF UNITED NATIONS ORGANS art. 22, paras. 52, 104-107 (1955); STRENGTHENING THE UNITED NATIONS, *supra* note 92, at 5, 36, 79.

[95] Advisory Opinion on Certain Expenses of the United Nations (Article 17, para. 2, of the Charter), [1962] I.C.J. 151.

K. Withdrawal of Israeli Forces

Israel should eventually withdraw its forces to the armistice lines of 1949 which constituted its *de facto* boundary before the six-day war. International law forbids a state to maintain armed forces in the territory of a foreign state without its consent, unless authorized by United Nations decision or required by defensive necessity. The doctrine asserted by Secretary of State Stimson in refusing to recognize any change of rights from the Japanese occupation of Manchuria in 1931 in violation of its obligations under the Kellogg-Briand Pact was accepted by the League of Nations, which held that the occupation also violated Japan's obligation under article 10 of the Covenant.[96] The concept of "no fruits of aggression" implying a duty to withdraw forces from illegally occupied territory has been generally accepted.

Article 51 of the United Nations Charter goes further. It recognizes the inherent right of individual or collective self-defense, in the event of an armed attack, only "until the Security Council has taken measures necessary to maintain international peace and security." This implies that an occupation of foreign territory, even if justified as a defensive necessity, must be withdrawn when peace and security have been restored. Consequently, in the Suez incident of 1956, the United Nations insisted, without deciding who was the aggressor, that the forces of Israel, France and the United Kingdom in Egyptian territory must be withdrawn under the cease-fire as the first step in establishing peace.[97]

After the Security Council had adopted cease-fire resolutions in the six-day war, the Soviet Union, supported by France, the Arab states, India and others, demanded on June 6, 1967, that Israel withdraw from occupied territories. Israel, however, supported by the United States and others insisted that such a withdrawal be accompanied by Arab renunciation of belligerency and perhaps of other polices inconsistent with international law such as exclusion of Israel shipping through the Suez Canal and the Straits of Tiran.[98]

While it is true that the Arab states would be hampered in negotiations as long as Israel occupied portions of their territory, it would seem that they should be ready to renounce policies in violation of international law contemporaneously with Israel's withdrawal. Return to the situation which has led to three Middle Eastern wars would not seem expedient. A package in which all agreed, not only to accept their obligations under international law and the United Nations Charter, but also to act in accordance with these obligations, would seem an essential condition of peace, as was recognized by the Security Council resolution of November 22, 1967.

---

[96] Wright, *The Stimson Note of January 7, 1932*, 26 AM. J. INT'L L. 342 (1932); LEGAL PROBLEMS IN THE FAR EASTERN CONFLICT 153-56 (1941); *Recognition, Intervention and Ideologies, supra* note 42, at 97.

[97] G.A. Res. 997, *supra* note 82.

[98] See, *e.g.*, U.N. Doc. S/PV.1358 (1967).

L. Role of the United Nations

The responsibility of the United Nations under the Charter is clear. It should, as it has, demand a cease-fire as a provisional measure[99] and, if hostilities cease as a result, it should seek to restore international peace and security by achieving agreement among the parties. Neither the Security Council nor the General Assembly has power to make a binding decision settling the dispute, but either can make recommendations for settlement if the dispute or situation is one "the continuance of which is likely to endanger the maintenance of international peace and security" as the Middle Eastern situation certainly is.[100] Either can request Advisory Opinions from the International Court of Justice to determine legal obligations involved[101] and can recommend that the parties submit legal issues to the Court for binding judgment.[102] The Security Council may decide upon measures to enforce such a judgment.[103]

The United Nations has ordinarily made a return to pre-war boundaries part of a cease-fire demand.[104] The Soviet Union, the Arab countries, and others believe that Israel's failure to do so in the present instance constitutes a failure to meet its responsibilities.

These states also consider that the United Nations has a responsibility to determine the aggressor in the hostilities.[105] Such a determination, however, has usually been avoided because it is thought that it might complicate the problem of restoring peace. Provisional cease-fire measures are addressed to all belligerents and only if one or both parties refuse to accept a cease-fire, or after accepting violate its terms, does the Charter, and practice under it, require a determination of the aggressor.[106]

The fact that both Israel and the Arab states had failed to observe obligations under the Charter and international law gave a certain justification for the failure of the United Nations to demand immediate withdrawal of Israeli forces behind the cease-fire lines of 1949, although it has been recognized that "to conform to sub-

---

[99] U.N. CHARTER art. 40.

[100] Id., arts. 33, 36, 37, 11(2), 14.

[101] Id., art. 96.

[102] Id., art. 36.

[103] Id., art. 94.

[104] Withdrawal was demanded in cease fire resolutions pertaining to Kashmir (S.C. Res. 47 (1948), S.C. Res. 209 (1965)); Korea (S.C. Res. 82 (1950)); and Suez (G.A. Res. 997, supra note 82). Withdrawal was not demanded in the case of the Dominican Republic in 1965, nor that of Palestine in 1948, although in the latter situation, S.C. Res. 56 of August 19, 1948 declared that "No party is entitled to gain military or political advantage through violation of the truce."

[105] E.g., U.N. Doc. S/PV.1351, at 21-27, June 8, 1967.

[106] Such refusal or violation was considered in League of Nations practice to be the best test of aggression and was incorporated in "The General Convention to Improve the Means of Preventing War," opened for signature on September 26, 1931. 12 LEAGUE OF NATIONS OFF. J., Spec. Supp. 92, at 24 (1931). See also Wright, The Concept of Aggression in International Law, 29 AM. J. INT'L L. 373, 382 (1935); The Prevention of Aggression, 50 id. 514, 530 (1956); A STUDY OF WAR, supra note 62. Article 40 of the U.N. Charter contemplates this test. See WRIGHT, THE ROLE OF INTERNATIONAL LAW IN THE ELIMINATION OF WAR, supra note 69, at 62.

stantial justice the armistice should be proposed before the fighting has resulted in any substantial change in the *de facto* line of occupation and should be based on that line."[107]

Israel has suggested that the great powers, especially the United States, which had facilitated Israel's withdrawal of forces from the Aqaba area in 1957 by assuming that Egypt would open the Suez Canal and the Gulf of Aqaba to free navigation for all states including Israel, had a responsibility to take action when Nasser closed the Straits of Tiran in May 1967.[108]   President Eisenhower's statement of February 1957 suggested, however, a general interest in assuring Egypt's observance of its international obligations, rather than a specific commitment made by the United States to induce Israel to withdraw its forces.   Such a commitment, beneficial to Israel, would have been contrary to the principle of "no fruits of aggression."   Perhaps because of its involvement in Vietnam, the United States took no action in the 1967 crisis beyond a declaration of principle, and the Security Council proved unable to act because some of the great powers favored Israel and others favored Egypt.   Prompt action to open the Gulf to Israeli shipping might have prevented the war.

M. Determination of Aggression

Inasmuch as a cease-fire was obtained, it was unnecessary and probably undesirable for the United Nations to determine the aggressor in the hostilities and such a determination presented serious difficulties of fact and law.[109]   Israel claimed that Egypt's act in closing the Straits of Tiran was a blockade which constituted an act of war against Israel.[110]   Egypt's expulsion of the United Nations Emergency Force, and its mobilization of its own forces in the Sinai area and the Gaza strip on the Israeli frontier, was said further to indicate its aggressive intentions.   Israel thus claimed that it was the victim of "armed attack" in the broad sense, and was free to act defensively under article 51 of the Charter.   It, however, refused to permit UNEF to cross the armistice line to its territory.   It claimed at first that it did not actually use armed force against Egypt until the latter had initiated action against it

---

[107] Wright, *The Concept of Aggression in International Law*, supra note 106, at 394.

[108] Israel Information Service, N.Y. Bulletin, Feb. 5, 1968.

[109] See note 106 *supra* and accompanying text.

[110] In announcing the withdrawal of Israeli forces from the Aqaba area on March 1, 1957, that country's Foreign Minister said in the General Assembly:

"Interference, by armed force, with ships of Israel flag exercising free and innocent passage in the Gulf of Aqaba and through the Straits of Tiran, will be regarded by Israel as an attack entitling it to exercise its inherent right of self-defence under Article 51 of the United Nations Charter and to take all such measures as are necessary to ensure the free and innocent passage of its ships in the Gulf and in the Straits."

11 U.N. GAOR 1276 (1957).   To similar effect see U.N. Doc. A/PV.1536, June 19, 1967, at 42-46. An official Egyptian report, published on February 19, 1968, stated that President Nasser warned his close advisers in May 1967 that blockade of the Gulf of Aqaba meant certain war with Israel.   N.Y. Times, March 3, 1968, at 12, col. 1.

on the ground and in the air, and that defense against Egypt's blockade and the Arab effort to conquer Israel were its sole goals in using force.[111] It later admitted, in effect, that its air attack preceded Egyptian attack on its territory but claimed that Egypt's aggressive acts justified its attack as necessary defense.[112]

Egypt considered that the closing of the Straits of Tiran and the expulsion of UNEF were within its domestic jurisdiction; that mobilization was necessary for defense against Israeli mobilization on the Syrian frontier, of which it allegedly had intelligence reports; that it had no intention of initiating hostilities, and that it did not in fact take military action until Israeli air forces had bombed Egyptian airports, which was followed by simultaneous Israeli action in the Gaza strip, Sinai, Sharm el Sheikh and other areas. "[T]he dimensions of the Israeli attack are so wide," the Egyptian representative in the Security Council said, "that no one can doubt the premeditated nature of this aggression."[113]

Clear evidence of the facts would be important to determine the aggressor, but it would appear that the well-authenticated acts of Egypt, especially its insistence that a "state of war" existed and its policy to terminate the existence of Israel, accompanied by the closure of the Straits of Tiran and extensive mobilizations on the Israel frontier, could be regarded as amounting to an "armed attack" on Israel. On the other hand, Israel's refusal to permit UNEF to cross the armistice line into its territory, its superior military preparations, its continued occupation of Arab territory, and its annexation of old Jerusalem, suggest that Israel had intentions other than defense. Furthermore, its massive air and land attack initiated the war on June 5. The issue of which was the aggressor may not have to be decided in the process of restoring peace, but it may arise in subsequent controversies concerning reparation for injuries received during the hostilities, on the principle that the

---

[111] U.N. Doc. S/PV.1347, June 5, 1967, at 17-21.

[112] See remarks of Premier Eshkol quoted in N.Y. Times, July 8, 1967, at 4, col. 4. Israel apologized for its attack on the U.S. intelligence ship *Liberty* on the high seas on June 8, 1967, saying it thought it was an Egyptian ship. N.Y. Times, June 10, 1967, at 14, col. 6. Since the prolonged inspection of the ship by Israeli aircraft and its clear markings make this explanation improbable, it has been suggested that Israel hoped to destroy evidence acquired by the ship of Israel's priority in armed attack on Egypt. LIFE, June 23, 1967, at 29.

[113] Statements of the U.A.R. Delegation in the Security Council on May 29 and June 5, 1967, U.N. Docs. S/PV.1343, at 21-47; S/PV.1347, at 22-30.

Not only priority in initiating hostilities, but also aggressive intentions and superiority of preparation for attack were considered evidence of the aggressor by the Rumboldt Committee which investigated the Greco-Bulgarian incident of 1925 (see note 114 *infra*); by the Lytton Commission which investigated the Manchurian incident of 1931; and by the Nuremberg Tribunal. See Wright, *The Concept of Aggression in International Law*, supra note 106, at 380, 386, 388; INTERNATIONAL LAW AND THE UNITED NATIONS, supra note 92, at 89. On the Lytton Commission's suggestion that weight in determining the aggressor should be attached to the fact that the Japanese were better prepared than the Chinese when hostilities began on the night of September 18-19, 1931, the writer commented in 1935:

"Military efficiency may exhibit some correlation with aggressiveness, but it is doubtful whether the correlation is sufficient to justify the conclusion that the more efficient belligerent is invariably to be branded as the aggressor."

The Concept of Aggression in International Law, supra note 106, at 381.

aggressor should be liable to compensate his victims resulting from his act of aggression.[114]

V
Summation of Legal Issues

Reviewing the thirteen legal issues discussed, it appears that Israel was in the wrong on three: the annexation of Jerusalem, the continued occupation of Arab territory, and the failure to repatriate or compensate Arab refugees. Arab states were in the wrong also on three issues: the assertion of a state of war with Israel, refusal to recognize the latter's right to exist, and the closure of the Suez Canal and the Gulf of Aqaba to Israeli shipping. The Arab claims that the Balfour Declaration and the partition of Palestine violated their rights were probably originally valid, but became moot after the general recognition of Israel and its admission to the United Nations. The issue concerning the status of UNEF also became moot after its withdrawal, which seems to have been legally necessary. The responsibility of the United Nations and the Great Powers to insist that the Suez Canal and the Straits of Tiran be kept open continues, as does the responsibility of the United Nations to restore international peace and security. On two issues, those concerning the use of Jordan waters and determination of the boundaries of Israel, both the Arabs and Israelis have manifested imperfect respect for international law and for the necessity to reach agreement. On the issue of responsibility for initiating the six-day war, Egypt made threats and took hostile measures instigating the war, but Israel's large-scale attack on June 5 started the war. Both may be guilty of aggression.

VI
Prospects of the Future

Little progress toward a settlement of the situation had been made by March 1968 apart from establishing cease-fire lines. The Security Council in November recognized principles of settlement including withdrawal of Israeli forces from the occupied territory and Arab renunciation of belligerency, and provided for United Nations presence in the area for purposes of conciliation. Ambassador Gunnar Jarring has been seeking a basis for conciliatory action since December 1967. The General

---

[114] The principle was applied in art. 232 of the Treaty of Versailles which required Germany to make reparation to Belgium for *all* losses it had suffered as a result of the German invasion in view of Germany's explicit obligation to Belgium under the neutralization treaty of 1839, while reparations to other countries were in principle based on their losses resulting from German violations of the law of war. See Wright, *The Outlawry of War,* 19 Am. J. Int'l L. 76, 86 (1925). See also Articles of Interpretation of the Pact of Paris (Kellogg-Briand Pact): "A violating state is liable to pay compensation for all damage caused by a violation of the Pact to any signatory state or to its nationals." Int'l L. Ass'n, Report of Thirty-eighth Conference 1, 66, 68 (London 1934). Greece, found to be the aggressor in the Greco-Bulgarian incident of 1925, was required to make reparation for Bulgarian losses. See 37th Sess. of the Council, 12th meeting, 7 League of Nations Off. J. 172 (1925). See also Wright, *The Outlawry of War and the Law of War, supra* note 62.

Assembly has declared that Israel should renounce its annexation of Jordanian Jerusalem.

The Arabs have refused to negotiate and have strengthened their military position by importing Soviet arms, gaining assistance of Soviet advisers and benefiting by the presence of Soviet naval force in the eastern Mediterranean. Israel has declared the annexation of old Jerusalem, has refused to evacuate the occupied territories, at least until other issues are settled, and hopes for the support of the United States, which also has naval forces in the eastern Mediterranean. The United States, however, has been seeking to maintain an impartial position by urging settlement of the refugee problem and asserting that Israel's withdrawal from occupied areas must be contingent on Egyptian renunciation of belligerency, recognition of Israel, and opening of the waterways. It also has sought to maintain the military balance of power by giving arms to both Israel and Jordan.

Sporadic hostilities have occurred on the Syrian, Jordanian and Suez frontiers in violation of the cease-fire agreements, as well as by Arab guerrillas inside the occupied territories. The Suez Canal continues blocked and another round of major hostilities between Israel and the Arabs, which might escalate into general war, seems likely unless effective international action, preferably through the United Nations, breaks the deadlock.

It has been suggested that termination of Vietnam hostilities might induce the Soviet Union and the United States to exert influence in common toward realization of the Security Council resolution of November 22, 1967. Both of the superpowers seem anxious to continue their *détente*, which has been hampered by the Vietnam intervention, and to establish peace in the Middle East. The ambivalence of their Middle Eastern policies in the past is notable. Both accepted the Balfour Declaration and the British Mandate for Palestine, and the Soviet Union promptly followed the United States in recognition of Israel in May 1948. They were together in supporting the United Nations cease-fire in 1956, and in insisting upon withdrawal of the British and French forces, and the evacuation by Israel of the territories it had occupied, as the first step toward settlement of the Suez problem.

However, after the United States had affronted Arab opinion by the Eisenhower doctrine of 1957,[115] thought by the Arabs to manifest United States support of imperialism and Zionism, the Soviet Union has manifested a pro-Arab position, par-

---

[115] This doctrine, by declaring that "The United States is prepared to use armed force to assist any such [Middle Eastern] nation or group of such nations requesting assistance against armed aggression from any country controlled by international communism" (71 Stat. 5 (1957)), convinced the Arab countries, which had just experienced aggression, not from International Communism but from Israel, Great Britain, and France, that the United States had changed its policy which had opposed the latter aggressions. Only Lebanon, under a western-oriented government, among the Arab states accepted the Eisenhower doctrine, and that government was changed by revolution in 1958 partly because of this position conflicting with the Arab policy of "neutralism." See Wright, *United States Intervention in the Lebanon, supra* note 50, at 124. For further discussion of the Eisenhower Doctrine, see 5 M. WHITEMAN, DIGEST OF INTERNATIONAL LAW 1137-56 (1965).

ticularly after communist-oriented parties had developed, especially in Syria and
Iraq.

The United States has usually sought to be impartial in the Middle Eastern
controversies. It has been anxious to maintain friendly relations with the Arabs
because of the interest of American corporations in Middle Eastern oil and a general
interest in peace, but domestic politics have urged a pro-Israel policy because of the
extensive Zionist influence in such critical areas as New York City. Furthermore,
the cold war obsession of Americans has induced the Government to oppose the
Soviet Union and Middle Eastern states which accept Soviet aid. After the Soviet
Union had given financial and technical support to Egypt to build the Aswan Dam,
following United States repudiation of its offer to give such support in June 1956,
United States antagonism to Egypt increased.[116]

The positions of Great Britain and France have also been ambivalent. Great
Britain has favored the Jewish national home in Palestine, developed it as Mandatory
Power for nearly thirty years, and was responsible for placing the serious situation
which had developed in 1947 before the United Nations for solution. This resulted
in partition of Palestine as desired by the Zionists at that time. Great Britain was
also responsible for intervention in Egypt following Israel's invasion in 1956. It has,
however, supported the Arab League and the independence of Arab states.

France was allied with Israel and Britain against Egypt in the intervention of
1956 and had followed a pro-Israeli policy until the recent crisis during which it
has tended to support the Arab position.

The position of the Great Powers, therefore, seems somewhat flexible and elements
in the situation of both Israel and the Arabs militate against excessive rigidity. Arab
nationalism, especially Egyptian nationalism, urges avoidance of excessive dependence
upon the Soviet Union for arms, and experience in the three wars with Israel suggests caution in getting into another. Some Arab countries such as Tunisia and to
a lesser degree Jordan have urged accommodation with Israel.

Israel had a population, within the 1949 armistice lines, which included a majority
of oriental Jews most of whom speak Arabic, who feel discriminated against by the
government, controlled by European and American Jews, and who, with the two
hundred thousand resident Arabs, have favored accommodation with Arab neighbors.[117] It, therefore, would face a serious domestic problem if it attempted to
assimilate the recently occupied areas with more than half a million Arabs. If these

---

[116] See text accompanying note 21 *supra.* President Eisenhower wrote in his memoirs that the
Aswan loan was withdrawn because the Soviet offer was "blackmail" and that arms were refused to
Israel to balance those sent to Egypt by the Soviet Union for the same reason. DWIGHT D. EISENHOWER,
THE WHITE HOUSE YEARS: WAGING PEACE 1956-1961, at 25, 31 (1965). See also ANTHONY EDEN, FULL
CIRCLE 470 (1960).

[117] They professed their solidarity with Israel during the six-day war and appeared to support retention
of the occupied areas by Israel, but complained of discrimination in Israel's immigration and welfare
policies. See *Israel's Oriental Problem,* a monthly bulletin distributed by the Council of the Sephardi
Community, vol. 3, no. 1, at 4-5 (1967).

eas were retained with their present inhabitants, apart from the issue of legality, ιe western Jews now in control would be a minority of the population of Israel ;pecially if, as has been suggested, the refugee problem were liquidated by settling ιl the refugees in these areas. If these areas were accorded a semi-colonial status, Israel ιould jeopardize its claim to be a democracy unless a true federation of the Arab rea with Jewish Israel could be effected. If the present population of the recently ιccupied areas were deported or driven out, the refugee problem would be accentuated ιnd world opinion would be shocked. Annexation of Jerusalem was shocking to Christian and Moslem opinion as indicated by the large majority in the General Assembly opposing it. It seems doubtful whether the strategic advantages of holding the recently occupied territories can compensate for the internal and external difficulties Israel would encounter.

The suggestion that Jews abroad should not be admitted to Zionist organizations unless they promise to migrate to Israel within five years would not only militate against favorable support for Israel among American Jews, who do not usually wish to migrate, but suggests an effort to maintain a majority of westernized Jews to neutralize the influence of the Oriental Jews[118] and the Arabs in Israel, perhaps to fill the recently occupied areas if their inhabitants are expelled.

Both the Jews and the Arabs would undoubtedly benefit by reaching an accommodation and establishing peace in the Middle East. The Soviet Union, the United States and the world would all profit by eliminating the escalating possibilities of Middle Eastern hostilities. The Security Council's unanimous recommendation, on November 22, 1967, of a settlement, based on mutual recognition of the legal rights of both Israel and the Arabs, indicates a first step. A further step has been suggested by the leaders of the Oriental Jewish Community in Israel. They have proposed establishment of an "autónomous Palestinian Arab Entity in the occupied area in which all the refugees would be settled."[119] Many of the refugees of 1948 and 1949 are already there. A federation of Israel with such a Palestinian Arab state and perhaps with Jordan was proposed but considered impracticable in 1947. But political independence of these states with economic union was recommended by the United Nations and accepted by the Zionists in 1947 and, after military defeat in 1949, by the Arabs. Return to this proposal, repudiated by the victorious Zionists in 1949, might be considered.[120]

---

[118] Id.
[119] Id. at 7-8.
[120] Cf. note 53 supra.

A BINATIONAL APPROACH TO THE PALESTINE CONFLICT

DON PERETZ*

I

BINATIONALISM VERSUS EXCLUSIVITY

Binationalism as a possible solution to the bitter conflict between Arab and Jewish nationalisms in Palestine is not a novel conception. Thirty and even forty years ago there were Zionists such as Dr. Judah Magnes[1] and leaders of the *Ha-Shomer ha-Zair* movement[2] who conceived of binationalism as a middle way toward resolution of the conflict. However, neither Palestine Arab nationalists nor most Zionist leaders found such proposals meritorious. By the end of World War II when the Biltmore program[3] calling for a Jewish Commonwealth in Palestine had become accepted Zionist policy, and establishment of the country as an independent Arab state was the generally proclaimed goal of Palestine's Arab leaders,[4] a binationalist compromise seemed even more remote. Extermination of ninety per cent of Europe's Jews, and intensification of Arab nationalism deepened the rift between the two groups of peoples. Zionists, with the support of most organized world Jewry, by and large declared willingness to accept less than all of Palestine rather than surrender to a shared sovereignty. They preferred a smaller but exclusive Jewish state in part of the disputed area to a diluted control within a larger region. Without complete sovereignty, they believed, it would be impossible to achieve their total national

---

* B.A. 1945, University of Minnesota; M.A. 1952, Ph.D. 1955, Columbia University. Professor of Political Science and Director of the Southwest Asia North Africa Program, State University of New York at Binghamton, N.Y. Author, ISRAEL AND THE PALESTINE ARABS (1955); THE MIDDLE EAST TODAY (1963); THE MIDDLE EAST: SELECTED READINGS (1968).

[1] Dr. Judah Magnes was an American Zionist leader who became the first president of the Hebrew University in Jerusalem. He was among the first and leading proponents of an Arab-Jewish or binational solution to the Palestine problem. He died in 1948, shortly after the partition of Palestine. Dr. Magnes' position is set forth in J. MAGNES & M. BUBER, ARAB-JEWISH UNITY, TESTIMONY BEFORE THE ANGLO-AMERICAN COMMISSION FOR THE IHUD (UNION) ASSOCIATION (1947).

[2] *Ha-Shomer ha-Zair* (The Young Guard) is a Zionist youth movement established in Eastern Europe. Its founders became the leaders of the Mapam political party, a left wing Zionist socialist movement now represented in the Israel Parliament and government. It no longer supports binationalism. *See* 1 & 2 PALESTINE, A STUDY OF JEWISH, ARAB AND BRITISH POLICIES (published for the Esco Foundation for Palestine, Inc.) (1947).

[3] The Biltmore Program was adopted at a Zionist conference held at the Biltmore Hotel in New York City during May 1942. It called for establishment of Palestine "as a Jewish commonwealth." 2 *id.* at 1014.

[4] The principal leader of the Palestine Arab nationalists, Haj Amin al-Husayni, Mufti of Jerusalem and leader of the Palestine Arab Higher Committee, declared that "Zionists must not have an inch of this country" in 1947 at the time he and his followers organized a boycott and demonstrations against the inquiry into the dispute undertaken by the United Nations Special Commission on Palestine (UNSCOP). J. HUREWITZ, THE STRUGGLE FOR PALESTINE 294 (1950).

aspirations and to guarantee the unlimited immigration of Jews to Palestine which had become a major goal following Hitler's extermination of their coreligionists.

Arab nationalists, too, aspired to exclusive jurisdiction of Palestine. This was evident in their rejection of binationalist proposals and by their insistence that Jewish immigration be so curbed that an Arab majority in the country would be guaranteed in perpetuity.[5] It was so dangerous for any Arab of consequence to express public support for Magnes or his views that binationalism was labeled as merely another form of Zionist intrigue. Magnes himself has related that more than one of his Arab friends who dared openly to support binationalist views was either assassinated or otherwise effectively silenced through the use of violence.

The majority of United Nations members in 1947 recognized, in effect, Arab and Jewish demands for exclusivity of jurisdiction when they recommended partition of the disputed land.[6] Whereas most Palestine Jews and their supporters abroad joyfully accepted this supposed compromise, the country's Arab majority and their co-nationalists insisted that denial of complete sovereignty violated indigenous rights.[7] While the United Nations recommendation failed to effect any measure of real compromise, it (for all practical purposes) made a binationalist solution politically unrealistic. By the end of the 1948 Palestine war the concept of exclusivity was further strengthened since the new nation of Israel was almost an exclusive Jewish state, with only a tiny, politically ineffective Arab minority.[8] The remnants of geographic Palestine were exclusively Arab since no Jews remained in Egyptian occupied Gaza or what was to become the Hashemite Kingdom of Jordan's West Bank. Very soon most of the former proponents of binationalism accepted the new status quo and now characterized the idea as anachronistic.

There was little reason for political realists to remain loyal to the binationalist concept. It received no public support from any respected Arab leader or political group. On the contrary, the stated goal of most Arab nationalists remained re-creation of an Arab Palestine to include the territory of the Jewish state.[9] Both Arabs and Zionists retained the goal of complete sovereignty.

---

[5] *Id.*

[6] By its resolution 181(II) the General Assembly endorsed the proposal of UNSCOP by a vote of 33 to 13 with 10 abstentions on November 29, 1947. The resulting Plan of Partition with Economic Union proposed to divide Palestine into a Jewish state of 5,500 square miles (about 55% of the total area), an international enclave to include Jerusalem and an Arab state comprising the rest of Palestine. 2 U.N. GAOR, Resolutions 131, 132, U.N. Doc. A/519 (1947).

[7] The Arab Higher Committee condemned the partition proposal as "null and void" and announced that it would refuse to participate in its implementation, calling on the British Government which held the Mandate for Palestine to turn the country over "to its Arab people." J. HUREWITZ, *supra* note 4, at 310.

[8] During the Palestine war of 1947-48, some 725,000 Arabs fled from areas occupied by Israel, leaving approximately 161,000 within Israel's armistice frontiers out of a total population of 1,173,000. STATISTICAL ABSTRACT OF ISRAEL 27 (1961).

[9] Although between 1949 and 1964 some Arab governments supported a compromise solution to the Palestine problem based on the U.N. partition resolution, at the Cairo Summit Conference of Arab Chiefs of State attended by delegations from Jordan, Algeria, Sudan, Iraq, Saudi Arabia, the United Arab Republic,

Experience elsewhere since World War II is hardly encouraging to binational or multi-national concepts. In new states created since the war, and in older, long established countries formed from two or more national, ethnic, linguistic, or religious groups, it is difficult to find supportive evidence for harmonious relationships resulting from their fusion within a single state. Among the new African countries one can readily find discouragement for multi-national concepts in the recent history of Nigeria, the insurrection of southern Negro peoples against the Arab Sudanese government, the revolt of the Buganda tribesmen against Uganda, the disruption of the Congo, and the collapse of the Mali Federation caused by the withdrawal of Senegal in 1960. In Asia recent experience is no more encouraging. Until today Burma is torn by conflicts between the Rangoon authorities and groups such as the Shans, Kachins, Karens, and others. Moving down the list of new Asian states to Indonesia, Vietnam, Laos, Thailand, Malaysia, and India the picture is also one of discontent, upheaval and failure by central authorities to maintain political equilibrium. Within the Middle East itself, the conflicts between Arabs and Kurds in Iraq, and between Greeks and Turks in Cyprus, indicate the extent of dissatisfaction within multi-national states.[10]

The longer-established Western nations offer little, if any, more hope. In recent months Canada and Belgium have captured world attention through their internal ethnic conflicts. And from the Soviet Union and Yugoslavia are heard rumors of dissent and dissatisfaction based upon national differences. It seems that one of the major political dilemmas facing the modern world is how to reconcile the claims of diverse groups within effectively centralized multi-national states.[11]

Returning to Palestine, we are here faced with similar dilemmas. On the one hand evidence from both Arabs and Jews during the last half century seems to point overwhelmingly to the impossibility of shared jurisdiction within a single political entity. Their continued demands for exclusive jurisdiction in the disputed territory of Palestine militate against compromise. Yet without compromise over the crucial question of jurisdiction, even an easing of tensions, to say nothing of solution, does not seem to be in view. Continuation of the status quo in political relationships

Yemen, Kuwait, Lebanon, and Libya (*i.e.*, all Arab League states except Tunisia and Morocco), during January 1964, those present unanimously agreed to organize "the people of Palestine to enable them to liberate its homeland and determine its future." *See* L. KADI, ARAB SUMMIT CONFERENCES AND THE PALESTINE PROBLEM (1936-1950) (1964-1966) (Palestine Books No. 4, 1966) (Research Center, Palestine Liberation Organization, Beirut).

[10] For a survey of the question "Can two or more self-differentiating culture-groups co-exist within a single political structure?" see Connor, *Self-Determination*, 20 WORLD POLITICS 30 (1967).

[11] In Nigeria, for example, it is difficult not to sympathize with the plight of the Biafrans, for their secessionist state is formed from an attractive, intelligent, and creative people. If allowed to pursue its own policies free from outside intervention, Biafra may well have developed into a viable and progressive country. Yet international opinion has overwhelmingly supported the central government in Lagos in opposition to Biafran claims for exclusive national jurisdiction within their territory. Most African nations, Nigeria's former British administrators and the major world powers of both East and West oppose the secessionist state. Does this implicitly mean support for multi-nationalism as the lesser and least disruptive of choices?

threatens not only Arabs and Israelis, but the political equilibrium of the entire international community.   While Arab and Zionist nationalist claims remain irreconcilable, the superpowers and even lesser states with aspirations for influence in the Middle East are attracted to support one side or the other.   The result is that Palestine has become a major area of tension in the competition and conflict among world powers and among nations which aspire to become powers.

Often the key issue in the Palestine conflict has been lost sight of, and symptoms have been regarded as causes of continued tension.   Most obvious in this diversion has been the attempt to isolate subsidiary or secondary issues such as the refugee problem, borders, the status of Jerusalem, and division of the region's scarce water resources.   But, failure to bring Arabs and Israelis to agreement on any of these issues is symptomatic of the key problem of jurisdiction over the territory of Palestine.[12]

II

A BINATIONAL PLAN FOR THE FUTURE OF PALESTINE

The Arab-Israeli war of June 1967 radically altered the dimensions of this jurisdictional conflict, although not its essence.   The Israeli victory placed Zionist nationalism in a position where it controls and for the time being has exclusive jurisdiction over all the disputed territory.   On the other hand, victory radically altered the demographic aspect of the problem.[13]   The territory under Israeli jurisdiction is no longer inhabited by a nearly exclusively Jewish population.   It is now inhabited by two principal national groups, Jews and Arabs.[14]

---

[12] The literature on these various aspects of the Palestine problem is vast.   For a summary statement on their significance, see Peretz, *Israel and the Arab Nations*, in J. THOMPSON & R. REISCHAUER, MODERNIZATION OF THE ARAB WORLD 166 (1966).

[13] The territory occupied by Israel during the June 1967 six-day war included the Gaza Strip and the West Bank of Palestine between the armistice frontiers and the Jordan River.   The former was Egyptian-occupied territory, while the latter had been incorporated into the Hashemite Kingdom of Jordan during 1949.   In addition, Israel occupied the Sinai Peninsula and the Golan Heights of Syria. The total occupied area was thus three or four times that of Israel.   According to the latest issue of the Israel statistical yearbook published by the Israeli Government in Jerusalem, as of September 1967, the population of the state, including East Jerusalem, totaled 2,758,400 people, of whom 2,371,100 were Jews.   The population of the occupied areas, according to a government census, totaled 995,000, of which 599,000 lived in the West Bank; 365,000 in the Gaza Strip; 33,000 in Northern Sinai, and 6,400 in the Golan Heights.   This was considerably smaller than the Arab population of these areas before June 4, 1967, due to the exodus of about 250,000 refugees, mostly from the West Bank.   *See* ECONOMIC PLANNING AUTHORITY, PRIME MINISTER'S OFFICE, THE WEST BANK: AN ECONOMIC SURVEY (Hebrew) (Jerusalem, 1967).

[14] There are many who argue that the Jews are not a national group but a religious group. This, however, seems to be a rather theoretical argument that non-Israelis may fruitfully discuss in a philosophic vein. The Jews of Israel do constitute a national group in the light of all modern concepts of the term nation, that is, they are a group with a common language, and religion, and even more fundamentally, a group which identifies with a common past, present, and future, a self identified group.   Jews abroad may or may not choose to identify with their coreligionists in Israel as an extension of the "Jewish *nation*."   Many have chosen to be so identified, a few have renounced such national identification, and most others remain ambivalent and confused about their identity with fellow Jews in Israel. Ironically, many Zionists dispute Arab claims to national status, charging that the Arab world is a

While the June war brought great tragedy to the region, increasing by thousands the number of dead and wounded victims of the conflict, and greatly increasing the number of refugees and displaced persons, both Arabs and Jews, it may also offer hope of an alternative to continued strife over the exclusive jurisdiction of Palestine.[15] Failure to take advantage of this opportunity will probably lead to renewed warfare, thousands of additional victims and increased numbers of refugees.[16]

The approach to an easing of tensions that I propose here is not intended as a definitive solution to the Arab-Israel conflict. Nor am I hopeful that it will find support among any substantial number of Arabs or Jews. My intention in making these suggestions is to stimulate new lines of thought. It might be useful for those concerned with this conflict to think in other than conventional terms about its solution. I realize the obstacles and difficulties in turning to new lines of thought in connection with this or with any major international problem so beclouded by emotion and fierce partisanship. In the case of Palestine discussion of solutions which go beyond the conventional framework of a Jewish or an Arab state is often suspect and therefore cast aside as irrelevant. Thus there are few Jews and even fewer Arabs who have begun to re-examine the conflict in the hope that some new approach may be applied.[17] I would like to further encourage those somewhat visionary individuals who have thought in unique terms about solutions, and to encourage others to give more serious thought to their ideas and suggestions.

Obviously Israeli Jews and Palestine Arabs will not, nor could they, create a binational state tomorrow, or even perhaps within the next decade. The deep suspicions, mistrust, and hatreds that separate them would be enough to prevent their cooperation in any effort which so closely touches their vital existence. Furthermore, there are great practical obstacles to fusion in a single political entity in the near future. The economic and cultural gap between Israeli Jews and Palestine Arabs is far wider than the gaps which separate other disparate groups which have unsuccessfully tried to unite politically in recent years. Israel is today a Western

---

diverse region devoid of any real national character. But the same standards apply to Arabs as well as Jews. By and large the Arabs are self-identified as a national group with common attributes in language, a historical past, present and future, despite their division into a congeries of many different political forms.

[15] There have only been estimates of Arab casualties in the June war. They indicate that Egyptian, Syrian and Jordanian military dead and wounded totaled tens of thousands. These included some 5,000-10,000 Egyptian soldiers killed in Sinai and about 6,000 Jordanian soldiers killed or missing in the West Bank. Israeli dead were approximately 700 and seriously wounded only about 2,500. *See Facts on File, Keesings Contemporary Archives*, and the *New York Times* for June through October 1967.

[16] The total number of refugees is estimated at about 250,000 in Jordan, 125,000 in Syria, 30,000 in the United Arab Republic, and 300,000 displaced persons from the Suez Canal Zone. The number is not constant since there was a continuing displacement of Arabs from Israel to Jordan at the rate of 7,000 per week in the months immediately after the war. *See* Peretz, *Israel's New Arab Dilemma*, 22 THE MIDDLE EAST JOURNAL 45 (1968); Report of the Secretary-General Under General Assembly Resolution 2252 (ES-V) and Security Council Resolution 237 (1967), U.N. Docs. A/6797 and S/8158 (1967).

[17] For various approaches by different Israeli groups to the problems following the six day war, see volumes 10 and 11 of *New Outlook*, a Middle East monthly published in Tel-Aviv, Israel. For a new Arab viewpoint, see Hourani, *The Moment of Truth*, ENCOUNTER, Nov. 1967, at 3.

oriented, European nation. Its vital statistics in matters such as literacy, birth and death rates, level of per capita income, occupational distribution, taxation, social welfare and public expenditure, indicate that it is much more of the West than of the Arab world.[18] While tens of thousands of Palestinians have made great strides in improving their individual material status, in increasing the level of their technological and scientific sophistication, and in broadening their world outlook during recent decades, the Palestine Arab community is still largely a rural, peasant community, more of Asia than of the West. Although tens of thousands of Palestinians have acted as leavening agents in the progress of the Arab world since the 1950s, the greater number of Palestinians who remained in Jordan, and in the areas now occupied by Israel, are members of a traditional community with an outlook on the world and a philosophy of life which are quite at variance with those of their Israeli neighbors.

Therefore no political realist could conceive that these two disparate groups of people could be hastily fused into a single state—even if such fusion were the only answer to their conflicting claims for the territory which they both hold dear.

Although these groups are so vastly different, the fact that they live so closely and in some places so intermixed, necessitates their interaction. Until today, interaction between them has been marked more by violence or the threat of violence than by peaceful cooperation. Because each side has feared its ultimate national extinction, each has demanded, and has fought for, exclusive jurisdiction over its territory and the people within that territory. For each side the struggle has been a matter of national life or death. With Israel's victory in June, the concept of Palestine as a national entity, a state in which Palestinian Arabs would have exclusive sovereignty, seems to have died—thus the rallying cries by most Arab nationalists of support for Palestinian underground fighters. There is the hope that violent actions will keep alive the sparks of a Palestinian national consciousness, and the concept of a Palestinian Arab political entity.[19]

However, is the absolute sovereignty for which Zionists and Arab nationalists have been fighting a *sine qua non* for realization of their ultimate goals, or for continued existence? Could the Arab life or the Jewish life toward which nationalists aspire be lived in a state where the respective groups do not have exclusive political jurisdiction, in a state where political sovereignty is shared? Are a Palestine Arab army, or a Jewish military complex, a predominantly Arab or Jewish parliament or civil service, essential to guarantee that Arab children go to Arab schools, that Jews lead fully Jewish lives, that cultural images and symbols and historical nostalgias are not forgotten?

---

[18] For a comparison of differences between Israel and West Bank Arab demographic and economic status, see Sheshkin, *Economic Structure of the West Bank*, NEW OUTLOOK, Sept.-Oct. 1967, at 20.

[19] Shammas, *Armed Struggle is the Only Way*, Beirut Star, Feb. 4, 1968, an article on possibilities of merging Arab commando units. *See also No Alternative* (editorial), Beirut Star, Feb. 25, 1968.

It seems that continuation of present tensions will lead to renewed warfare in which the creative aspects of Jewish and Arab culture will become secondary to military culture. In their quest for political exclusivity, both peoples will be forced to surrender many constructive aspects of their national lives. As the science of warfare and military technology become increasingly complicated and prohibitively expensive, ever larger amounts of indigenous talent, national wealth, and public effort will have to be channeled into defense of exclusive political rights. It would indeed be an ironic twist of history if for the sake of maintaining an exclusively Jewish army to protect an exclusively Jewish state, traditional Jewish learning were lost. Yet this is no remote possibility. Today both Israel and its Arab neighbors must make great sacrifices to keep the right of exclusive national jurisdiction. In less than a week in June 1967 the United Arab Republic alone lost military equipment and supplies whose value was nearly that of the High Nile Dam,[20] a project in which that nation had invested a decade of its best talents and major resources. The cost of the war to Israel has been estimated at nearly one-third that amount, or the price of several Hebrew Universities, a landmark, which if it is permitted to endure, will be of far greater significance to the world as a symbol of Jewish accomplishment than victory in the Six Day War, or than the Jewish army which exists to defend exclusive political jurisdiction.

Switzerland is an instructive historical case in which political jurisdiction does not necessarily mean dilution of cultural or religious life. If sovereignty in Palestine were shared in a similar fashion between Jews and Arabs the billions spent to defend or to acquire exclusive jurisdiction could be used to raise substantially both Jewish and Arab national prestige and to preserve and strengthen Jewish and Arab national cultures through greatly expanding the number of Hebrew and Arab universities, the Hadassah medical complexes, and the High Nile, Euphrates, and Jordan dams.[21]

However, as history has shown, where great emotional commitments and investments have been made, even the most rational men often find that that which is rational seems to be beyond their accomplishment. Indeed, it may often seem to be irrational since it does not conform to their own conception of orderly processes

---

[20] Estimates of the value of military equipment lost by Egypt in the June war range between one and two billion dollars. President Nasser informed an interviewer from *Look* magazine that 80% of the Egyptian army was lost. Israel's finance minister reported the cost of the war to Israel at about $750 million. 1967 FACTS ON FILE 500; Attwood, *Nasser Talks*, LOOK, March 19, 1968, at 61.

[21] Under the Swiss system, governmental powers are divided or shared by federal authorities and twenty-three cantons which make up the Swiss federation. There are major linguistic, religious and economic differences between the cantons so that each canton or group of cantons has vital interests and cultural orientations which are distinctive from those of its neighbors. While under the old confederation from 1291 to 1798, there were serious disagreements among these diverse groups, occasionally resulting in war between them, since the mid-nineteenth century they have been able to reconcile their differences in a federation that has withstood the strains of European wars between nations which had the sympathies of one or another group of Swiss. *See* THE FEDERAL CONSTITUTION OF SWITZERLAND (C. Huges ed. 1954).

and ideal solutions. Therefore, I do not propose that Arabs and Israelis meet to-morrow at a drafting table to plan the liquidation of their exclusive national claims.

While a binational state in Palestine is unattainable in the immediate future, there are steps toward such a solution that many could accept who otherwise disagree with the binational principle. One such step has already been taken in placing the disputed territory and its strategic hinterlands under a single political authority. In ordinary circumstances this step could not easily have been realized. It is one of many results of a cataclysmic disaster. Other results of the disaster cannot be modified, such as restoration of the thousands of lost lives, or replenishment of the billions of wasted dollars. The placing of Palestine under a single political juris-diction could be altered in a variety of ways. One would be to restore the status quo that existed on June 4, 1967. However, restoration of that status quo would not substantially improve the lot of most people affected by the conflict. Israel would gain little if anything by restoration of the pre-June military situation. Most of the Arab refugees would still be refugees, and those who were not would return to a situation still filled with tension, and the continued possibility if not probability of war. Another alternative, suggested by some Israelis is incorporation of all, or parts, of the so-called occupied territories within Israel. Obviously this is unacceptable to Arabs, as it is to many Israelis. It would not guarantee peace. On the contrary, it would lead to an upsurge of Palestinian Arab irredentism and the outbreak of in-creased guerrilla activity against the Government of Israel. A third alternative would be establishment of a binational state now. But since neither Palestinians nor Israelis are yet ready for the cooperation prerequisite to the peaceful operation of a binational state, this alternative is not now feasible.

An effective step at this time might be to change the juridical status of occupied Palestine with the consent of the people who live there and who consider it their home. Many local government functions are presently being carried out in the occupied territories by Palestinians who carried them out when the territory was governed by Jordan.[22] Might it not be possible to increase these functions with a view to developing a total system of self-government by Arab Palestinians? This could have appeal to inhabitants of the occupied territories only if the symbolism of occupa-tion ceased to exist. To win Arab cooperation for peaceful and mutually beneficial

---

[22] Prevailing policy of the Israeli military government is to comply with the 1949 Geneva Convention Relative to the Protection of Civilian Persons in Time of War. In essence this means continuation of the status quo in local administration and reflects the following general principles: (a) the limited and temporary nature of occupation, (b) that sovereignty is not vested in the occupation, (c) that the prime duty is the establishment of order in the occupied area, (d) that the minimum alteration should be made to the existing administration, economy, legal system and general life of the occupied community, and (e) that the minimum is to be determined by the restrictions and changes properly imposed for the security of the occupant's armed forces and civil administration.

Early in 1968 Israel stated that the territory occupied in June would no longer be called "enemy territory," leaving its status in limbo and arousing Arab suspicions that it would be incorporated into Israel. N.Y. Times, March 1, 1968, at 1, col. 4.

development of the West Bank, military occupation would have to be demilitarized. Planning for the occupied areas can be effective only if undertaken with Arab cooperation.[23] If it is merely imposed upon the inhabitants it will no doubt be resisted.

The Arabs of Palestine also have responsibilities if they desire to avert continued bloodshed and warfare. They cannot expect self-determination at the expense of Jewish lives or Israeli security. It would be unreasonable to expect termination of Israel's occupation policies without assurance that cessation of these policies will also mean an end of Arab guerrilla warfare against Jews. If there were to be a *quid pro quo* for ending the guerrilla warfare, it might be expected that Palestinian Arab leaders could terminate it in the interest of their own and their peoples' welfare.

Jerusalem is a key to improved relationships between Israelis and Palestinian Arabs. Few, if any, of the city's 65,000 or 70,000 Arabs have reconciled themselves to becoming Israeli citizens.[24] There is not one Arab leader who has accepted this status. Without an accommodation between the Arab and Jewish inhabitants of Jerusalem, accommodation elsewhere is hardly likely. A status imposed by one side on the city is not an accommodation and will only exacerbate the existing tensions, inflame irredentist sentiments, and encourage Arab guerrillas and their supporters. Accommodation is possible without rebuilding the barriers that walled off Jews and Arabs from contact during the past twenty years. However, it does not mean complete and utter submission to the conquerors. Jerusalem might well become the testing ground for binationalism by making it not merely a Jewish but a joint capital for the Jewish sections of Palestine now called Israel, and for the Arab sectors which could be made self-governing. Within Jerusalem, Arab city officials who were responsible for Arab sectors of the city before June could continue to be responsible in the same way and with the same authority that they held then. Jewish officials could continue to manage their sectors of the city without surrendering any of its Jewishness. A major difference would be that all Palestinians, Jews and Arabs, and all non-Palestinians who desire to visit any sector of the city would be permitted to do so. Many municipal services such as water, electricity, sanitation, and the like would be jointly planned and operated for the city as a whole. Palestinian Arabs would again become responsible for Arab education, and for maintaining cultural and religious aspects of life that had previously been their responsibility.

If Arabs and Jews could effectively cooperate in Jerusalem, reaching mutually satisfactory accommodation there, might not the example of their efforts be applied in other parts of Palestine where the Arab population is essentially similar in its

---

[23] In regard to Israeli plans for the occupied territory and failure to obtain consent of the Arab inhabitants, see Peretz, *Israel's Administration and Arab Refugees*, 46 FOREIGN AFFAIRS 336 (1968).

[24] On Jerusalem Arab attitudes toward the Israeli "integration" of Arab and Jewish Jerusalem, see statement by former Mayor of Jordanian Jerusalem, Rouhi al-Khatib, N.Y. Times, March 20, 1968, at 11, col. 1.

cultural-linguistic patterns and nationalist outlook? If accommodation fails in Jerusalem it is unlikely to succeed elsewhere for similar reasons.

A further step toward developing cooperation among the two peoples might be establishment of a Palestinian Arab parliament, to parallel the predominantly Jewish Knesset.[25] This parliament could be entrusted with forming a government for the largely Arab areas of Palestine, including those in Israel such as Nazareth or the Little Triangle adjoining the former Jordanian frontier. If this body were entrusted with responsibilities for education, social welfare, and other such matters on behalf of all Palestine Arabs, its authority need in no way derogate from the responsibilities which Jews feel they must necessarily carry in order to preserve their Jewish life and culture. I am not suggesting that this diffusion of responsibility take place tomorrow or the day after, but only after it has been attempted on a small pilot scale in Jerusalem where it could now be undertaken unilaterally with agreement by Israel and the Arab population of the city.

Certain national functions might be delegated by the Arab and Jewish parliaments to a central federal authority or third parliamentary body which would represent both Arab and Jewish communities. Representation in this body might be based on the present numerical division in the country between Jews and Arabs, or it might be fixed constitutionally so that both national groups had equal representation. What if a deadlock were to occur at the federal level between Jews and Arabs? I am sure that if such a system were imposed today, there would be deadlock. But if both Arabs and Jews realize within the next few years that their demands for exclusive jurisdiction will lead only to renewed warfare, and if both sides are willing to experiment with a peaceful accommodation in Jerusalem, then the way will be paved toward the binational entity that has been briefly outlined here.

A question may well be asked about the fate of Jordan in such a visionary scheme. It is Jordan which has suffered more than any other country from the June war. Even before Jerusalem and the West Bank were torn away from Jordan there was serious question about the country's viability. Now the question is even more serious whether Jordan can remain a viable state without half its population and the major source of its sparse foreign currency earnings.[26] An additional step in the long-term process outlined above might be inclusion of Jordan as a third partner in the proposed federal state of Palestine.[27] Jordan, with its large Palestinian population, and Arab Palestine might again become a single entity within the larger federation. In either case, Jerusalem could again become an Arab capital shared with Israel

---

[25] Although there have been five and eight Arabs in the 120-member Israel Knesset, they are either tied to the Zionist Mapam or Mapai party or to the Communist Party. Only the latter is considered by Arabs to represent Arab interests; therefore, although there is formal representation of the Arab community of Israel in parliament, it is not considered by most Arabs to be truly representative.

[26] See Report of the Secretary-General, supra note 16, at 76-89; Beeson, Hard Times for Jordan, Beirut Star, Feb. 5, 1968.

[27] The Swiss Cantonal system might be instructive. See generally THE FEDERAL CONSTITUTION OF SWITZERLAND (C. Huges ed. 1954).

under two flags. The establishment of a rudimentary common market between Israel, Jerusalem, the West Bank, and Jordan, authorized when Israel re-established trade and commercial links across the Jordan River, may be the first unwitting step toward the proposal which is outlined above.[28]

Modification of the concept of exclusive jurisdiction along the lines I have proposed would resolve many of the problems that have plagued the area in the form of the so-called "Palestine dispute." Steps toward shared sovereignty would resolve questions about Israel's borders disputed by its Arab neighbors since the 1949 armistice agreements. With Jerusalem as a joint capital, the dilemma of internationalizing the holy city and its surrounding holy sites could easily be settled since they would be the special preserve of no single religious group. Some eighty per cent of the Palestine refugees and their offspring would be home again in a binational Palestine within the borders of the present Israel-occupied territories.

To become a vital and effective political organism a binational Arab-Jewish state would have to guarantee complete equality to all its citizens, giving special prerogatives to no single group. Complete equality in cultural, religious, linguistic, and political affairs would in effect mean that a binational state would no longer be merely a Jewish, a Zionist, or an Arab state, but a nation of diverse but similar groups. Such a nation would no longer be that nation which has been the target of Arab nationalist antagonism for over two decades.[29]

A binational state could not come into existence unless there were peace between it and its Arab neighbors. Without peace, it would constantly be torn by religious and ethnic dissension as each group sought to impose its will on the other. Only if such a state could be guaranteed free access to all waterways, freedom of trade and communications, and security of its borders could it flourish. Great power guarantees ending the disastrously expensive arms race and assuring economic assistance to the old and new Arab refugees would be required.

If it were to flourish, such a state could make major contributions to economic, cultural and social development of the Middle East, for as Israeli scientists and scholars lend their services to other nations in Asia, Africa and Latin America today, they could in a peaceful Middle East as citizens of a binational Palestine lend their services to the whole Arab world. The Arab world could contribute much to a truly Middle Eastern binational Palestine by assisting it to integrate into and to become part of the region. The economic union envisaged between binational Palestine and Jordan giving the latter access to Mediterranean ports and to its agricultural, mineral, and industrial resources now in Israeli hands could well be the foundation for a greater Middle East common market.

True, this vision of a peaceful Middle East may seem as much a fantasy as a

---

[28] Trade barriers are being lifted gradually. See Ha-Aretz and Jerusalem Post, Aug. 1967—Feb. 1968.
[29] See Peretz, *Israel and the Arab Nations, supra* note 12, for discussion of causes of Arab animosity to Israel.

Soviet-American detente, or as a world without war. Is there, however, a peaceful alternative? Can peace be imposed on the Arabs by a militarily powerful Israel, or can an Israeli withdrawal imposed by a combination of world powers bring peace and security to the area? The region has been torn asunder by the continuous struggle between Zionist and Arab nationalisms for nearly half a century. Only if these two nationalisms can devise a new formula for living together can they avoid a fourth round of even more destructive war within five, ten or twenty years!

DIRECTIONS FOR A MIDDLE EAST SETTLEMENT— SOME UNDERLYING LEGAL PROBLEMS

Shabtai Rosenne*

I
Introduction

A. Legal Framework of Arab-Israeli Relations

The invitation to me to participate in this symposium suggested devoting attention primarily to the legal aspects and not to the facts. Yet there is great value in the civil law maxim: *Narra mihi facta, narabo tibi jus.* Law does not operate in a vacuum or in the abstract, but only in the closest contact with facts; and the merit of legal exposition depends directly upon its relationship with the facts.

It is a fact that as part of its approach to the settlement of the current crisis, the Government of Israel is insistent that whatever solution is reached should be embodied in a secure legal regime of a contractual character directly binding on all the states concerned.

International law in general, and the underlying international legal aspects of the crisis of the Middle East, are no exceptions to this legal approach which integrates law with the facts. But faced with the multitude of facts arrayed by one protagonist or another, sometimes facts going back to the remotest periods of prehistory, the first task of the lawyer is to separate the wheat from the chaff, to place first things first and last things last, and to discipline himself to the most rigorous standards of *relevance* that contemporary legal science imposes. The authority of the International Court itself exists for this approach: the irony with which in 1953 that august tribunal brushed off historical arguments, in that instance only going back to the early feudal period, will not be lost on the perceptive reader of international jurisprudence.[1]

Another fundamental question which must be indicated at the outset relates to the very character of the legal framework within which the political issues are to be discussed and placed. A close study of presentations made by Arab spokesmen

---

* LL.B. 1938, University of London; Ph.D. 1959, Hebrew University of Jerusalem. Ambassador, Deputy Permanent Representative of Israel to the United Nations. Member of the Israel bar, and of the International Law Commission and the Commission on Human Rights of the United Nations. Associate of the Institute of International Law. Author, The Law and Practice of the International Court (1965), and various works on the law of Israel and on international law.

Insofar as a person holding an official and representative position can maintain personal views, the opinions expressed in this article are not necessarily those of the government which the author has the honor to represent.

[1] Minquiers and Ecrehos Case, [1953] I.C.J. 47, 56. Note its reference to "historical controversies." Likewise, in the *Temple of Preah Vihear Case*, the court refused to regard as legally decisive various arguments of a "physical, historical, religious and archaeological character." [1962] I.C.J. 6, 15.

may lead to the conclusion that very frequently they fall back not on objective and established principles and rules of contemporary international law, but on subjective, vague and, on the whole, discredited theories of natural law and natural justice, whatever those terms might mean—indeed it is never clear whether they have in mind the so-called *jus naturae* or the *jus naturale*. The word "discredited" is used not in a disparaging sense—the great importance which the very concept of natural law played in the primitive period of the history of international law and in its evolution as a branch of science distinct from theology, in which its roots were once embedded, is well known. The expression is employed in the sense that natural law and natural justice are undisciplined and highly subjective concepts or, at most, concepts of an exclusively philosophical character meaning all things to all men. *Quot homines, tot sententiae!* With all its vagueness and imperfections, positive international law today does provide the generally accepted standards of international conduct: it is to positive international law, both conventional and customary, and only to positive international law, that rights and obligations, whether synallagmatic or not, are traced. This is not to imply that natural law concepts and natural law approaches are of no value. Very frequently, they inspire the development of the law—both the creation of new law and the evolution of existing law—and even more frequently what might be called the natural sense of the lawyer is an essential element in the interpretation and application of the law. However, in the present case, the so-called natural law appears as a meta-juridical element. It is not the law, and it creates neither rights nor obligations. To some it would appear that reliance on natural law is a recognition that there is no case in law.

This factor is significant with regard to the Middle Eastern crisis because the more one probes into the matter, the more one is shocked by the absence of an accepted legal framework common to Israel and the Arab States within which debate is conducted and by the manner in which the Arab spokesmen reject received law as the standard-setting agent. Even the Charter of the United Nations is brushed aside or accorded perfunctory attention by the Arab diplomats, who prefer arbitrary interpretations unsupported by commonly accepted canons of legal workmanship. In fact, at times one is left with the impression that all that remains as a framework of the debate are the Rules of Procedure of whatever organ might be discussing the matter at a given moment, and even these are as often breached as observed.

B. Role of the International Court of Justice

Criticism is frequently advanced by these same proponents of a natural law approach to the case by reason of the fact that although, on several occasions since 1947, legal questions have been formulated for the purpose of seeking an advisory opinion from the International Court of Justice, neither the Security Council nor the General Assembly has ever decided to request an advisory opinion.[2] (Paren-

---

[2] For details, see 2 S. ROSENNE, THE LAW AND PRACTICE OF THE INTERNATIONAL COURT 665 (Gen-

thetically it may be observed that before World War II, the Jewish side felt that the Mandatory Government was not properly applying the Mandate and that certain legal issues ought to have been put by the competent organs of the League of Nations to the Permanent Court of International Justice and this, too, was never done.)

Several observations can be made on this criticism. As a matter of common practice, it is characteristic of the United Nations that the political organs have, in general, and probably wisely, refrained from submitting legal questions for advisory opinion in the course of their handling of political issues. The reasons for this are deep. They can be found in the whole structure of the United Nations and in the limited and ambiguous role which the Charter envisages for the advisory opinion in the course of political action by the Security Council and the General Assembly. Experience of the use of the advisory opinion in political circumstances seems to indicate two things at least: (a) that before the advisory procedure can be put to fruitful use, there has to be some measure of general agreement that the judicial pronouncement, *whatever it might be*, would facilitate the political decisions; and (b) that in the circumstances there is a reasonable measure of agreement between the states concerned that procedures available under the Statute of the International Court of Justice would be appropriate for the determination of given and agreed issues. Here, the United Nations presents no analogy with the League of Nations where the requirement of unanimity ensured that both these factors were thoroughly examined before the Council of the League decided to request an advisory opinion.[3] Examination of the questions which have been proposed for submission to the Court on the Palestine question since 1947 shows above all that those who sponsored them made no effort whatsoever to see if agreed formulations could be reached. They were one-sided, loaded questions and were treated as such by the competent political organs.

Since the question of the possible role of the Court in the Middle East crisis has been raised, it might be useful to reiterate that of all the states concerned only Israel has accepted the compulsory jurisdiction of the Court in its Declaration dated October 3, 1956 which is still in force.[4] It is an elementary principle of the law of the Court that the consent of the parties, whether expressed formally or in some informal manner, constitutes the only effective basis for judicial action; and this is as true of the contentious jurisdiction as it is of the advisory competence.

The Government of Israel has in the past expressed its reserves towards proposed references to the Court. The fundamental reason has always been the absence of

---

eral Assembly) and 668 (Security Council) (1965). Two cases arising out of the situation in Palestine have nevertheless been brought before the court, namely the Advisory Opinion on Reparation for Injuries Suffered in the Service of the United Nations, [1949] I.C.J. 174, and the Case Concerning the Protection of French Nationals in Egypt, [1950] I.C.J. 59.

[3] 2 S. ROSENNE, *supra* note 2, at 658.

[4] 252 U.N.T.S. 301.

the necessary consensual basis in fact. The proposals have not been seen as sincere attempts to obtain judicial determination of controverted issues which the parties have agreed should be judicially determined as part of the process of the pacific settlement of those issues, but rather as attempts to employ the judicial process for unilateral advantage. It may easily be the assumption that in such circumstances, the Court would have found it improper for it to have taken part in such an abuse of the judicial machinery.

C. Historic Issues

It is commonplace that, because of the central place it occupies in the history of human evolution, the Middle East evokes a host of mixed reactions. Their roots can be traced to many causes, but predominant among them are undoubtedly religious and psychological motives, the implications of the long and difficult history of the relations between the Jewish and the Christian worlds and the equally complex history of the relationships between the Christian and the Muslim worlds, this latter being symbolized by the spell which to this day the Crusades and all they stood for (and incidentally they were a very black period in Jewish history) cast upon the psychology of the peoples of the Middle East. One must also not ignore that the annals of Jewish-Muslim relations are not simply an uninterrupted succession of golden ages, as is sometimes inferred, but they, too, are characterized by episodic antisemitism of an extremely virulent character.

Thus questions frequently arise such as: the right of Great Britain to have disposed of the territory of Palestine during World War I; the legality of the Balfour Declaration, its interpretation, and its compatibility with other binding undertakings said to have been given by the British Government to others; the compatibility of the Mandate for Palestine with Article 22 of the Covenant of the League of Nations; the legality of the manner in which the Mandate was implemented; the appropriateness of the decision of the British Government in 1947 to remit the question of the future government of Palestine to the General Assembly of the United Nations; of the legitimacy of the decision then reached by the General Assembly and embodied in its well known resolution 181(II) of November 29, 1947, and so on. Much has been written and much no doubt will continue to be written on these and similar questions.

Although their existence as genuine and relevant legal questions may be open to doubt, a few general observations about some of these issues may be made.

Before the Peace Treaties that put an end to World War I, Palestine was part of the Ottoman Empire which, in 1914, in a manner fully in conformity with the international law of the epoch, joined the war as an active belligerent on the side of the Central Powers. During the war, the Allied Powers made certain arrangements between themselves regarding the disposition of various territories of the Ottoman Empire in the event they should be victorious. That was then and has remained a normal phenomenon of relations between allied belligerents. Ottoman sovereignty over the territory of Palestine, as over many other of its territories, was ceded to the Allied Powers in the Peace Treaty. No obvious ground is seen for challenging the title thus acquired by Great Britain as Mandatory on behalf of the League of Nations over Palestine.

The Balfour Declaration, contained in a letter dated November 2, 1917 from the British Foreign Secretary for the attention of the Zionist Federation, was also a part of the wartime political arrangements envisaged for the eventuality of the defeat of the Ottoman Empire.[5] Its precise legal status at the time it was made may be open to discussion but that problem is secondary in view of the fact that the Council of the League of Nations incorporated its text into the Preamble to the Mandate for Palestine[6] as follows:

> *Whereas* the Principal Allied Powers have also agreed that the Mandatory should be responsible for putting into effect the declaration originally made on November 2nd, 1917, by the Government of His Britannic Majesty, and adopted by the said Powers, in favour of the establishment in Palestine of a national home for the Jewish people, it being clearly understood that nothing should be done which might prejudice the civil and religious rights of existing non-Jewish communities in Palestine, or the rights and political status enjoyed by Jews in any other country; and
>
> *Whereas* recognition has thereby been given to the historical connection of the Jewish people with Palestine and to the grounds for reconstituting their national home in that country.

The formal and substantive validity of the Mandate for Palestine, as of all the other Mandates, is hardly a matter of discussion. As far back as 1924, the Permanent Court of International Justice interpreted and applied that Mandate and thus necessarily acknowledged its validity.[7] The International Court of Justice has pointed out in connection with the Mandate for South-West Africa, that a Mandate cannot be correctly regarded as embodying only an executive action by the Council of the League in pursuance of the Covenant but, in fact and in law, is an international agreement having the character of a treaty or convention.[8] This was carried into the Charter of the United Nations through the transitory provisions of Article 80 according to which "nothing . . . shall be construed in or of itself to alter in any manner the rights whatsover of any States or any peoples or the terms of existing international instruments to which Members of the United Nations may respectively be

---

[5] For text see Cmd. No. 5479, at 22 (1937). See in general L. Stein, The Balfour Declaration (1961).

[6] Cmd. No. 1785 (1922), reprinted in 2 U.N. GAOR, Supp. 11, U.N. Doc. A/364, Add. 1, at 18 (1947).

[7] See in particular the judgment of the Permanent Court of International Justice of August 30, 1924 in the Mavrommatis Palestine Concessions Case, [1924] P.C.I.J., Ser. A, No. 2.

[8] South-West Africa Cases, Preliminary Objections, [1962] I.C.J. 319, 330.

parties. . . ."[9] As the International Court of Justice said on another occasion, Article 80 "presupposes that the rights of States and peoples shall not lapse automatically on the dissolution of the League of Nations. It obviously was the intention to safeguard the rights of states and peoples under all circumstances and in all respects."[10]

II

ROLE OF THE UNITED NATIONS 1947-1967

In 1947 the question of the future Government of Palestine was submitted by the Mandatory Government to the General Assembly of the United Nations,[11] the only body competent under the Charter to deal with the future of the territories formerly under League of Nations Mandate, and, after exhaustive examination of the problem,[12] the General Assembly recommended the termination of the Mandate and the partition of Palestine into a Jewish and Arab state which, together with an internationalized Jerusalem, would be linked in a plan of economic union.[13]

In the course of its examination of the issue, the General Assembly made appropriate arrangements to acquaint itself fully with the position of all sides. Both the Jewish Agency for Palestine[14] (a body whose establishment was authorized by the Mandate for Palestine and from which it derived its status) and the Arab Higher Committee,[15] which was commonly regarded as representative of the Palestinian Arabs, were invited to participate in accordance with the Rules of Procedure in the General Assembly's deliberations, quite apart from the fact that several Arab states themselves were already at that time members of the United Nations. The partition plan constituted the General Assembly's compromise solution for the conflicting claims to self-determination of the Jews and of the Arabs. All the claims and counterclaims had been carefully weighed and all the different interests as they then existed had been balanced.

The Jewish side accepted the compromise. The Arab side rejected it[16] and almost

---

[9] On the relationship between Article 80 and the rights of the Jewish people under the Balfour Declaration and the Mandate, in the conception of the San Francisco Conference, see Gilchrist, *Colonial Questions at the San Francisco Conference*, 39 AM. POL. SCI. REV. 982, 990-91 (1945).

In view of the attitude adopted at the time, it is curious today to hear Arab spokesmen relying on parts of the Balfour Declaration and the Mandate. *Nemo potest venire contra factum proprium!*

[10] International Status of South-West Africa Case, [1950] I.C.J. 128, 134.

[11] See J. ROBINSON, PALESTINE AND THE UNITED NATIONS, PRELUDE TO SOLUTION (1947) on the first phase.

[12] For the report of the United Nations Special Committee on Palestine (UNSCOP), see 2 U.N. GAOR, Supp. 11, U.N. Doc. A/364 (1947).

[13] G.A. Res. 181(II), 2 U.N. GAOR, Resolutions 131, 132, U.N. Doc. A/519 (1947).

[14] G.A. Res. 104(S-1), 2 U.N. GAOR, 1st Spec. Sess., Resolutions, at 6, U.N. Doc. A/310 (1947).

[15] G.A. Res. 105 (S-1), *id*. It might, however, be noted that on June 13, 1947 the Arab Higher Committee notified the Secretary-General of the United Nations that it would abstain from collaboration with UNSCOP. Report of UNSCOP, *supra* note 12, vol. 2, at 5. This was repeated on July 10, 1947. *Id*. at 8. And see paras. 32-34 of the Report of UNSCOP, *supra* note 12, vol. 1, at 4.

[16] *Cf*. the statements of the representatives of Saudi Arabia, Iraq, and Syria at the 128th Plenary meeting of the General Assembly on November 29, 1947, immediately after the adoption of resolution 181(II). 2 U.N. GAOR 1425-27 (1947).

from the outset openly used armed force to prevent its implementation. In its first special report to the Security Council of February 16, 1948, the United Nations Palestine Commission, which had been established to assist in the implementation of resolution 181(II), reported: "Powerful Arab interests, both inside and outside Palestine, are defying the resolution of the General Assembly and are engaged in a deliberate effort to alter by force the settlement envisaged therein."[17]

The Mandate over Palestine formally terminated at midnight of May 14-15, 1948 in conformity with the General Assembly's resolution and following the passing of the Palestine Act, 1948, by the British Parliament.[18] Simultaneously, the Jews of Palestine proclaimed the independence of Israel[19] which was immediately attacked not only by Arabs in Palestine but by the armed forces of the neighboring states. These forces rapidly advanced not only into the areas of Palestine which had been originally intended to form part of the Arab state, but beyond into parts of Palestine not destined for the Arab states, including Jerusalem. Thus at one and the same moment, the Mandate terminated, Israel proclaimed its independence, and the Arab-Israeli war began.

There is no formal declaration of war by the Arab states, it is true. A formal declaration of war in the sense of the third Hague Convention of 1907 would naturally have meant the recognition of Israel, something which the Arab states to this day have consistently avoided. But in lieu of the polite diplomatic communications customary even during World War II, there is a series of quite unambiguous statements made to different organs of the United Nations,[20] and these

---

[17] 3 U.N. SCOR, Spec. Supp. 2, at 11, U.N. Doc. S/676 (1948).

[18] Palestine Act of 1948, 11 & 12 Geo. 6, c. 27.

[19] For English translation, see 1 LAWS OF THE STATE OF ISRAEL 3 (authorized translation from the Hebrew). The principal operative paragraph of the Declaration contains the following sentence: "Accordingly, we . . . are here assembled . . . and, by virtue of our natural and historic right and on the strength of the resolution of the United Nations General Assembly hereby declare the establishment of a Jewish State . . . ." As Ben Gurion wrote later:

"[A] proposal was approved . . . to establish a Jewish state on the basis of the partition of the country. And once again the approved proposal was not acted upon until the Jews of the country proclaimed their independence, established their state, and defended it with their armed strength against all the Arab countries."

Jewish Survival, in ISRAELI GOVERNMENT YEAR-BOOK 1, at 32 (1953).

[20] See cablegram of May 15, 1948 from the Secretary-General of the League of Arab States to the Secretary-General of the United Nations, 3 U.N. SCOR, Supp., May 1948, at 83, U.N. Doc. S/745 (1948); cablegram of May 16, 1948 from the King of Transjordan to the Secretary-General of the United Nations, *id.* at 90, U.N. Doc. S/748 (1948); cablegram of May 15, 1948 from the Minister for Foreign Affairs of Egypt to the President of the Security Council, read into the record of the 292nd meeting of the Security Council on May 15, 1948. 3 U.N. SCOR, No. 66, at 2-3, U.N. Doc. S/743 (1948). Note, too, the answers given at the Council's 301st meeting on May 22, 1948 by the representatives of Egypt, Syria, Iraq and Lebanon to a questionnaire addressed to them by the Security Council. *Id.*, No. 72, at 6-17. For the questionnaire, see *id.*, Supp. May 1948, *supra*, at 90, U.N. Doc. S/753. For the reply by Saudi Arabia, see *id.* at 95 (U.N. Doc. S/772). For the refusal of Transjordan to reply, see U.N. Doc. S/760 (mimeographed only). Apparently the questionnaire was ignored by the Yemen. A similar questionnaire was addressed to the "Jewish Authorities in Palestine," and a reply, emanating from the Provisional Government of Israel, was given to the Security Council by a person designated in the *Official Records* as the representative of the Jewish Agency for Palestine, in the course of the 301st meeting. 3 U.N. SCOR, No. 72, at 8 (1948).

statements were accompanied by quite unambiguous actions. The Arab states have, each in its own way, made clear their position, that they regard themselves as being at war, in a state of belligerency with Israel. The absence of declarations of war is merely the absence of irrelevant formalities.

In that way, what Israel calls the War of Independence and which, as has regrettably transpired, was merely the first phase in a state of war which has now lasted for some twenty years, commenced. The Arab states partly succeeded in their objective. By dint of their efforts, they thwarted the implementation of that part of the General Assembly's resolution which aimed to give satisfaction to Arab aspirations and meet Arab claims for self-determination. Instead of Palestine being divided into an Arab state and a Jewish state, linked under the umbrella of an over-all economic union, the Arab parts of the country came under the occupation of Jordan and Egypt, respectively. This should be remembered today, when the right of the Arabs of Palestine to self-determination is asserted. It was they who rejected it in 1948. On the other hand, the Jews succeeded in beating off the Arab attacks on them.

This phase of the war was brought to an end by a series of armistice agreements negotiated directly by the parties under the chairmanship of a United Nations representative during the first seven months of 1949.[21] The central feature of those armistice agreements was their declared intention to form a transition to permanent peace, and their detailed provisions regarding the establishment and demarcation of the armistice lines to serve as a temporary expedient pending the drawing up of agreed frontiers. The armistice regime was a temporary stopgap measure which was supposed to bring an end to that military phase and constitute the basis for a peaceful settlement of all outstanding problems, including of course the Arab refugee problem.[22] The work of producing the peace settlement was conferred on the parties directly concerned, assisted by a three-power Palestine Conciliation Commission (United States, France, and Turkey), whose broad terms of reference were laid down by the General Assembly in its resolution 194 (III) of December 11, 1948.[22a]

It is not necessary now to trace in detail the tortuous paths followed by the Palestine Conciliation Commission. It is sufficient to state that by the end of 1951 it was leading nowhere.[23] Already by that time, the armistice agreements were coming under severe strain, and a very fundamental divergence of approach between

---

[21] See S. ROSENNE, ISRAEL'S ARMISTICE AGREEMENTS WITH THE ARAB STATES (1951); N. BAR-YAACOV, THE ISRAEL-SYRIAN ARMISTICE, PROBLEMS OF INTERPRETATION (1967). No comparable works of Arab provenance are known to us. For the official texts of the agreements, see 42 U.N.T.S. 251 (Egypt), 287 (Lebanon), 303 (Jordan), and 327 (Syria).

[22] Thus the Security Council, in its resolution 73 of August 11, 1949, after noting with satisfaction the conclusion of the agreements, expressed the hope that the governments concerned would by negotiations seek to extend their scope and seek agreement by negotiations on the final settlement of all outstanding questions.

[22a] 3 U.N. GAOR, pt. 1, Resolutions 21, U.N. Doc. A/810 (1948).

[23] Cf. Progress Report of the United Nations Conciliation Commission for Palestine covering the period from January 23 to November 19, 1951. 6 U.N. GAOR, Supp. 18, U.N. Doc. A/1985 (1951).

Israel and the Arab states—symptomatic of the fundamental differences on the very nature of the legal framework between them to which allusion has been made— began to make its presence felt as a matter of political reality. If this, which is ostensibly a question of interpretation, is mentioned now, it is because it seems that of all the many and complicated legal issues which lie behind the different strands of the Middle East situation, this is one of the most significant, both in terms of the concrete political situation which we face and in terms of the larger issues with which this symposium is concerned, namely, the test of international law in the contemporary world.

That difference of interpretation can be briefly summarized. I think it would be fair to the Arab states if their position were put in these words—it should be explained that the writer had the opportunity of discussing this very problem with an eminent lawyer in the service of Egypt in 1951, Mr. Waheed Raafat, at the time the greatest Egyptian authority on the law of the Suez Canal. He explained it in this way. Under the established law of nations, he said, an armistice is an incident of war, and the state of war continues until it is replaced by a peace treaty. The jural relations between the states concerned are governed by the laws of war. In support of this view, he adduced a number of learned authorities and many decisions of the Allied Prize Courts after the two World Wars. The only limitation on belligerent rights, the only contraction of the state of war which he could recognize, were those which flowed directly and specifically from the terms of the armistice agreement narrowly interpreted. This, in a nutshell, was the Arab view by 1951 and they seem to have held that view consistently all the time to this day, because a very similar doctrine was expounded by the representative of the United Arab Republic in the Security Council, at the end of last May.[24] Since then, the Khartoum Arab Summit Conference on September 1, 1967 reaffirmed the main principles of Arab policy, namely: no peace with Israel, no recognition of Israel, and no negotiations with it.[25] On the other hand, the Arab position does not apparently give any recognition to the principle of reciprocity, which occupies a central place in international legal relationships and one which is left untouched by the Charter.

Israel has not, as far as I am aware, expressed any views on what might have been the rules of international law before the League of Nations. What we do contest is that this is the law today, at all events as between members of the United Nations.[26] As a matter of principle we believe that the very existence of a state of war is utterly incompatible with membership in the United Nations and the obligations imposed by the Charter. We note that even the Council of the League took this view, in

---

[24] Cf. the statement of Ambassador El Kony at the 1343rd meeting of the Security Council on May 29, 1967. U.N. Doc. S/PV.1343, at 36 (1967).

[25] N.Y. Times, Sept. 2, 1967, at 1, col. 5.

[26] For an authoritative non-official Israeli exposition of that thesis, see N. FEINBERG, THE LEGALITY OF A "STATE OF WAR" AFTER THE CESSATION OF HOSTILITIES UNDER THE CHARTER OF THE UNITED NATIONS AND THE COVENANT OF THE LEAGUE OF NATIONS (1961).

connection with the dispute between Poland and Lithuania over Vilna,[27] and surely the Charter is not a retreat from the Covenant. That is a major premise. We go on to say that even regardless of that, the armistice agreements meant what they said and that they prohibited entirely any continuation of the state of war and any attempt to exercise belligerent rights on land, on sea or in the air, whether by regular military forces or by para-military forces and irregulars. This view, it seems to us, was forcefully upheld by the Security Council after a detailed discussion on this very issue, in its resolution 95 of September 1, 1951, as reaffirmed in a consensus decision of 1955.[28]

This is not a doctrinal refinement. It might be were it only a matter for academies and books. But when, on the one hand, it is juxtaposed with the subjective natural law concepts which are characteristic of so much of the Arab exposition on the legal and philosophical plane, and when, on the other hand, it is coupled with actions which under no circumstances are compatible with peaceful relations and are only to be explained as manifestations of claims of belligerency, of an *animus belligerendi*, it will be seen that the apparently technical issue of interpretation goes to the very roots of Arab-Israeli relations. For reduced to essentials, it is a symbol for the real crisis in the Middle East, a crisis which in substance has not changed from 1948 to this day. On the level of practical politics, the two theses are utterly irreconcilable and their existence side by side is a guarantee for political instability, to put it at its lowest, and a prescription for a fighting war when the tension reaches boiling point.

That is precisely what has happened. Scarcely was the ink dry on the armistice agreements when the old story of forays, raids, infiltration, acts of banditry and sabotage from across the armistice lines into Israel recommenced. The provocations were deliberate and were strong and when they became too much, Israel responded with deliberate but controlled force directed against the bases and centers from which the raiders and infiltrators proceeded. Whereas the Israeli Government acknowledged responsibility for its decisions and for the acts of its armed forces, the Arab Governments repeatedly disclaimed all responsibility for their decisions and for any of these acts emanating from their territories, under the pretext that they were perpetrated by irregulars and persons not amenable to their control. One result of this has been that in the Security Council, a number of resolutions have been adopted purportedly condemning Israel for this defensive use of her armed forces while the Arab states, behind the shield of the Soviet veto, have been virtually always protected against expressions of disapproval, even in the mildest of terms, by the organ responsible for the maintenance of international peace and security.[29] In

---

[27] 9 LEAGUE OF NATIONS OFF. J. 176-78 (1928).

[28] 10 U.N. SCOR, 688th meeting, paras. 98-102, at 20 (1955).

[29] As an example, see the proceedings of the 1319th meeting of the Security Council on November 4, 1966, when the Soviet veto prevented the adoption of a mild draft resolution which would have invited the Government of Syria to strengthen its measures for preventing that type of incident. Much

fact, in all the period from 1955 onwards, it was not until the Security Council's resolution 248, adopted on March 24, 1968, that the Security Council pronounced itself on these Arab acts and even then it used very indirect language.[30]

By 1956 the Israeli Government reached the conclusion that the constant violation of the armistice agreement by Egypt, its exploitation as a cover for perpetrating armed attacks against Israel on the basis of this continuation of the state of war doctrine, distorted the motive and purpose of the armistice agreement and deprived it of all its functions. The Egyptian attitude and actions constituted an unjustified repudiation of the agreement so that no useful purpose would be served by returning to it. It informed the Secretary-General of the United Nations of this and, through him, the Egyptian Government.[31] The arrangements which were then made to restore tranquility to the region took account of this at least in a *de facto* way. For instead of the armistice agreement and the special machinery for supervising its implementation, the UNEF was created and stationed along the sensitive areas of Sinai, that is, along the borders of the Gaza Strip and at the headland which forms the Strait of Tiran.[32] However, no direct agreement was then made between Israel and Egypt. All rested on indirect, and sometimes imprecise and unformulated, understandings, sometimes on a government-to-government basis, and sometimes on an individual basis.[33]

For several years the present Secretary-General of the United Nations had been drawing attention to the general fragility of the status of UNEF in the absence of progress towards the settlement of outstanding questions.[34] Furthermore, the question of UNEF, of its very constitutionality in United Nations terms, became entangled in another question which at the time loomed larger but in retrospect appears to have been of less long-term significance. I am referring to the question of the

---

earlier, in resolution 101 of November 24, 1953, the Security Council had admonished Jordan in those terms. In resolution 107 of March 30, 1955, it suggested ways in which "infiltration could be reduced to an occasional nuisance."

[30] See the discussion at the 1401st to 1407th meetings of the Security Council, between March 21 and 24, 1968. U.N. Docs. S/PV.1401-1407 (1968).

[31] Aide-mémoire of November 3, 1956. 11 U.N. GAOR, Annexes, Agenda Item No. 5, at 9, U.N. Doc. A/3279 (1956).

[32] Cf. UNEF, Report of the Secretary-General, 12 U.N. GAOR, Annexes, Agenda Item No. 65, at 1, U.N. Doc. A/3694 and Add. 1 (1957). Annual reports were submitted subsequently until 1966.

[33] The confusion over the legal basis for UNEF's operation was increased in 1967. The views of the present Secretary-General are contained in Report of the Secretary-General on the Withdrawal of the United Nations Emergency Force, U.N. GAOR, 5th Emer. Spec. Sess., Annexes, Agenda Item No. 5, at 4, 9, U.N. Doc. A/6730 and Add. 1-3 (1967). Nevertheless, the matter is still highly controversial.

[34] "It is an unhappy statement to have to make, but it is a reality all too apparent that, despite almost a decade of relative quiet along the long line on which UNEF is deployed, relations between the peoples on the opposite sides of the line are such that if the United Nations buffer should be removed, serious fighting would, quite likely, soon be resumed."

UNEF, Report of the Secretary-General, 21 U.N. GAOR, Annexes, Agenda Item No. 21, at 2, U.N. Doc. A/6406 (1966). That same year U Thant pointed out that the presence of a force like UNEF might actually free the parties "from any pressing obligation to exert a really serious effort towards a settlement of their differences." Introduction to the Annual Report of the Secretary-General on the Work of the Organization, June 16, 1965-June 15, 1966, *id.*, Supp. 1A, at 5, U.N. Doc. A/6301/Add. 1, at 17 (1966).

Congo and the issue of the interpretation of a number of cardinal provisions in the United Nations Charter which led to the crisis of the nineteenth session of the General Assembly in 1964.[35]

After a temporary but precarious respite, the same situation returned with even greater intensity, and already by 1965 it became evident that unless something was done crisis would again creep upon the Middle Eastern world. Yet nothing was done about it. The old story repeated itself. What is more the Arab states, and especially Syria and Egypt, encouraged by Soviet backing and by their own deteriorating relations with the West, and heavily armed, grew more arrogant and truculent. When the Egyptian Government decided in May 1967 to request the peremptory removal of UNEF,[36] the vacuousness of the settlement of 1957 as it related to Israel and Egypt and the shifting sands on which the pacification of the area rested became evident. The real and urgent threat posed to Israel's very existence by the massed armies of her immediate neighbors, backed by all the other Arab states, led straight to the third phase of the Arab-Israeli war, which goes by the name already of the Six Days War of June 1967.

III

THE SECURITY COUNCIL RESOLUTION OF NOVEMBER 22, 1967

A. Background and Scope

The principal events since then are fresh in everyone's mind. The fighting terminated after Israel, Egypt, Jordan, Iraq, Lebanon, and Syria had accepted on the basis of reciprocity a series of resolutions adopted by the Security Council calling for a cease-fire "as a first step." Although all the Arab states had in one way or another signified their participation in the Arabs' war on Israel, some of them even participating actively in it, it will be noted that the acceptance of the cease-fire was in fact limited to the four limitrophe states together with Iraq, which had been most actively concerned. Kuwait unabashedly rejected the cease-fire in a formal communication to the Secretary-General of the United Nations, and the other Arab states—including Algeria, from which country units had participated in the fighting and which is today a member of the Security Council—made no response at all.[37] The Security Council's call for a cease-fire was unconditional. Furthermore, the Council had rejected, as did the emergency special session of the General Assembly shortly thereafter, all attempts to attribute responsibility for the breakdown of peace to one side or another. All proposals tending to attribute to Israel

---

[35] Advisory Opinion on Expenses of the United Nations, [1962] I.C.J. 151.

[36] See Report of the Secretary-General on the Withdrawal of UNEF, *supra* note 33.

[37] On the status of the acceptance of the cease-fire resolutions, see U.N. Docs. S/7985 and S/8279, of June 15 and November 30, 1967, respectively. For the cease-fire resolutions themselves, see Security Council resolutions 233, June 6, 1967; 234, June 7, 1967; and 235, June 9, 1967. Iraq's acceptance of the cease-fire was couched in very roundabout terms. 22 U.N. SCOR, Supp. April-June 1967, at 260, U.N. Doc. S/7990. For the refusal of Kuwait, see U.N. Doc. S/7968 (mimeographed only).

responsibility for "aggression" were flatly rejected.[38] As a result, the cease-fire took effect on the basis of the military lines as they existed on the dates in question. It is unnecessary to describe those lines in detail: the Suez Canal with Egypt, the River Jordan with Jordan, and the Golan Heights with Syria.

The establishment of the cease-fire was followed by a long period of difficult negotiations which culminated in the Security Council's resolution 242 of November 22, 1967, adopted unanimously by all its fifteen members. Carefully drawn up in the English language,[39] after every word had been weighed, that resolution reads

The Security Council,

Expressing its continuing concern with the grave situation in the Middle East,

Emphasizing the inadmissibility of the acquisition of territory by war and the need to work for a just and lasting peace in which every State in the area can live in security,

Emphasizing further that all Member States in their acceptance of the Charter of the United Nations have undertaken a commitment to act in accordance with Article 2 of the Charter,

1. *Affirms* that the fulfilment of Charter principles requires the establishment of a just and lasting peace in the Middle East which should include the application of both the following principles:

(i) Withdrawal of Israeli armed forces from territories occupied in the recent conflict;

(ii) Termination of all claims or states of belligerency and respect for and acknowledgment of the sovereignty, territorial integrity and political independence of every State in the area and their right to live in peace within secure and recognized boundaries free from threats or acts of force;

2. *Affirms further* the necessity

(a) For guaranteeing freedom of navigation through international waterways in the area;

(b) For achieving a just settlement of the refugee problem;

(c) For guaranteeing the territorial inviolability and political independence of every State in the area, through measures including the establishment of demilitarized zones;

3. *Requests* the Secretary-General to designate a Special Representative to proceed to the Middle East to establish and maintain contacts with the States concerned in order to promote agreement and assist efforts to achieve a peaceful and accepted settlement in accordance with the provisions and principles in this resolution;

4. *Requests* the Secretary-General to report to the Security Council on the progress of the efforts of the Special Representative as soon as possible.

[38] See in particular the voting at the 1360th meeting of the Security Council on June 14, 1967 (U.N. Doc. S/PV.1360) and at the 1548th Plenary meeting of the General Assembly on July 4, 1967, A/PV.1548). See also the statement of the representative of Israel at the 1618th meeting of the General Assembly on December 4, 1967, U.N. Doc. A/PV.1618, at 133.
[39] For the original draft, see U.N. Doc. S/8247 (1967).

This resolution indicates the major problems the solution of which will, in the unanimous view of the members of the Security Council, lead to a just and lasting peace in the Middle East. It is an entity in itself and is not to be eroded away by selective and tendentious interpretations and choosiness. A few words about some of the legal aspects underlying it would now be appropriate.

In the first place, even if this smacks a little of legal technicalities, it may be mentioned that the resolution was proposed and adopted within the general framework of chapter VI of the United Nations Charter.[40] The significance of this would be that technically the resolution has the status of a recommendation of the Security Council. It is to be regarded essentially as a series of guidelines and signposts pointing in the direction of peace.

Looked at in more historical perspective, it is significant—a point which is often overlooked—that it is the first resolution in all the long history of the United Nations dealing with the Middle East situation that emphatically and deliberately calls for 'a just and lasting peace." The political implications of the difference of interpretation to which allusion has been made, and the voting strength of the Arab states and their friends in the United Nations, had succeeded in keeping the word "peace" virtually unused in United Nations jurisprudence regarding the Middle East.[41] The body which has the primary responsibility for the maintenance of international peace in fact abdicated its function to maintain peace in the Middle East. It was content to let things drift, with the consequences all too familiar to us. Two major legal problems underlie this. In the first place it is often thought that multilateral diplomacy through common membership in a political organization such as the United Nations could provide an adequate general juridical framework for bilateral

[40] *Cf.* the reference by the sponsor, the representative of the United Kingdom, to chapter VI of the Charter when he introduced the draft resolution at the 1379th meeting of the Security Council on November 16, 1967. U.N. Doc. S/PV.1379, at 6.

[41] The relevant pronouncements make curious reading. The Security Council, in its resolution 62 of November 16, 1948, called upon the parties to negotiate the armistice agreements "in order to eliminate the threat to the peace in Palestine and to facilitate the transition from the present truce to permanent peace." In resolution 73 of August 11, 1949, taking note of the conclusion of the armistice agreements, it urged the parties to extend their scope and by negotiation to achieve agreement on the final settlement of all outstanding questions. In its resolution 89 of November 17, 1950, it reminded the parties of their obligations under the Charter and under the armistice agreements to settle their outstanding issues. In its resolution 93 of May 18, 1951, it expressed some concern at the lack of progress. In its resolution 95 of September 1, 1951, a similar reference appears. In its resolution 101 of November 24, 1953, it reaffirmed the necessity to make progress towards the settlement of outstanding questions. General Assembly resolution 186(S-2) of May 14, 1948 (U.N. GAOR, 2d Spec. Sess., Resolutions 5, U.N. Doc. A/555 (1948)) included among the terms of reference of the U.N. Mediator in Palestine to "promote a peaceful adjustment of the future situation of Palestine." Resolution 194(III) of December 11, 1948 called upon the parties to seek agreement with a view to the final settlement of all questions outstanding between them. For citation see note 22a *supra.* This sentiment was repeated in resolutions 394 of December 14, 1950 (5 *id.*, Supp. 20, at 24, U.N. Doc. A/1775 (1950)) and 512 of January 26, 1952 (6 *id.*, Supp. 20, at 11, U.N. Doc. A/2119 (1952)), which also considered that the governments concerned have the primary responsibility for reaching a settlement of their outstanding differences. Resolution 1125 of February 2, 1957 referred to "achieving situations conducive to the maintenance of peaceful conditions in the area." 11 *id.*, Supp. 17, at 62, U.N. Doc. A/3572 (1957).

relations between individual members of the Organization. Israel's experience shows that this is not so. In a way it can be said that the armistice agreements attempted to fill this juridical need, and of course they did for a time. With their disappearance, which is now tacitly acknowledged by the Security Council—for not one of the resolutions adopted in 1967 makes any reference to them[42]—the void has become all the more glaring. The Charter of the United Nations may provide a series of general principles upon which the international relations of all states should be oriented. But these principles by themselves are not sufficiently closely woven together to provide an adequate juridical framework for any sort of bilateral relations, so long as neither general international law nor United Nations machinery provides other means of bridging the gap save negotiations and agreement *inter partes*. The question here cannot be assimilated to the more familiar situation in which states have temporarily broken off diplomatic relations with each other. In those circumstances, the general framework of international law, whether customary law or conventional law, operates to retain all the essential elements of juridical relationships despite the temporary obstacles of an essentially political character. In the Middle East situation, however, the general rules of international law have not been allowed to operate at all. This is symbolized on the general level by the refusal of the Arab states to recognize Israel,[43] and on the particular level by a series of carefully drawn reservations which the Arab states attach to their participation in general multilateral treaties, and intended to prevent any form of treaty relationship coming into force between them and Israel.[44]

In the second place, it must be recalled that one of the fundamental principles for the effective operation of international law in any circumstance is the principle of reciprocity. The rules of international law are abstractions until they come to be reciprocally applied in concrete circumstances. If one were to criticize the legal tenet of the Government of Israel in relation to the problem of interpretation of the armistice agreements mentioned earlier, it could fairly be said that it attached insufficient weight to this element of reciprocity. As a result of the events which led to the final collapse of the armistice system in the early part of 1967, it has become necessary to give greater weight to this element of reciprocity. So while we continue to hold that, in principle, the maintenance of a state of war is incompatible with obligations under the Charter, the principle of reciprocity, which is certainly not excluded by the Charter, leads to the conclusion that if the Arab states insist on placing their juridical relations with Israel on that basis, Israel for its part is entitled,

---

[42] The only comment on this was made by the Permanent Representative of Syria in his letter to the Secretary-General of the United Nations of July 25, 1967. U.N. Docs. S/8094, A/6775 (1967). Determining is the absence of reaction by any member of the Security Council.

[43] Reiterated in the Khartoum resolution of the Arab Summit Conference of September 1, 1967, referred to above. See note 25 *supra*.

[44] For a convenient illustration of this, compare *Depositary Practice in Relation to Reservations, Report of the Secretary-General*, 2 Y.B. INT'L L. COMM'N 74, 87, U.N. Doc. A/5687 (1965).

if not obliged, to meet them on the same ground. It cannot be accepted that one side is entitled to base its policies and actions on the law of war and on claims of belligerency, and the other side not.

B. Withdrawal of Forces

The Security Council's resolution commences with a reference to what it calls "the inadmissibility of the acquisition of territory by war." Something must be said about that because in one form or another this idea occupied a prominent place in the discussions of 1967.

Those words reformulate a Spanish expression which has become almost epi-grammatic in United Nations circles, namely *"La victoria no da derechos."* This notion is one which, in that form, appears in a number of important treaties of Latin America. It lies behind the so-called Stimson Doctrine[45] and the Briand-Kellogg Pact of August 27, 1928,[46] and traces of it are also found in Article 2, para-graph 4, of the United Nations Charter. But the idea did not originate with them. In fact, it is nothing more than the established rule of international law that only a formal agreement, and more particularly after a war, usually a treaty of peace, is competent to transfer territory from one country to another. It is certainly in that sense, and in a juridical context that embodied the doctrine of *uti possidetis*, that the Spanish expression was first used by the Minister for Foreign Affairs of the Argentine, Sr. Mariano Varela, in his note of December 27, 1869 in connection with the war between Argentina, Brazil and Uruguay on the one hand and Paraguay on the other. The Argentine Government then argued that military victory by itself did not give rights to territory, and that the disposition of territory could only follow from an international agreement between the parties concerned, and the Spanish phrase, now aphoristic, is but a small part of a much longer contention.[47]

---

[45] See 26 AM. J. INT'L L. 342 (1932).

[46] 94 L.N.T.S. 57.

[47] For the text of that Note, see REPUBLICA ARGENTINA, MEMORIA DE RELACIONES EXTERIORES DE LA REPUBLICA 164 (1870). The relevant passage reads as follows:

"La República Argentina cree y sostiene, apoyada en títulos incontestables, que el territorio que se cuestiona le pertenece esclusivamente, y que su posesion por parte del Paraguay ha sido una usurpacion á derechos nuestros. Residiendo ese territorio por la victoria del las armas aliadas, su ocupacion ha sido un hecho natural y lójico. Sin embargo, el Gobierno Argentino ha sostenido hace muy poco tiempo en discusiones con el representante de S.M. el Emperador del Brasil, que la victoria no dá derecho á las naciones aliadas, para declarar por sí, límites suyos los que el tratado señala.

"Cree mi Gobierno, hoy como entonces, que los limites deben ser discutidos con el Gobierno que se establezca en el Paraguay, y que su fijacion será establecida en los tratados que se celebren despues de exhibidas por las partes contratantes, los títulos en que cada uno apoye sus derechos."

In this connection, attention is called to the following:

The Special Committee on Principles of International Law Concerning Friendly Relations and Co-operation Among States in Accordance with the Charter of the United Nations at its 1967 session discussed the principle that states shall refrain in their international relations from the threat or use of force against the territorial integrity or political independence of any state or in any other manner inconsistent with the purposes of the United Nations, *i.e.*, the interrelationship, above all, of Article 2, paragraph 4, and Article 51 of the Charter. In the course of the discussion there was general agreement that the principle

In the context in which the Security Council used that expression, this seems to be the only possible meaning because it is immediately followed by an emphatic statement on the need to work for a just and lasting peace in which every state in the area can live in security.

As already indicated, the law does not operate in a vacuum. The Security Council was not throwing out maxims like the well-known maxims of equity, but was making a concrete recommendation to deal with a concrete set of circumstances. In doing that it seems to have recalled, in a form which in the particular circumstances was politically attractive, an established rule of international law which, as far as is known, is fully operative throughout the whole world up to the present day.

In point of fact any attempt to read too much into that assertion by the Security Council, or into the Spanish phrase from which it may have originated, is not likely to be fruitful in terms of advancing concrete solutions to concrete problems. If the acquisition of territory by war is inadmissible as a general proposition, it could be recalled that the United Arab Republic has no title to the Gaza Strip and the Kingdom of Jordan no title to the West Bank and the part of Jerusalem it formerly occupied. One could even go further and point to many defects in the political map of the world which would follow from any blind and unquestioning acceptance of the bald statement that victory does not give rights.

It is in that context that the question of the withdrawal of Israeli forces has to be viewed. The relevant portion of the English text of the Security Council resolution should be carefully scrutinized. It does not say "withdrawal of *the* Israeli armed forces from *the* territories occupied in the recent conflict" (even though that is a possible interpretation of some of the other language versions of the resolution). It refers to "withdrawal of Israeli armed forces from territories occupied in the recent conflict." It does not say *what* is to be withdrawn. It does not say to *where* the Israeli forces are to withdraw. It does not say *when* they are to withdraw. This is no accident. In the first place, and this remark is directed particularly to those who are attracted by the process of historical interpretation, it may be recalled that

---

applied in relation to present or existing boundaries of a state. On the other hand, a discussion arose as to whether international lines of demarcation were the equivalent of boundaries for this purpose. The difference was not reconciled, and the Committee's Report contains the following statement from the Report of the Working Group of the Drafting Committee:

"7. *Military occupation and non-recognition of situations brought about by the illegal threat or use of force*

"There was no agreement on the inclusion of a statement to the effect that the territory of a State may never be the object of military occupation or other measures of force on any grounds whatsoever.

"Nor was there agreement whether a statement should be included requiring that situations brought about by an illegal threat or use of force would not be recognized."

See the Committee's Report, to be published in the official records of the twenty-second session of the General Assembly, Annexes, Agenda Item No. 87, para. 107; for provisional version, see U.N. Doc. A/6799, at 62 (1967).

both the Security Council and the General Assembly had rejected all draft resolutions the intent of which was to require the withdrawal, immediate or otherwise, of all Israeli forces back to the lines they occupied on June 5, 1967.[48] There is widespread recognition that those lines are not satisfactory as permanent frontiers and that the establishment of just and lasting peace requires the establishment of new and more viable frontiers.[49] The Security Council did not attempt to spell out what those new frontiers should be. It left that to be elaborated by the normal free play of diplomatic processes. Here, it might be added, the Security Council was acting much in the way it had acted in 1948 when it adopted resolution 62 calling for negotiations for armistice agreements. Then, too, it did not attempt to spell out what the armistice lines should be. In fact the greater part of the negotiations for those armistice agreements consisted in detailed and direct discussion between the delegations as to what the appropriate lines should be, having regard to actual conditions on the ground.

In the structure of the Security Council's resolution the withdrawal of Israeli armed forces does not imply necessarily any corresponding advance of the armed forces of any Arab State, nor by itself does it imply the determination of territorial sovereignty over the affected areas. The resolution also refers specifically to the possibility of establishing demilitarized zones. This, too, follows the experience of the armistice agreements as well as more general international experience. The demilitarized zones created as a result of the armistice agreements were not notably successful. One of the reasons is that because at the time everybody concerned believed the armistice agreements would be of short duration, many of the practical details of the demilitarized zones were left unsettled, pending the peace treaty which was thought to be not far off. However, that unhappy experience does not preclude the establishment of new demilitarized zones as part of a wider agreement and settlement, but one of the essential conditions for this would be not again to leave more things unsaid than said.

In that way the Security Council indicates that what is required is, the establishment of secure and recognized boundaries in which all the states of the area can live in political independence and peace, free from threats and acts of force. This is to be accompanied by the termination of all claims and states of belligerency, and respect for the sovereignty, territorial integrity, and political independence of all states in the area. This points directly back to the element of reciprocity which, as already explained, is one of the linch-pins of international law.

The Security Council's resolution mentions certain other problems, although its list is by no means an exhaustive catalog of all the outstanding problems in the area.

---

[48] See in particular the meetings mentioned in note 38 *supra*.

[49] *Cf.* these words by President Johnson on June 19, 1967: "The nations of the region have had only fragile and violated truce lines for 20 years. What they now need are recognized boundaries that will give them security against terror, destruction and war." 57 DEP'T STATE BULL. 31, 33 (1967).

C. International Waterways

Foremost among these is the necessity for guaranteeing freedom of navigation through international waterways in the area.

This refers to three important international waterways, two of which have been much discussed, and the third of which has only recently come into international prominence. The first two are the Suez Canal and the Strait of Tiran, and the third is the Strait of Bab-el-Mandeb, where the Red Sea joins the Indian Ocean by Aden and the Island of Perim.[50]

---

[50] On the Gulf of Aqaba and the Strait of Tiran, see Kennedy, *A Brief Geographical and Hydrographical Study of Bays and Estuaries the Coasts of Which Belong to Different States*, 1 UNITED NATIONS CONFERENCE ON LAW OF THE SEA, OFFICIAL RECORDS, 198, at 208, U.N. Doc. A/CONF. 13/15 (1958). On Bab-el-Mandeb, see Kennedy, *A Brief Geographical and Hydrographical Study of Straits Which Constitute Routes for International Traffic, id.* at 114, 115, U.N. Doc. A/CONF. 13/6 and Add. 1 (1958). And see, more generally, the British Admiralty publication, RED SEA AND GULF OF ADEN PILOT (1955). At the 1382nd meeting of the Security Council on November 22, 1967, the Israeli Foreign Minister referred to the necessity for "guaranteeing free navigation for all shipping, including that of Israel, in all the waterways leading to and from the Red Sea." U.N. Doc. S/PV.1382, at 46.

One of the Arab arguments in relation to the Strait of Tiran is that Israeli possession of any part of the coastline of the Gulf of Aqaba constitutes a breach of the armistice agreement with Egypt. That Agreement distinguished between what it called the Western Front and the Eastern Front (see Article VII and Annex 2). It made provision for the Egyptian controlled and Israeli controlled parts respectively of the Western Front only but was completely silent regarding the Eastern Front. This means that the specifics of what is there called the Eastern Front, which included what became the southern part of Israel down to Eilat (except for the actual frontier of Egypt itself), were not covered by the Egyptian agreement but remained for settlement later when the Jordan agreement should be concluded.

Very shortly after the signing of the Israel-Egyptian agreement, early in March 1949, Israeli forces advanced south to the littoral. Jordan complained to the Acting Mediator that this advance was a breach of the truce of July 15, 1948. There was no breach of the Israel-Egyptian Agreement, and no complaints of any kind were made by Egypt.

In the Acting Mediator's report of March 23, 1949, after investigation by United Nations observers, the following appears:

"1. Since 8 March 1949 Israeli military forces at considerably more than normal patrol strength have moved into the area between the Dead Sea and the Gulf of Aqaba in Palestine, and have taken up positions at several points which they had not previously occupied.

"2. There has never been anything in the nature of a military line in this area. It appears that Arab forces in small strength have recently patrolled in parts of the area, as have small Israeli patrols, in violation of the truce in both cases.

"3. The main movement of Israeli troops has been down the road in the Wadi Araba, which road runs for its whole length inside Palestine but close to the Palestine-Transjordan frontier.

"4. The complaint that Israeli troops crossed the Transjordan border could not be verified. On 18 March, the senior United Nations observer at Amman reported that no Israeli post existed at that time on the Transjordan side of Wadi Araba.

"5. The report that one body of Israeli troops entered Umm Reshresh (MR 145 885) by a road from the Egyptian side of the frontier could not be verified. No complaint of such movement has been received from Egyptian authorities though it has been established by the observers that an Israeli force reached Umm Reshresh by way of Ras En Negeb on the Egyptian frontier. The Egyptian-Israeli General Armistice Agreement defines the western half of this area, *i.e.*, west of a line running midway between the Egyptian and Transjordan frontiers, as the western front, in which only Israeli defensive forces, based on the settlements, may be maintained. The eastern half of this area, or the eastern front, pending the conclusion of an armistice agreement with Transjordan, remains fully subject to the existing truce."

And

"It is clear on the evidence available to me as a result of the investigation by United Nations observers since 7 March that Israeli forces have effectively occupied this area since that date.

This is not the time or place to discuss the detailed legal questions of these international waterways. It is sufficient to recall that the Suez Canal regime is governed essentially by the Constantinople Convention of 1888,[51] and the two straits are

Previous to 7 March Transjordan forces had lightly patrolled at least parts of the area, and it is contended by Transjordan sources that they had maintained fixed positions at Gharandal, Bir Qattar (MR 137 890), Ain El Weinba and Meliha (MR 162 968). It has not been possible to verify on the basis of a check by United Nations observers when such positions were established by Transjordan forces, but it is established that no Transjordan forces are now on the Palestine side of the frontier in this area. No fighting ever having taken place in that area before and no significant forces of either side having been concentrated there, it had not been necessary to place it under close observation or to define any truce lines.

"I am quite convinced that, other than those at Aqaba, any positions established in this area either by Transjordan or by Israeli forces have all been established since the existing truce came into effect on 18 July 1948, with the possible exception of Transjordan positions at Ain Habd and Kurnub, and have, therefore, been established contrary to the terms of that truce. Similarly, patrolling activity and reinforcement of pre-truce forces on either side of the frontier in this sector are in conflict with truce conditions which have been accepted by both sides."

4 U.N. SCOR, Supp. March 1949, 44, 46-48, U.N. Doc. S/1295 & Corr. 1 (1949).

This position was consolidated by the armistice agreement with Jordan as appears clearly from Article V and the annexed map. See also the report by the Acting Mediator, after the conclusion on March 11, 1949 of a cease-fire agreement between Israel and Jordan, in U.N. Docs. S/1284 and S/1284/Corr. 1 (1949) (mimeographed only).

On May 23, 1949, Egypt submitted a complaint to the Mixed Armistice Commission on the occupation of Umm Reshresh and Bir Qattar. On February 8, 1950 the Commission, by a majority vote, decided that "[t]he advance of Israeli Forces of 10 March 1949 to the Gulf of Aqaba area and the occupation of Bir Qattar is a violation of the Egyptian-Israeli General Armistice Agreement." However, the contention that the advance of Israeli Forces on March 10, 1949 and occupation of Umm Reshresh were another violation of the agreement, was rejected by a majority vote of the Commission. Both sides appealed against parts of the decision to the Special Committee established by Article X of the agreement. On March 20, 1950, the Special Committee, by a majority vote, confirmed the decision of the Mixed Armistice Commission. Under the provisions of the agreement, this decision was final, but the Israeli Government found unacceptable the decision about Bir Qattar mainly on the ground that it was based upon a misinterpretation of Article VII of the agreement. This interpretation placed the Bir Qattar in the area of the Western Front, covered by Article VII, para. 4, from which all Israeli Forces were excluded, apart from defensive forces based on the settlements. The views of the Government of Israel on this subject were formulated officially in a letter from the Minister for Foreign Affairs to the Chief of Staff of UNTSO of June 23, 1950. In spite of the fact that this issue was not mentioned in the original Egyptian complaint to the Security Council regarding expulsion of Arabs from the Negev (5 U.N. SCOR, Supp. Sept.-Dec. 1950, at 23, U.N. Doc. S/1790 (1950)), it was, nevertheless, discussed in the 511th, 514th, 517th, 518th, 522nd, and 524th meetings of the Council. In the course of the 522nd meeting of the Council, Mr. Eban explained that following the "assurances and clarifications" which emerged from conversations with the Chief of Staff securing Israel's interests, Israel was able to modify its attitude as regards Bir Qattar. Consequently, the Security Council, in its resolution 89 of November 17, 1950, *inter alia* took note of the Government of Israel's statement that "Israeli forces will evacuate Bir Qattar pursuant to the 20 March 1950 decision of the Special Committee . . . and that the Israeli Armed Forces will withdraw to positions authorized by the Armistice Agreement." In his letter dated March 12, 1951 to the President of the Security Council, the Chief of Staff informed the Security Council that "a United Nations observer visited Bir Qattar on January 3, 1951 and found no evidence of military positions there, and former defence works had been filled in." 6 U.N. SCOR, Supp. April-June 1951, at 11, U.N. Doc. S/2049 (1951).

Egypt did not pursue the question of Aqaba and Umm Reshresh any further and thus left the status of the area, including that of Umm Reshresh, outside the scope of the Israel-Egyptian armistice agreement, recognizing it to be within the area covered by the Israel-Jordan agreement.

[51] For the authentic French text, see 61 Brit. & For. State Papers 293 (1887-88). For a contemporary English translation by the British Government, see Great Britain, Parliamentary Papers, 1889, Commercial No. 2, C. 5623. For a later translation by the United States Government, see The Suez Problem, July 26-September 22, 1956, U.S. Dep't of State, Pub. No. 6392, at 16 (1956).

under the legal regime of international straits of customary international law or, which is much the same thing, the codified law particularly as embodied in Article 16 of the United Nations Convention on the Territorial Sea and Contiguous Zone of 1958.[52] Naturally these two sets of legal regimes are different in their details but they have in common an underlying conception which links back to the basic question of the juridical relationships *in toto* subsisting between Israel and the Arab States concerned. It is clear from all international experience that freedom of navigation through this type of international waterway cannot be guaranteed to anyone so long as any of the territorial states concerned adopts the subjective attitude that it is in a state of war with another state. It is in this respect that the Constantinople Convention of 1888 has proved inadequate because in practice the operation of the Canal has not been insulated from the politics of the territorial state;[53] and judging from the Tiran experience, much the same can be said regarding the general international law on the question of the innocent passage of ships through natural waterways linking two parts of the high seas or linking the high seas to the territorial sea of another state.

The issue of free navigation through international waterways of the Middle East has been one of the crucial issues of the smoldering Middle East crisis during the last twenty years. It twice provoked major outbreaks, in 1956 and in 1967. This aspect of the Middle East crisis may not be as spectacular as some of its other aspects. However, it it nonetheless real and pressing, and when I ponder on the problems which face us and direct my attention to the waterway problem, I cannot put out of my mind that the question of the freedom of the seas was a major issue in two world wars and found a place both in President Wilson's Fourteen Points[54] and in the Atlantic Charter.[55]

D. Refugees

The Arab refugee problem, too, is mentioned in the Security Council's resolution which affirmed the necessity for achieving a just settlement of the refugee problem.

Let it be stated quite frankly that this problem is not only tragic—there is an element of banality in that—but in some respects the most baffling of the individual problems which together combine to make up the crisis of the Middle East. It impinges pressingly on Israel's most vital interests.

Certain relatively secondary aspects of the problem may be disposed of first.

---

[52] 516 U.N.T.S. 205.

[53] S.C. Res. 118 (1956).

[54] The second of President Wilson's Fourteen Points referred to "[A]bsolute freedom of navigation upon the seas outside territorial waters, alike in peace and in war, except as the seas may be closed in whole or in part by international action for the enforcement of international covenants." 56 CONG. REC. 680 (1918).

[55] In the Atlantic Charter of August 14, 1941, the seventh of the common principles on which the future peace of the world should be based stated that "such a peace should enable all men to traverse the high seas and oceans without hindrance." 5 DEP'T STATE BULL. 125 (1941).

From the point of view of the existence of the problem, the question of how many refugees there are is not a matter of great moment because the fact remains that there are large numbers of refugees. Some of the exaggerated figures advanced from time to time may be contested, and some of the statistical data compiled by the United Nations or by other sources may be disputed. But that does not affect the broad political issue.

Again, while there may be technical distinctions between "old" and "new" refugees, the latter being those who became refugees after last June, it is doubtful if this goes to the fundamentals. Nevertheless, in both cases it has to be recognized that from one point of view the Arab refugee problem cannot be divorced from the general demographic problems of the State of Israel in which even before last June, Arab citizens constituted at least ten per cent of the total population and were increasing at a far higher rate than the Jewish majority. This, in turn, links it directly to the major problem of Israel-Arab relations.

That having been said, the refugee problem has two main aspects. The first is the welfare problem, which, serious though it is, should not be exaggerated and which is largely being handled by the United Nations Relief and Works Agency for Palestine Refugees with the assistance of governments including the Government of Israel. The second is the political problem, what the Security Council calls finding a "just settlement" of the refugee problem.

In brief, the Israeli view is that the just settlement of the refugee problem, which is earnestly desired, cannot be separated from the overall problem of the Middle East crisis. As far as I can understand the Arab position, it is based on two main elements. One is the so-called right of self-determination (of natural law origins) and the other is said to be based on the General Assembly resolution 194(III) of December 11, 1948.[56] Both these elements are an attempt to rationalize the refusal of the Arab governments, in which they have persisted since 1948, to cooperate in any manner, shape or form in the international efforts to produce a solution to the refugee problem through the traditional processes of resettlement in the different communities in which they now live. The Arab insistence on the absolute "right" of the refugees to return to their homes is regarded as a transparent attempt to win international support for the objective of planting a Trojan horse in Israel's midst. The Arab spokesmen, in their attempt to give legal verisimilitude to their approach, rely particularly on the following paragraph in General Assembly resolution 194(III):

> The General Assembly . . .
> *Resolves* that the refugees wishing to return to their homes and live at peace with their neighbours should be permitted to do so at the earliest practicable date, and that compensation should be paid for the property of those choosing not to return and for loss of or damage to property which, under principles of international law or in equity, should be made good by the Governments or authorities responsible;

---

[56] *Supra* note 22a.

Instructs the Conciliation Commission to facilitate the repatriation, resettlement and economic and social rehabilitation of the refugees and the payment of compensation, and to maintain close relations with the Director of the United Nations Relief for Palestine Refugees and, through him, with the appropriate organs and agencies of the United Nations.

Much could be said about that paragraph although probably all that there is to be said about it already appears in the records of the General Assembly. For that reason the present exposition will be limited to a few observations only.

It will, of course, be appreciated in the first place that this resolution as a whole has a status no different from that of any other resolution of the General Assembly. While there may be some ambiguity over the precise status, in legal terms, of a resolution of the General Assembly, one thing is, it is believed, generally accepted and that is that a General Assembly resolution is not legally a dispositive text. It neither creates rights nor does it take rights away. It is a political statement.

In the second place, Israel was not a member of the United Nations in 1948, although it participated in the committee meetings when the question was discussed. Those of the Arab states which then were members of the United Nations displayed little enthusiasm for that paragraph 11 and on some of the votes, even voted against it.

That paragraph itself is one paragraph out of a 15-paragraph resolution which established the Palestine Conciliation Commission and gave it broad terms of reference designed to carry through the transition to permanent peace initiated a little earlier by the Security Council when it called for the armistice negotiations. It was in that context that the two alternative solutions to the refugee problem, namely, return or resettlement with compensation, were placed. The assumption of the resolution was that the details would be elaborated by intergovernmental agreement. By a long process of erosion which is part and parcel of the whole Arab concept that their relations with Israel are relations of war, paragraph 11 became detached from its context. As a result the belief has been sedulously fostered that the Arab refugee problem exists and can be solved on its own, without intergovernmental agreement, and that paragraph 11 of the 1948 resolution, taken in an absolute fashion, indicates the only way in which the problem can be solved.

There is very little that the law can say on this. The Security Council's resolution of last November has recognized the real place of the refugee problem in the overall political context and it is in that context that its solution has been called for.

IV

CONCLUSION

This paper is confined to the major outstanding problems as they appear through the Security Council's resolution of last November. There are, of course, many others. I could mention by way of example all the questions of war damages, which are considerable; the question of compensation for the large numbers of Jewish refugees from the Arab states who have found refuge in Israel in a kind of population exchange and were forced to abandon their property in the Arab countries, in which, however, Israel accepted the moral and material responsibilities of a humane host-country and the Arab states did not; the questions of the Holy Places which give rise to extremely complex issues extending beyond the horizons of Israeli-Arab relations; and many technical questions relating to matters coming within the competence of the technical organs of the United Nations and of the Specialized Agencies. The list could be expanded *ad infinitum*. There is hardly a branch of international law or of United Nations law which does not come into play. But to do this would be a self-defeating task, because it would detract attention from the essentials.

The long drawn out crisis in the Middle East can be taken as a case study of the dangers to international peace which are created by a too loose and unthoughtful reliance on abstractions and general principles. It may come as a shock to realize that the principles of the United Nations Charter are of little value by themselves unless they are properly brought into a fully worked out context of political, military and legal relationships which correspond to the needs of the situation. It was too easily thought in the early days of the Middle East crisis that the United Nations Charter itself supplied a sufficiently taut legal regime which would be vigorous enough to protect all the states of the area from the threat or use of armed force against their political independence. It is this hope which has been disappointed. It is in this defect of contemporary international law and organization that the challenge to the international lawyer and political scientist lies. It is the inability of the contemporary legal order to provide any effective substitute for peaceful relations other than direct agreement between the states concerned that has led the government of Israel to the conviction that only full and direct contractual relationships, freely arrived at, are the essential prerequisite for the establishment of a just and lasting peace in the area.

THE ROLE OF THE UNITED NATIONS VIS-À-VIS THE PALESTINE QUESTION

MUHAMMAD H. EL-FARRA[*]

I

A SHORT REVIEW OF THE MAIN PROBLEM

The present Middle East Crisis is part and parcel of the Palestine problem, which has defied all efforts for a solution for the past fifty years. This is because, in attempting to solve the problem, no adequate weight was given to the rule of law, which embodies the right of every people to self-determination.

A review of this question shows that from the very beginning the law of nations was disregarded. Its first defiance took place in 1897 when the leaders of the Zionist movement resolved at Basle, Switzerland, to establish a Jewish state in Palestine.[1] It was later defied in 1917 when Lord Balfour, British Secretary of State for Foreign Affairs, promulgated the Balfour Declaration,[2] promising to facilitate the establishment of a national home for the Jewish peoples on Arab land without reference to the will of the vast majority of the legitimate inhabitants. No matter how we look at this promise it came from one who was giving what he did not own.

I would like to emphasize in this connection that the phrase "a national home for the Jewish people" provoked much controversy.[3] But, regardless of whether it was intended to mean creating a Jewish state or a "homeland," it conflicted with Arab rights. In 1937, twenty years after the Declaration was issued, the Palestine Royal Commission, after a thorough examination of the records bearing upon the question, came to the conclusion that

> His Majesty's Government could not commit itself to the establishment of a Jewish State. It could only undertake to facilitate the growth of a Home. It would depend mainly on the zeal and enterprise of the Jews whether the Home would grow big enough to become a State.[4]

The Zionist leaders got the hint and planned for the usurpation of Palestine through their zeal, ability, and enterprise, reflected in an organized campaign of

[*] LL.B. 1950, Suffolk University; LL.M. 1951, Boston University; S.J.D. 1958, University of Pennsylvania. Ambassador Extraordinary and Plenipotentiary, Permament Representative of the Hashemite Kingdom of Jordan to the United Nations.

[1] *See* 1 PALESTINE: A STUDY OF JEWISH, ARAB, AND BRITISH POLICIES (Esco Foundation for Palestine, Inc.) 40-42 (1947); C. SYKES, CROSSROADS TO ISRAEL 10-11 (1965).

[2] The text of the declaration is officially quoted in PALESTINE ROYAL COMMISSION, REPORT, CMD. No. 5479, at 22 (1937).

[3] *See* references cited note 1 *supra*.

[4] CMD. No. 5479, *supra* note 2, at 24.

political action, fund-raising, and propaganda. This organized campaign ignored all Arab rights including the reservations embodied in the Balfour Declaration that:

> [N]othing shall be done which may prejudice the civil and religious rights of existing non-Jewish communities in Palestine, or the rights and political status enjoyed by Jews in any other country.

The Arabs of Palestine own 94.6 per cent of Palestine, and it is obvious that any attempt to establish a state conflicts with existing Arab rights. The Zionists, therefore, turned to President Truman and other Americans to commit another injustice in defiance of the legitimate rights of the Arab people of Palestine.

Thus, again, international law was utterly ignored when the question of Palestine became an issue of domestic politics in the United States, and American governors, senators, congressmen, mayors, and every conceivable aspirant for public office, with a few notable exceptions, pledged the establishment of a Jewish state in Palestine.

It might be noted in this connection that President Wilson, in his address of 4 July 1918, laid down the following as one of the four great ends for which the associated peoples of the world were fighting:

> The settlement of every question, whether of territory, of sovereignty, of economic arrangement, or of political relationship, upon the basis of the free acceptance of that settlement by the people immediately concerned, and not upon the basis of the material interest or advantage of any other nation or people which may desire a different settlement for the sake of its own exterior influence or mastery.[5]

It should be stressed that the Arab peoples were among the associated peoples who fought with the United States, as allies and friends, for this principle, and who were promised complete independence only to be betrayed later on by their very allies and friends.

What is more, international law was disregarded when duress and pressure took the place of law and equity during the United Nations debate of 1947 that led to the recommendation calling for the partition of Palestine against the will of its people in violation of their inherent right to self-determination. Indeed, international law was disregarded when the General Assembly in 1947 rejected a request of Sub-Committee II of its Ad Hoc Committee on the Palestinian Question to the effect that, before recommending any solution to the Palestine problem, the International Court of Justice should be requested to give an advisory opinion on certain legal questions connected with or arising from the problem, including questions concerning the competence of the United Nations to recommend or enforce any solution contrary to the wishes of the majority of the people of Palestine.[6]

Why has the United Nations side-stepped international law by refusing to submit

---

[5] W. WILSON, *Four Factors of World Peace*, in SELECTED ADDRESSES AND PUBLIC PAPERS OF WOODROW WILSON 266, 268 (A.B. Hart ed. 1918).

[6] 2 U.N. GAOR, Ad Hoc Comm. on the Palestine Question 203 (1947). *See* remarks by Sir Mohammed Zafrullah Khan, 2 U.N. GAOR 1373 (1947).

basic legal issues in the Palestine case to the International Court of Justice? Is it not because it was clear to all political forces at the United Nations that, like Lord Balfour, the United Nations could not grant sovereignty to a Jewish state since the United Nations itself does not possess the sovereignty in order to be able to dispose of it, and, therefore, usurpation through votes, force and politics should be the answer?

II
THE PRESENT CRISIS

I have so far spoken about the past. But it is the past which makes and conditions the present, and it is the present which molds the future. Let us now turn to the present crisis.

On 5 June, 1967 Israel, in a surprise attack, destroyed the Egyptian air force as well as that of Syria and Jordan. It subsequently occupied all of Sinai, all of the Gaza Strip, all of the West Bank of Jordan and a part of Syrian territory.

This Israeli attack is in most respects no different from the Sinai Campaign of 1956. The one factual difference is that Israel this time occupied both Jordanian and Syrian territories in addition to Sinai and the Gaza Strip. In 1956 only Sinai and Gaza were occupied.

But despite the gravity and the nature of the Israeli attack, a short comparison between the action of political forces in the United Nations vis-à-vis the 1956 invasion and the present one would show a different behaviour on the part of some of the big powers vis-à-vis this crisis. Thus, international law which was upheld in 1956 was trampled on in 1967.

On the Sinai invasion of 1956, firm and strict adherence to the rule of the Charter was championed by the overwhelming majority of members of the United Nations. The United States played a leading role in this matter. Former President Eisenhower said to the nation: "[A]s I review the march of world events in recent years, I am ever more deeply convinced that the processes of the United Nations represent the soundest hope for peace in the world."[7] Neither Zionist pressure, in an American election year, nor any other consideration was able to prevail in substituting political expediency for accepted norms of international law.

The basic facts in the present crisis are the same—the invasion, the occupation, the designs, the tactics, the planning, and the election year. And both Israeli invasions were intended to bring about further expansion.

The 1956 Sinai Campaign was preceded by the Israeli attacks on Gaza in February 1955 which led to a United Nations resolution calling once more upon Israel to take all necessary measures to prevent the recurrence of such actions.[8]

The 1967 Israeli invasion of the three Arab territories was preceded by many

---

[7] PUBLIC PAPERS OF THE PRESIDENTS OF THE UNITED STATES: DWIGHT D. EISENHOWER, 1956, at 1065.
[8] S.C. Res. 106 (1955).

acts of provocation culminating in the Israeli invasion of Es Samu' in 1966 which led to a United Nations resolution of condemnation censuring Israel for "this large-scale military action."[9]

In both the 1956 and the 1967 cases the attempt was made by Israel to retain control of occupied areas. In 1956 the attempt failed. The outcome of the 1967 attempt is still pending before the United Nations.

There is a risk today threatening the very integrity of the United Nations. It may not be an exaggeration to state that the future of the United Nations and the rule of law would be at stake if the practice of 1947 is repeated and political expediency, in an American election year, is allowed to play a role. One wonders whether it would be in the interest of the United States to be part of such an attempt, or lend its support to it.

International law today is facing a real test. So is the United Nations which is the organization created to uphold the rule of law and safeguard the values enshrined in its Charter. Members of the world organization, scholars, and students of law know what brought about the end of the League of Nations. The memory of the Italian occupation of Ethiopia and the action of the King of Italy in declaring himself Emperor, as a result of this conquest, is still very vivid in the minds of these people. They are rightly disturbed about the future of the United Nations.

International law on the present Middle East Crisis is very clear. It is axiomatic that, by an illegal act, no legal result can be produced, no right acquired; no fruits for aggression. No reminder is needed of the "Stimson Doctrine" of 1932, nor of the position of the United States regarding the invasion of China by Japan in 1932. Equally well known is the position of the American states which, in 1936, declared the following as an accepted principle in the "American Community of Nations": (a) "Proscription of territorial conquest and that, in consequence, no acquisition made through violence shall be recognized."[10] This is part of what is known as the Buenos Aires Declaration of 1936. Again in 1938 the American states adopted the Lima Declaration, in which they reiterated: "[T]he occupation or acquisition of territory or any other modification or territorial or boundary arrangement obtained through conquest by force or by non-pacific means shall not be valid or have legal effect."[11] The Charter of the Organization of American States[12] signed at Bogotá on 30 April, 1948 embodies in Article 17 thereof the following: "No territorial acquisitions or special advantages obtained either by force or by other means of coercion shall be recognized."

---

[9] S.C. Res. 228 (1966).

[10] Report of the Delegation of the United States of America to the Inter-American Conference for the Maintenance of Peace, Buenos Aires, 1936, pp. 227, 228, quoted in 5 M. WHITEMAN, DIGEST OF INTERNATIONAL LAW 880-81 (1965).

[11] Report of the Delegation of the United States of America to the Eighth International Conference of American States, Lima, 1938, pp. 132, 133, quoted in 5 M. WHITEMAN, *supra* note 10, at 881.

[12] 119 U.N.T.S. 3 [1948] 2 U.S.T. 2394; T.I.A.S. No. 2361.

In July 1967, while the Middle East situation was being debated in the General Assembly's Special Session, and before any action was taken, Israel proceeded nevertheless to take steps to annex the City of Jerusalem and face the United Nations with a *fait accompli*. The General Assembly met this challenge with a resolution No. 2253 (ES-V) on 4 July, 1967, adopted by 99 votes with abstentions unfortunately including that of the United States.[13] This resolution in effect affirmed the above principles of international law:

The General Assembly,
Deeply concerned at the situation prevailing in Jerusalem as a result of the measures taken by Israel to change the status of the City,
1. *Considers* that these measures are invalid;
2. *Calls upon* Israel to rescind all measures already taken and to desist forthwith from taking any action which would alter the status of Jerusalem;
3. *Requests* the Secretary-General to report to the General Assembly and the Security Council on the situation and on the implementation of the present resolution not later than one week from its adoption.[14]

In the face of Israel's defiance of this United Nations resolution, the General Assembly adopted another resolution on 14 July, 1967, deploring the failure of Israel to implement the first resolution and reiterating its request. The resolution reads as follows:

The General Assembly,
Recalling its resolution 2253(ES-V) of 4 July 1967,
Having received the report submitted by the Secretary-General,
Taking note with the deepest regret and concern of the non-compliance by Israel with resolution 2253 (ES-V),
1. *Deplores* the failure of Israel to implement General Assembly resolution 2253 (ES-V);
2. *Reiterates* its call to Israel in that resolution to rescind all measures already taken and to desist forthwith from taking any action which would alter the status of Jerusalem;
3. *Requests* the Secretary-General to report to the Security Council and the General Assembly on the situation and on the implementation of the present resolution.[15]

The Israeli answer was, in effect, that Jerusalem is not negotiable.[16]

At a later stage, Jordan raised the question of Jerusalem before the Security Council, and after lengthy deliberations the Council adopted resolution 252 (1968) of 21 May, 1968. It deplored the failure of Israel to comply with the above General Assembly resolutions. It considered all Israeli measures which tend to change the legal status of Jerusalem invalid, and requested the Secretary-General to report on the implementation of the present resolution.

---

[13] U.N. Doc. A/PV. 1548, at 102-05 (1967).
[14] G.A. Res. 2253 (ES-V), U.N. GAOR 5th Emer. Spec. Sess., Supp. 1, at 4, U.N. Doc. A/6798 (1967).
[15] *Id.*
[16] *Cf.* Jones, *The Status of Jerusalem: Some National and International Aspects,* in this symposium, p. 169.

This Security Council resolution reads as follows:

The Security Council,

Recalling General Assembly resolutions 2253 (ES-V) and 2254 (ES-V) of 4 and 14 July 1967,

Having considered the letter (S/8560) of the Permanent Representative of Jordan on the situation in Jerusalem and the report of the Secretary-General (S/8146),

Having heard the statements made before the Council,

Noting that since the adoption of the above-mentioned resolutions, Israel has taken further measures and actions in contravention of those resolutions,

Bearing in mind the need to work for a just and lasting peace,

Reaffirming that acquisition of territory by military conquest is inadmissible,

1. *Deplores* the failure of Israel to comply with the General Assembly resolutions mentioned above;

2. *Considers* that all legislative and administrative measures and actions taken by Israel, including expropriation of land properties thereon, which tend to change the legal status of Jerusalem are invalid and cannot change that status;

3. *Urgently calls upon* Israel to rescind all such measures already taken and to desist forthwith from taking any further action which tends to change the status of Jerusalem;

4. *Requests* the Secretary-General to report to the Security Council on the implementation of the present resolution.

III
THE JEWS AND THE WAILING WALL

An example of Zionist tactics and designs for expansion is afforded by consideration of the Wailing Wall Area. How did the Jewish claim to the area start? Did they have any title or any right of possession to the Wailing Wall and the adjacent area in the Arab City of Jerusalem?

The Government of Great Britain, the Administering Power, stated to Parliament in a White Paper, in November 1928, the following:

The Western or Wailing Wall formed part of the western exterior of the ancient Jewish Temple; as such, it is holy to the Jewish community, and their custom of praying there extends back to the Middle Ages and possibly further. The Wall is also part of the Haram-al-Sharif; as such, it is holy to Moslems. Moreover, it is legally the absolute property of the Moslem community, and the strip of pavement facing it is Waqf property, as is shown by documents preserved by the Guardian of the Waqf.[17]

It is thus clear that the Mandatory Power never doubted the exclusive legal ownership of the Wall and the adjacent pavement by the Moslem community.

Moreover, in 1930 an ad hoc international tribunal was appointed to determine the rights and the claims of both the Moslems and the Jews in connection with that area. This Tribunal consisted of three jurists—from Sweden, Switzerland and the

---

[17] THE WESTERN OR WAILING WALL IN JERUSALEM: MEMORANDUM BY THE SECRETARY OF STATE FOR THE COLONIES, CMD. No. 3229, at 3 (1928).

Netherlands: Eliel Löfgren, formerly Swedish Minister for Foreign Affairs, member of the Upper Chamber of the Swedish Riksdag (to act as Chairman); Charles Barde, Vice-President of the Court of Justice at Geneva, President of the Austro-Roumanian Mixed Arbitration Tribunal, and C. J. van Kempen, formerly Governor of the East Coast of Sumatra, member of the States-General of the Netherlands.

The Tribunal held twenty-three meetings, during which it heard the arguments of both sides and engaged in hearing evidence. It heard fifty-two witnesses, twenty-one presented by the Jewish side, and thirty by the Moslem side and one British official called by the Tribunal.

In its verdict, the Tribunal emphasized that the "Jews do not claim any proprietorship to the Wall or to the Pavement in front of it."[18] But the Tribunal nonetheless "considered it to be its duty to inquire into the question of legal ownership as a necessary basis for determining the legal position in the matter."[19] As a result of thorough investigation, it reached the conclusion that

> [T]he ownership of the Wall, as well as the possession of it and of those parts of its surroundings that are here in question, accrues to the Moslems. The Wall itself as being an integral part of the Haram-esh-Sherif area is Moslem property. From the inquiries conducted by the Commission [same Tribunal] partly in the Sharia Court and partly through the hearing of witnesses' evidence, it has emerged that the Pavement in front of the Wall, where the Jews perform their devotions, is also Moslem property.[20]

The Tribunal went a step further and ascertained that "the area that is coincident with the said Pavement was constituted a Moslem Waqf by Afdal, the son of Saladin, in about the year 1193 A.D."[21]

It was also found that, in about 1320 A.D., what is known as the Magharba Quarter buildings were put up "to serve as lodgings for Moroccan pilgrims, those buildings were also made Waqf by a certain Abu Madian."[22]

The Moslem inhabitants of Jersualem have always objected to any Jewish acts calculated to change the status quo whereby to allege legal possession or ownership.

In 1911, the Guardian of the Abu Madian Waqf, *i.e.*, the Magharba Quarter, had complained that "the Jews, contrary to usage, had placed chairs on the pavement, and he requested that 'in order to avoid a future claim of ownership' the present state of affairs should be stopped."[23] The Administrative Council of Jerusalem thereupon decided that it was not permissible to place on the pavement any article that

---

[18] Report of the Commission appointed by His Majesty's Government . . . with the approval of the Council of the League of Nations, to determine the rights and claims of Moslems and Jews in connection with the Western or Wailing Wall at Jerusalem, Dec. 1930, at 5-6 (London, 1931) (distributed in the United Nations as U.N. Docs. S/8427/Add. 1 and A/7057/Add. 1).

[19] *Id.*

[20] *Id.* at 39-40.

[21] *Id.* at 40.

[22] *Id.*

[23] *Id.* at 45.

could be "considered as indications of ownership."[24]   The Commission found that
the evident motive for the petition and the decision was to prevent any future Jewish
claim to ownership or possession.[25]   It is this same Magharba Quarter which was
recently bulldozed in utter disregard of law, equity, and indeed any moral or religious
values and despite United Nations resolutions on this matter.   It is clear now that the
apparently innocent carrying of chairs, lamps and curtains by the Jewish worshippers
was the first sinister step to deprive Arabs of their title.   The present bulldozing
of the whole Magharba Quarter proves that Arab apprehension was justified.

IV

Other Arab Territories

What is more (and in pursuance of their theory that might gives right), the
Israelis established Jewish settlements and expropriated lands in newly occupied Arab
territories, with no legal basis for this other than force and conquest.   But in international law, the present military supremacy cannot create new rights where none
previously existed.   The late Dag Hammerskjöld, as Secretary-General of the
United Nations, said in a report concerning the 1956 crisis:

> The United Nations cannot condone a change of the *status juris* resulting from
> military action contrary to the provisions of the Charter.   The Organization must,
> therefore, maintain that the *status juris* existing prior to such military action be
> re-established by a withdrawal of troops, and by the relinquishment or nullification of
> rights asserted in territories covered by the military action and depending upon it.[26]

It is evident that Israel cannot dictate its conditions for withdrawal.   Military
conquest cannot be the framework within which peace terms may be negotiated.
How can Arabs be expected to accept any conditions for Israeli withdrawal from
undisputed Arab territory?   This has no justification in law or equity.   It takes us
to the law of the jungle.   The Israeli request implies recognition of rights of conquest, and conquest conveys no right but imposes a duty.   Yes, a duty on the conquered if no measures are taken by the world Organization to check this aggression,
to liberate the homeland from the invaders.   This Israeli behaviour should not be
encouraged.   Israel should receive no support in its dangerous and continued in-
fringements on international law.   The rule of law must be upheld, and, on this point,
we entirely subscribe to the United States views, expressed on 16 November, 1956
by Mr. Herbert Hoover, the Under-Secretary of State, who reminded the Assembly
that:

---

[24] Decision described *id.*

[25] *Id.*   These findings about Moslem legal rights and property vis-à-vis the Western (Wailing) Wall
and adajecent areas were incorporated under: "Palestine (Western or Wailing Wall) Order in Council
1931," which appeared in the *Official Gazette of the Government of Palestine* in an extraordinary
gazette, Supplement No. 8/1931, 8 June, 1931.   This Order came into force on 8th June, 1931.

[26] Report of the Secretary-General in pursuit of General Assembly Resolution 1123, 11 U.N. GAOR,
Annexes, Agenda Item No. 66, at 47, U.N. Doc. A/3512 (1957).

The basic purpose of the Charter is peace with justice. The United States is convinced that the United Nations is the best instrument for achieving this end. Peace
alone is not enough, for without justice, peace is illusory and temporary. On the
other hand, without peace, justice would be submerged by the limitless injustices of
war.[27]

The same theory was reaffirmed by another United States Representative, Ambassador Lodge, when he said:

We do not believe that any Member is entitled to exact a price for its compliance
with the elementary principle of this Organization that: all Members shall refrain
from the use of force against the territorial integrity of any State, or in any other
manner inconsistent with the purposes of the United Nations.[28]

While debating the tripartite invasion before the General Assembly on 1 March,
1957, Mr. Lodge said:

[T]he United States has sought a solution which would be based on justice and
which would take account of the legitimate interests of all the parties. The United
States position was manifested from the very beginning in its draft resolution before
the Security Council [S/3710], which called upon Israel to withdraw and which
called for the withholding of assistance to Israel if it did not withdraw. The United
States views in this respect have been steadfast. They were most recently and
most authoritatively set forth by President Eisenhower in his public address of
20 February 1957. In this endeavour we have recognized that it is incompatible
with the principles of the Charter and with the obligations of membership in the
United Nations for any Member to seek political gains through the use of force or
to use as a bargaining point a gain achieved by means of force.[29]

Thus, if this Israeli theory is permitted to prevail, it will destroy the United
Nations, the effectiveness of its Charter and the sanctity of international law. It
certainly leads to more tension, more complications and more invitations to war in the
future.

The Arab point of view, in the current crisis, is not different from the stand which
the United States adopted in 1956.

Ambassador Goldberg, the distinguished United States representative on the
Security Council and permanent United States representative to the United Nations,
while arguing the case for the United States prior to the Israeli victory, said in
May 1967 that restoration of the status quo is the first essential to peace.

I said that the short-range problem was restoration of the *status quo ante* in the
Strait of Tiran—the status which has existed for eleven years—so that the Council,
enjoying the breathing spell, the cooling-off period that the Secretary-General has
suggested, could consider the underlying problems and arrive at a fair, just and
honourable solution of these problems.[30]

---

[27] 11 U.N. GAOR 91 (1956).
[28] *Id.* at 1052-53.
[29] *Id.* at 1277.
[30] U.N. Doc. S/PV. 1344, May 30, 1907, at 56.

Today, students of international law will certainly ponder the utter inconsistency between the United States policy announced in May and that announced in June of the same year, that is, after the Israeli victory, which said:

> What the Near East needs today are new steps toward real peace, not just a cease-fire, which is what we have today; not just a fragile and perilous armistice, which is what we have had for eighteen years; not just withdrawal which is necessary but insufficient.[31]

Prior to the hostilities, Ambassador Goldberg stated to the Security Council that meaningful peace negotiations could not take place unless the Gulf of Aqaba was reopened to Israeli shipping thereby restoring the *status quo ante*. He added that it would not be possible to negotiate and explore the underlying causes of the Arab-Israeli dispute in the tense atmosphere created by the closing of the Gulf of Aqaba.[32]

Following the Israeli victory the United States adopted an entirely contrary position. Ambassador Goldberg called the *status quo ante*, a "prescription for renewed hostilities."[33]

This attitude, to a great extent, brought about the inaction of the Security Council, which encouraged Israel to refuse to withdraw. Israel now even insists on individual negotiations, *i.e.* under duress and coercion. This is what the Rt. Hon. Anthony Nutting called the doctrine of "divide and conquer" and these are what he called "conquerors' terms."[34]

The Arab position is very clear. We maintain that a military solution or any forced solution is a "prescription for war." I need not remind the reader of the consequences of the Versailles Treaty, nor of the Munich Agreement, nor of what happened when Hitler became intoxicated by his victories. Where did his desire for expansion lead him? He occupied almost all of Europe. He reached Stalingrad and was on the outskirts of Moscow. His influence spread through North Africa and his troops reached the borders of Egypt. None of these territories accepted surrender as the solution or negotiations at gunpoint. His illegal occupation, conquest, and continued expansion did not improve his image. And where is Hitler now? Where is Nazism, and where is Fascism?

In our present case, then, should we accept the substitution of power for justice, might for right, or should justice and right and international law be our guiding principles?

---

[31] U.N. Doc. S/PV. 1358, June 13, 1967, p. 51.
[32] *See* U.N. Docs. S/PV. 1343, May 29, 1967, at 6-21, and S/PV. 1344, May 30, 1967, at 52-58.
[33] U.N. Doc. A/PV. 1527, June 30, 1967, at 16-17.
[34] Anthony Nutting, The Tragedy of Palestine from the Balfour Declaration to Today, address delivered at the annual conference of the American Council for Judaism, Nov. 2, 1967, at 6.

SOME INTERNATIONAL CONSTITUTIONAL ASPECTS OF THE PALESTINE CASE

JOHN W. HALDERMAN*

I

RELEVANT THEORIES OF THE CHARTER

The early Palestine case in the United Nations demonstrated the inadequacy of the prevailing theory as to how the Organization would deal with disputes and situations as part of its major function of maintaining peace and security. The case practically forced upon world attention the outline of another approach believed to have greater potential for the development of law, and actually more in keeping with the Charter as written, than the predominant theory. Subsequent developments in the U.N. handling of the case did not, however, on the whole, contribute to the development of this theory or, indeed, any consistent theory, but rather contributed to the present state of confusion as to the true nature of the powers of the world Organization in respect to the handling of disputes and situations.

The predominant theory of the Charter was sometimes expressed as embodying the combination of power with responsibility for the preservation of peace. It was thought that the desired combination could be achieved by giving permanent seats on the Security Council to the five major wartime allies, and by placing primary responsibility upon that organ for the maintenance of peace and security. The requirement of unanimity among the five, written into the Charter, was a manifestation of the fact, obvious enough in retrospect, that they regarded themselves as continuing to be fully sovereign in the traditional sense, and, consequently, of the essentially political approach, as distinguished from what might be called a legal or constitutional approach, upon which the predominant theory of the Charter was based.

This theory was also manifested by the intention that "enforcement measures" would be the principal power of the Organization for the maintenance of peace and security. This was the power given to the Council to apply sanctions—military measures or measures short of force—to the extent necessary for the maintenance of peace and security. As thus defined, the enforcement power could include the right to decide substantive issues in dispute and to enforce such decisions, with the effect

* LL.B. 1931, University of Oregon. Research Associate, Rule of Law Research Center, Duke University. Member of Secretariat, U.N. Conference on International Organization, San Francisco, 1945; served as a legal adviser to U.S. delegations to U.N. Preparatory Commission, 1945, first session of General Assembly, 1946, and other U.N. meetings; worked on Palestine case in Office of U.N. Political Affairs, U.S. Department of State, 1948-50. National War College Graduate, 1951; U.S. Foreign Service, 1951-59. Author, THE UNITED NATIONS AND THE RULE OF LAW (1966).

of forcing changes in the relationships of states, internal and external, without their consent.

The predominant theory of the Charter thus carried the possibility that the Organization might impinge upon the proposition, basic since the beginning of the modern state system, that there is no higher law-making authority than the states themselves.

This potential collision of basic concepts was treated rather ambivalently during discussions leading to the Charter.[1] The prevailing view of the enforcement function was that this was the essential power which was to enable the Organization to deal with aggressions such as had led to the Second World War. From this point of view, the question of resolving substantive issues in dispute between states was not directly relevant. It was regarded, as it always had been, as being primarily the responsibility of the parties to the disputes. With respect to the power of the Organization to contribute to the peaceful settlement of disputes, the Dumbarton Oaks Proposals advocated that it should have power to recommend procedures of settlement when the parties had failed to settle a case by means of their own choice.[2] When it was proposed by the British Delegation at San Francisco that the Council should be empowered to recommend actual terms of settlement,[3] there was a reluctance due to traditional fears of wrongful interference, intensified by recent memories of Munich. As to this British proposal, Mr. Dulles is reported as stating, in effect, in a United States Delegation meeting:[4]

[U]nder the Dumbarton Oaks Proposals it had been generally understood that the Security Council would act only as a policeman and would not itself have the function of settling disputes on the basis of merit. The British proposal goes very much farther by making the Security Council the arbiter of the world.

In a Four-Power Consultative Meeting, a United States spokesman, after indicating opposition to the British proposal, went on to say: "As matters now stand the Council can in any case take enforcement action if the dispute is not settled."[5] That the satisfactory handling of a dispute might require the solution of the substantive issue was indicated as follows by an advisor in a United States Delegation meeting, speaking of what was to become Chapter VII of the Charter defining the enforcement function:[6]

---

[1] *See, e.g.,* Minutes of the Eighteenth Meeting of the United States Delegation, San Francisco, April 26, 1945, [1945] 1 FOREIGN REL. U.S. 418-26 (1967).

[2] Ch. VIII, sec. A, para. 5. The text of the Proposals may be found in [1944] 1 FOREIGN REL. U.S. 890, 896 (1966).

[3] Minutes of the Second Four-Power Consultative Meeting on Charter Proposals, San Francisco, May 3, 1945, [1945] 1 FOREIGN REL. U.S. 565 (1967).

[4] Minutes of the Twenty-Eighth Meeting of the United States Delegation, San Francisco, May 3, 1945, *id.* at 577.

[5] Minutes of the Third Four-Power Consultative Meeting, *supra* note 3, at 586.

[6] Minutes of the Eighteenth Meeting of the United States Delegation, *supra* note 1, at 418.

[U]nder paragraph 1, Section B of Chapter VIII [of the Dumbarton Oaks Proposals] the authority to recommend procedures and terms of settlement would lie in the Security Council if it was determined that a threat to the peace exists. The Security Council under this paragraph would have unlimited powers to avert a threat to international peace and security and could even impose the terms of settlement. Perhaps this provision goes too far, but this is a possible interpretation.

A United States Delegate pointed out in the same meeting:[7]

[T]he matter had been discussed endlessly in the State Department, and then the question had been taken to Dumbarton Oaks and the controversy had raged again there. It was his belief that the problem would still come up in the Organization if it were not clarified in the Charter.

The matter was, in fact, clarified in the Charter through the adoption of the proposal, which became Article 37, authorizing the Council to recommend terms of settlement of disputes. It was emphasized at the time that this power was limited to that of recommendation, and would have no binding force.[8]

As to the enforcement function, language had been proposed at Dumbarton Oaks, and was carried into the Charter as Article 1, paragraph 1, which can readily be read either as including or excluding the power to enforce decisions on the merits. Article 1, paragraph 1, provides:

The Purposes of the United Nations are:

1. To maintain international peace and security, and to that end: to take effective collective measures for the prevention and removal of threats to the peace, and for the suppression of acts of aggression or other breaches of the peace . . . .

In Chapter VII, the introductory provision is consistent with this definition, authorizing the Council to determine the existence of threats to peace, breaches of peace and acts of aggression, and, in the event of such finding, to make recommendations for settlement, and, if necessary, decide upon measures of force or measures less than force to deal with the situation.

The limitation of the Organization's peaceful settlement function to the power of recommending terms of settlement meant, of course, that it could not make legally binding decisions. The collective measures function should have been correspondingly interpreted as excluding the power to enforce such decisions.

However, the adoption of this language did not, in fact, suffice to change the prevalent thinking. The problem did come up in the Organization, and notably in the Palestine case.

That case came into the United Nations when Great Britain decided to give up

---

[7] *Id.* at 423.
[8] Report of Rapporteur of Committee III/2 to Commission III, Doc. 1027, III/2/31 (1), 12 U.N.C.I.O. Docs. 159, 162 (1945), reprinted in UNITED NATIONS CONFERENCE ON INTERNATIONAL ORGANIZATION: SELECTED DOCUMENTS 756, 759 (1946).

the Mandate of Palestine with which it had been entrusted by the League of Nations, and called upon the United Nations to provide for the future government of that country.[9] The General Assembly, by resolution of November 29, 1947,[10] undertook to fulfill this request by recommending the Plan of Partition with Economic Union of Palestine. Under this Plan, Palestine was to be divided into three parts: an Arab state, a Jewish state, and the Jerusalem area which was to be placed under an international regime administered by the United Nations. The whole of Palestine was to constitute an economic union.

As a result of indications that the Arabs of Palestine and the surrounding Arab states would reject any plan envisioning partition of Palestine, the Assembly majority proceeded to incorporate in its resolution the requests that

> (b) The Security Council consider, if circumstances during the transitional period require such consideration, whether the situation in Palestine constitutes a threat to the peace. If it decides that such a threat exists, and in order to maintain international peace and security, the Security Council should supplement the authorization of the General Assembly by taking measures, under Articles 39 and 41 of the Charter, to empower the United Nations Commission, as provided in this resolution, to exercise in Palestine the functions which are assigned to it by this resolution;
> (c) The Security Council determine as a threat to the peace, breach of the peace or act of aggression, in accordance with Article 39 of the Charter, any attempt to alter by force the settlement envisaged by this resolution . . . .

The Commission referred to was the U.N. Palestine Commission, which was given the function of implementing the Plan. Articles 39 and 41 of the Charter provide for the use of force to deal with threats to peace or breaches of peace. The above-quoted paragraphs thus tended to convey the impression that the United Nations might undertake enforcement of the Plan as such, provided that the situation was deemed to constitute a threat to international peace. Sponsors of the paragraphs made it clear that the purpose they had in mind was implementation of the Plan as such.[11] The United States Delegation insisted that the decision whether a threat to peace exists must, under the Charter, rest with the Security Council in the exercise of its independent judgment.[12] However, the language of paragraph (b), which that Delegation supported, indicates that, once a threat to peace had been found to exist, resulting action would have the purpose of enforcing the Plan as such. Arab delegations requested to have submitted for adjudication the question whether the

---

[9] Letter from the United Kingdom Delegation . . . , U.N. GAOR, 1st Spec. Sess., vol. I, Annex I, at 183, U.N. Doc. A/286 (1947).

[10] G.A. Res. 181, 2 U.N. GAOR Resolutions 131 (1947), U.N. Doc. A/519 (1948).

[11] 2 U.N. GAOR, Ad Hoc Comm. on the Palestinian Question 166 (1947) (New Zealand); id. at 170 (Denmark); id. at 221 (Canada). The Danish Delegation introduced the paragraphs in question. Annexes 20 and 20a, id. at 266-67, U.N. Docs. A/AC.14/43 and A/AC.14/43/Rev. 1 (1947).

[12] 2 U.N. GAOR, Ad Hoc Comm. on the Palestinian Question 221 (1947); 3 U.N. SCOR, 260th meeting 401 (1948).

Council had the power to enforce the Plan.[13] This request was overridden with little discussion.[14]

Other statements tending to convey the impression that the Council had the power to enforce the Plan as such were made by the Secretary-General, in a statement to the first meeting of the Palestine Commission,[15] and by that Commission in requesting the provision of force by the Council, so that it could carry out its task.[16] This last request was made because of rising violence in Palestine as the end of the Mandate approached.

As a result of these pronouncements and others,[17] there appears to have been a widespread expectation that the Plan would be enforced if necessary.[18]

However, the issue between Arabs and Jews finally went to the arbitrament of force and the Security Council did not undertake enforcement measures of any kind, for any purpose. The Plan of Partition with Economic Union collapsed.

The reason it was not enforced may well have been stated by the Indian Delegation to an ensuing special session of the General Assembly:[19]

> It had been said that any solution would require force, but this ignored the difference between the temporary employment of force to maintain law and order and the perpetual use of force to uphold an arrangement unacceptable to the majority of the population. The only permanent solution could come through agreement.

Along the same line, certain members of the United States Department of State asked how it would be possible to enforce the economic union, which was an integral part of the Plan.[20]

Recognition of the inadequacy of the "enforcement" function implied the inadequacy of the predominant theory of the Charter. A move toward a different theory is indicated in the following explanation of the United States Representative to the Security Council of his delegation's decision to abandon enforcement of the Plan as such:[21]

> The recommendations of the General Assembly have great moral force which applies to all Members regardless of the views they hold or the votes they may have cast on any particular recommendation . . . .
>
>   . . . .
>
> The Security Council is authorized to take forceful measures with respect to

---

[13] Report of Subcommittee 2 to the Ad Hoc Comm. on the Palestinian Question, 2 U.N. GAOR, Ad Hoc Comm. on the Palestinian Question 270, 299-301, U.N. Doc. A/AC.14/32 (1947).

[14] The principal discussion and only votes took place at the committee stage. 2 U.N. GAOR, Ad Hoc Comm. on the Palestinian Question 201-03 (1947).

[15] U.N. Doc. A/AC.21/SR.1 (1948).

[16] 3 U.N. SCOR, Spec. Supp. 2, at 10, 18-19, U.N. Doc. A/AC.21/9 (1948).

[17] See, e.g., Soviet statement in 3 U.N. SCOR, 270th meeting 143 (1948).

[18] See, e.g., N.Y. Times, Feb. 25, 1948, at 1, col. 6.

[19] U.N. GAOR, 2d Spec. Sess., 1st Comm. 64 (1948).

[20] N.Y. Times, March 4, 1948, at 10, col. 4.

[21] 3 U.N. SCOR, 253d meeting 265-67 (1948).

Palestine to remove a threat to international peace. The Charter of the United Nations does not empower the Security Council to enforce a political settlement whether it is pursuant to a recommendation of the General Assembly or of the Security Council itself.

What this means is this: The Security Council under the Charter can take action to prevent aggression against Palestine from outside. The Security Council, by these same powers, can take action to prevent a threat to international peace and security from inside Palestine. But this action must be directed solely to the maintenance of international peace. The Security Council's action, in other words, is directed to keeping the peace and not to enforcing partition.

It was argued that this distinction was unreal since, if force had been applied strictly for the purpose of restoring peace, it would have had to be directed against the Arabs, who were resisting partition, and thus would have enabled the Jewish state to be set up and would have amounted, in effect, to enforcement of this vital part of the Plan.[22] Since this analysis was apparently correct, the question is suggested whether it would not have been the desirable course to state candidly that the real purpose of Security Council measures was to enforce the Plan as such.

II

A THEORY OF POSSIBLE POTENTIAL

The answer to this question, inherent in the main thesis of the present discussion, may take as its starting point the proposition that this phase of the Palestine case proved that the predominant theory of the Charter was inadequate. It did so in a way that resulted in the United States Representative moving over, at least temporarily, to a second theory which can be said to find its principal Charter statement in Article 37, authorizing the Council to recommend terms of settlement, and under which the central prerequisite becomes not enforcement through the collaboration of the major powers, but the willingness of parties to abide by United Nations recommendations for the substantive solutions of disputes.

By the time of the Palestine case there had already been strong indications in the German, Korean, Iranian and Greek cases, and in the Czech case which arose at this time, that the great power collaboration upon which the predominant theory of the Charter rested was not to be forthcoming. Also, the major powers had failed in negotiations on the agreements contemplated by Article 43 of the Charter, to be concluded between member states and the Security Council, concerning the troops and facilities to be provided to enable the Council to carry out its enforcement function. The Palestine case proved a point that still needed to be proved, namely that, at least in a case of this severity, the Council did not have the enforcement capability to fulfill its major purpose of maintaining peace and security even when the five permanent members were in accord. When, in these circumstances, the United States Representative stressed a moral obligation on the part of the Arab states

---

[22] See, e.g., id. 261st meeting 12-13 (1948).

to accept the Assembly's recommendation of terms of settlement, he was pointing out what was, in fact, the essential requirement for the fulfillment of this major purpose. However, the requisite moral force to bring about acceptance of the resolution was in fact lacking. The Arab states regarded the Plan as immoral and wrongful, and considered themselves perfectly justified in rejecting and resisting it.

If the Assembly's recommendation had been complied with, notwithstanding Arab disapproval of it, such acceptance would have constituted strong evidence of the existence of the kind of moral force that the United States Representative said existed. The ability of the United Nations to gain acceptance for its recommendations in this and similarly serious disputes would also have signified the existence of real law. It is fruitless, in this area, to distinguish moral obligations from legal obligations. Law means moral force, and both entail the requisite consensus of public opinion as to the meaning of justice.

Thus, the Palestine case, in its early phase, provided considerable proof that the predominant theory of the Charter, based on the ideas of power combined with responsibility and of great-power collaboration, and which regarded the enforcement function as the essential power of the Organization, was inadequate. While reason was thus given for governments and peoples to look for a new theory which might lay the basis for the successful achievement of the Organization's principal objective, such a course was discouraged by the growing east-west struggle. Western states, which had the greatest interest in the success of the Organization, were forced to look to their defenses, thus reinforcing the traditional approach to international relations based on power and politics. This tendency has increased in ensuing years.

If governments and peoples had then undertaken, or should still undertake, the search for a new theory to enable the Organization to fulfill its major purpose, what might be the nature of such a theory?

Although emphasis has been placed above upon the necessity of gathering moral force behind the recommendations of the United Nations on substantive issues in dispute, this line of thought may have greater relevance to the question of means than to that of the goal itself. It is indeed difficult to foresee a time when states will be willing to accept recommendations requiring sacrifices of what they regard as their vital interests. What is required, rather, would seem to be a transformation of thinking on the part of all concerned—a growth of consensus as to the meaning of justice—to the point where such differences will no longer exist to the extent of being able to cause wars.

The actual content of recommendations and, more broadly, the mode of handling actual disputes and situations by the United Nations, is believed to have a potential contribution to make to the achievement of this objective because of the public attention focused upon such matters.

An ultimate objective of endeavors properly to use the United Nations in concrete cases is, from this point of view, the growth of confidence in the system. Of practically equal importance is the development in the public mind of a consistent and workable set of principles and procedures, forming an adequate system for handling disputes and situations. It is not to be expected, in many cases, that there will be agreement as to what the correct applicable principles and procedures are—particularly, substantive principles. It is for this reason that emphasis is placed upon the effort made to decide correctly, rather than upon the actual application of correct principles. Efforts made, and seen to be made, by competent authorities to cause the United Nations to do justice in accordance with identifiable principles dispassionately applied should be expected, in time, to develop confidence in the system, and contribute to the emergence of the general outline of the system's structure.

On the other hand, the goal would seem inevitably to be set back to the extent that public efforts to deal with an important case tend to cause confusion as to relevant principles and powers. In this connection, the original predominant theories which were carried into the United Nations were inherently confusing. On one hand, there was a deliberate continuance of the traditional refusal of states to recognize a higher law-making authority; on the other, it was considered that the Organization should have a power of enforcement enabling it to do whatever was necessary for the maintenance of peace and security.

It is submitted that what has been referred to above as a second, potential theory of the Charter furnishes a consistent and workable outline which can be built upon. As it was outlined in the statement of the United States Representative above quoted, which finds a basis in the Charter as written, it would include a peaceful settlement function embracing a power of persuasion on the part of the Organization; and a collective measures function authorizing the application of measures of force or less than force for dealing with aggressions, other breaches of peace and threats to peace, but not, of course, including the power to enforce decisions on the merits as such.

The Palestine case has furnished perhaps more opportunities than any other case to come before the United Nations for utilizing the Organization in such manner as to advance or set back the prospects of developing law and the Charter. Some aspects of the case bearing on such matters may be briefly considered, evaluating them against the theory of the Charter just referred to.

A. Peaceful Settlement Function

Attention may first be given to the peaceful settlement function of the United Nations. While, as has been indicated, the Charter specifically provides that this should be essentially a power of persuasion, an important aspect of the function in practice consists in continuing efforts to make it appear as embracing the power to decide substantive issues with legally binding effect. Notwithstanding the proof of its inadequacy given by the failure of the Plan of Partition with Economic Union, as indicated above, parties to the Palestine dispute continued to assert the rule in question. Thus Israel claimed that the Assembly's resolution of November 29, 1947, recommending the Plan, was "the only internationally valid adjudication on the question of the future government of Palestine."[23] As to Jerusalem, however, which, under the same Plan, was to become an international city, the Israeli position was different. It was now holding the western part of the city, and claimed the right to continue to do so on the ground that the Arab attack on the city had invalidated that part of the Plan.[24] The Arabs, on the other hand, claimed that the part of the Plan calling for partition was a mere recommendation which they were entitled to reject;[25] however, the Israeli seizure of the western portion of Jerusalem was characterized by the Arabs as a violation of the Assembly resolution in question.[26]

The next phase of the case relevant to the present discussion concerned the refusal of Egypt to allow passage of Israeli-connected ships and cargoes through the Suez Canal. By its resolution of September 1, 1951,[27] the Security Council "called upon" Egypt to terminate these restrictions. Whereas clarity as to United Nations powers being exercised would seem indispensable to building an effective set of principles and procedures with roots in public opinion, the phrase "calls upon" seems calculated to cause uncertainty as to whether the Council was purporting to decide with binding effect or merely to recommend that Egypt take the desired action. The body of the resolution was also ambivalent, indicating in part that the Egyptian restrictions were in violation of existing legal obligations, and in part that they were wrong on grounds of equity and justice. The accusation that the measures violated existing law could have been decided only by the International Court of Justice or other competent tribunal and only if the parties agreed to submit the question; the proper role of the Council on this point would have been to recommend such submission. If the purpose were, on the other hand, to propose that Egypt change its regulations on grounds of equity and justice, neither the Council nor any other organ has been empowered to make binding orders to such effect. The relevant power which has been agreed to by all members of the United Nations is that of recommendation.

Two years later Israel asserted that Egypt had "defied" the resolution of September 1, 1951, "in contravention of Article 25 of the Charter."[28] Article 25 provides that member states agree to carry out decisions of the Security Council. However, under the Charter as written, the provision could not be intended to apply to proposals for changing existing legal relationships because it is specifically provided else-

---

[23] 3 U.N. GAOR, Supp. 11, Annex I, at 24, U.N. Doc. A/648 (1948).

[24] 3 U.N. GAOR, pt. 1, 1st Comm. 644-45 (1948).

[25] U.N. GAOR, 2d Spec. Sess., 1st Comm. 22-23 (1948).

[26] 4 U.N. GAOR, Ad Hoc Political Comm. 269 (1949).

[27] S.C. Res. 95.

[28] Letter dated 9 September 1953 . . . , 8 U.N. SCOR, Supp. July-Sept. 1953, at 75, U.N. Doc. S/3093 (1953).

where in that instrument that the relevant power is that of recommendation.[29] Again in 1954 an Israeli spokesman asserted that Egypt was continuing to "defy" the "verdict" of the Council represented by the resolution of September 1, 1951.[30] Other states also, in these debates, indicated that they regarded that resolution as legally binding.[31] In 1956 the Secretary-General referred to it as having "adjudicated" the controversy.[32]

Such expressions no doubt encouraged later actions and expressions tending to convey the impression of a power on the part of the United Nations to enforce decisions on the merits, including even such a power on the part of the General Assembly.[33] Such indications tend to be confusing because they conflict with the general knowledge that no such power was incorporated in the Charter, and that states have not tacitly accepted any such power with a scope that would permit general application. The indications referred to on the part of the General Assembly, which probably derived in part from the handling of the early Palestine case, also conflict with the position maintained officially by the United Nations and others that that organ is without power to do more than make recommendations in the handling of disputes and situations. Finally, since the efforts in question have proved generally unavailing, they must have damaged the prestige of the Organization by creating the impression that the states or regimes in question were successfully defying binding decisions of the United Nations.

There has been, in fact, little or no evidence of willingness on the part of states to accept a power of binding decision on such substantive issues when directed against themselves. Indeed, when states direct their attention toward the procedure of peaceful settlement as such, they tend to emphasize that parties should have freedom of choice as to methods of solution.[34]

The peaceful settlement function as written into the Charter, authorizing the Organization to attempt to persuade the parties to come to agreed solutions, lying between what might be called the two extreme positions just referred to, furnishes a solid starting point for development in that it is a power deliberately conferred

[29] L. GOODRICH & E. HAMBRO, CHARTER OF THE UNITED NATIONS 209 (2d rev. ed. 1949); R. RUSSELL & J. MUTHER, A HISTORY OF THE UNITED NATIONS CHARTER 665 (1958); D. BOWETT, THE LAW OF INTERNATIONAL INSTITUTIONS 32 (1963). But cf. McDougal & Reisman, *Rhodesia and the United Nations: The Lawfulness of International Control*, 62 AM. J. INT'L L. 1, 11 (1968).
[30] 9 U.N. SCOR, 658th meeting 25 (1954).
[31] A draft resolution which would have called upon Egypt "in accordance with its obligations under the Charter to comply" with the resolution of September 1, 1951, 9 U.N. SCOR, Supp. Jan.-March 1954, at 44, U.N. Doc. S/3188 and Corr. 1, would have passed except for a Soviet veto. 9 U.N. SCOR, 664th meeting 12 (1954). See remarks of delegations in *id.*, 663d meeting 3-4, 9.
[32] 11 U.N. SCOR, Supp. April-June 1956, at 52-53, U.N. Doc. S/3596 (1956).
[33] G.A. Res. 1761, 17 U.N. GAOR, Supp. 17, at 9, U.N. Doc. A/5217 (1962); G.A. Res. 1807, *id.* at 39-40. The over-all tendency in the handling of such cases as those concerning *apartheid* in South Africa and Portuguese overseas territories (to which the resolutions just cited respectively pertained) and Rhodesia is indicated by the evident fact that the Security Council's sanctions in the latter case are widely regarded as having the purpose of enforcing substantive decisions.
[34] U.N. Doc. A/6799, September 26, 1967, at 165.

upon the United Nations, and is accepted as generally applicable by all concerned. After the adoption of the Plan of Partition, the Arab states relied to a considerable extent on the assertion that it was merely a recommendation which they were perfectly entitled to reject.[35] This is of course true, and is believed to represent a strength of the recommendatory power from the standpoint of developing law and the Charter in world opinion. It provides greater flexibility than would a decision-making power. The failure of the Plan of Partition was a setback for the United Nations in large part because the impression had been created that it would be enforced if necessary and that, therefore, it had been adopted with legally binding effect. The rejection of a recommendation should not involve any comparable loss of United Nations prestige, and it is herein considered that the effort should be made, in the handling of cases, to have the right of rejection fully understood and accepted. The potential of this procedure in developing moral force behind the actions of the United Nations is believed to lie in the impact made on public opinion as the result of efforts to use the power properly, in a dispassionate search for justice.

Pursuing the theory that correct applications of the peaceful settlement function to concrete disputes may contribute to the growth of law, it is when we turn from questions of procedure to those of substantive principle that it is necessary to emphasize the importance of the effort made, rather than the correctness of the principles applied, as the decisive factor. This is because it is frequently impossible to know with certainty what substantive principle or principles ought to be applied in a given situation.

The early Palestine case, in which the Organization recommended the partition of the country, is an example. It will be a long time, if ever, before dispassionate people are able to say with any certainty what was the course of true justice in that situation. While the Plan of Partition overrode the principle of self-determination, the force of Zionism at the time was such as would undoubtedly have brought about partition in any case; the Plan, if carried out, would have had the advantageous tendency of lessening tensions, by providing for an economic union, and for free access of all concerned to Jerusalem.

The case also illustrates that the principle applicable to a case may change with passage of time, not only from one case to another but even within the same case. Such a change occurred between the Balfour Declaration and the end of the Mandate due to increased Jewish immigration, the intensification of Arab nationalism and other, interrelated, factors.[36]

The case also provides a corrective to undue optimism as to the possibility that competent authorities, however willing, will be able to embark upon the dispassionate search for justice without the intrusion of extraneous political factors. For example, during and after the Second World War, political factors extraneous to the Middle

---

[35] Cf. note 25 supra and accompanying text.
[36] See C. SYKES, CROSSROADS TO ISRAEL 19 (1965); R. CROSSMAN, A NATION REBORN 60-68 (1960).

East compelled British Governments to take different positions on the Palestine case from that represented by the Balfour Declaration of 1917 and the Mandate of 1922.[37]

Despite the difficulties of the case from the standpoint of the substantive solution to be sought, it is believed that the debates did bring out the issues for the benefit of world opinion, and that the recommendation of Partition with Economic Union was not, per se, a setback to the prospect of developing an effective system based on law.

Perhaps the substantive principle most desired to be applied by the Arab states in the present Middle East crisis is the rule, implied in Article 2, paragraph 4, of the Charter, that for a state to gain territory through the use of force is wrongful. This provision is as follows:

> All Members shall refrain in their international relations from the threat or use of force against the territorial integrity or political independence of any state, or in any other manner inconsistent with the Purposes of the United Nations.

This rule, sometimes regarded as the most important of the Charter, has been upheld in some cases by the United Nations (e.g., Greece, Korea, Hungary, and the Suez crisis of 1956); in other, and more recent, cases its application has been defeated, even by the votes of some states which now desire its application against Israel.

When, in December 1961, India used force to annex the Portuguese colonies of Goa, Damão, and Diu, a majority of the Security Council supported a draft resolution[38] which would have cited inter alia the above-quoted Article 2, paragraph 4, of the Charter, deplored the use of force by India, and called for a cessation of hostilities, the withdrawal of Indian forces and the search for a solution by peaceful means.[39] The resolution was defeated by the Soviet veto. The three other votes against it included that of the United Arab Republic.[40] The latter country co-sponsored another proposal[41] which would have declared that the mere existence of the Portuguese colonies in question constituted a threat to international peace.[42] It was defeated, receiving only the votes of the UAR, the USSR, and two other members.[43] While the proposed resolution was thus without direct impact, the attempted justification of the use of force by India would seem calculated to strengthen, in the eyes of world opinion, the claim of Israel in the 1967 crisis justifying its action as necessary to meet a threat to peace and to its security. On the basis of

---

[37] See, e.g., C. SYKES, supra note 36, at 179-200, 307; G. KIRK, SURVEY OF INTERNATIONAL AFFAIRS: THE MIDDLE EAST 1945-1960, at 200 (1954); R. CROSSMAN, PALESTINE MISSION: A PERSONAL RECORD 54-58, 188-200 (1947).

[38] U.N. Doc. S/5033 (1961).

[39] 16 U.N. SCOR, 988th meeting 21-22 (1961).

[40] Id. at 26-27.

[41] U.N. Doc. S/5032 (1961).

[42] 16 U.N. SCOR, 988th meeting 22 (1961).

[43] Id. at 26.

evidence known to the world, the threat in this case—the blockading of a waterway deemed vital by Israel, and artillery fire from Syrian onto Israeli territory—was obviously of an altogether different order of magnitude than the alleged threat posed by the Portuguese colonies to India, in the earlier case.

In the West Irian case Indonesia threatened the use of force, if necessary, to take over the territory in question, which it claimed as its own.[44] This question of sovereignty was in dispute, however, and a proposal that it be referred for adjudication was rejected by Indonesia.[45] Among various proposals for settlement in the United Nations, the one which would have involved the peaceful settlement function of the United Nations as such, and which came to vote, had as its central issue the Charter principle of self-determination. The vote was thus not directly upon the issue concerning the use of force, as in the Goan case; the object of the resolution was, of course, both to avoid force and to solve the case through application of the correct substantive principle. The resolution failed for lack of the necessary two-thirds majority,[46] and the paragraph specifically recognizing the principle of self-determination was similarly defeated in a separate vote.[47] Voting against in both cases were the United Arab Republic, Syria, Iraq, Jordan, Lebanon and the USSR. Later, the West Irian case was settled by agreement handing the territory over to Indonesia prior to consultation of the wishes of the inhabitants.[48] This settlement (of which the United Nations was caused to express its appreciation[49]) was said by some delegations to represent a yielding to Indonesia's threat of force.[50]

Other uses of force and threats of force during the period since the adoption of the United Nations Charter could, of course, be mentioned. The Goan and West Irian cases have been discussed as illustrating a point relevant to the present discussion. This is that if the Arab states and the Soviet Union desired the existence of a stronger and more effective rule against the seizure of territory by force to apply against Israel in the 1967 Middle Eastern crisis, those voting in the Goan and West Irian cases could have contributed to that end by voting against the use and threat of force in those respective cases.

B. Collective Measures Function

Turning from the peaceful settlement function to that of collective measures, the concluding phase of the discussion will consider how the application of United Nations force in the Palestine case may have affected the prospects of developing an effective system based on law.

---

[44] 16 U.N. GAOR 848, 849 (1961).
[45] Id. at 848.
[46] Id. at 875.
[47] Id. at 873.
[48] 437 U.N.T.S. 273 (1962); 17 U.N. GAOR, Annexes, Agenda Item No. 89, at 2, U.N. Doc. A/5710 and Add. 1 (1962).
[49] G.A. Res. 1752, 17 U.N. GAOR, Supp. 17, at 70, U.N. Doc. A/5217 (1962).
[50] See, e.g., 17 U.N. GAOR 51, 54, 57 (1962).

The theory of the Charter herein being pursued as having a potential with respect to the development of law would envision the endeavor to develop a United Nations collective measures function coming as close as possible to the ideal of a nonpolitical police function.

While it is not thought that this function has the potentiality of the peaceful settlement function, either as a part of an ultimate system or as contributing to its development, tangible pressures are sometimes applied by the United Nations, and they naturally attract considerable public attention. It is highly desirable that they be used within a framework that will encourage the growth of law. The idea of the police function is valuable for two reasons: first, because it is generally understood by all concerned; secondly, because a function of this general constitutional nature can be conceived as forming a component, useful part of an ultimate system based on law.

As noted above,[51] there appears to be only one authorization to be found in the Charter, as written, for the application of such measures as direct means of handling international disputes and situations. It empowers the United Nations, in the event of an aggression, other breach of peace or threat to peace to apply measures of force or measures short of force (such as diplomatic and economic sanctions) for the purpose of maintaining peace and security. These provisions could theoretically form the basis of a comprehensive function comparable, in constitutional status, to the normal police function.

The United Nations Emergency Force (UNEF) initiated by the General Assembly to serve in the Suez crisis of 1956 conformed to these objective criteria; that is, it was an application of tangible pressure deployed by the United Nations to deal with a situation known to be a threat to peace—an actual breach of peace at the time it was deployed.[52] As to whether it was actually an application of tangible pressure, it is to be observed that it was a military force deployed as such; it was not designated as falling within any non-military category such as that of an observer corps; it had the right to defend its assigned positions in some situations[53]—a power going beyond the customary right of self-defense against wrongful attack; and it had the power of arrest in some situations.[54]

UNEF was not, however, officially regarded as falling within the collective measures function. The reason can be said to have been the persistence of the original predominant theory which regards that function as being the monopoly of the Security Council and as having the purpose of dealing with aggressions such as

[51] See p. 80 *supra*.
[52] *See, e.g.*, G.A. Res. 1000, U.N. GAOR, 1st Emer. Spec. Sess., Supp. 1, at 2, 3, U.N. Doc. A/3354 (1956).
[53] Summary Study of the experience derived from the establishment and operation of the Force . . . , 13 U.N. GAOR, Annexes, Agenda Item No. 65, at 8, 31 (para. 179), U.N. Doc. A/3943 (1958); Schachter, *The Relation of Law, Politics and Action in the United Nations*, 109 ACADEMIE DE DROIT INTERNATIONAL, RECUEIL DES COURS 165, 210 (1963-II).
[54] Summary Study, *supra* note 53, at 17 (para. 70).

gave rise to the Second World War and, therefore, as involving the probability of combat operations. One definition of the relevant Charter function, by the International Court of Justice in 1962, simply ignored the part of the Charter definition which authorizes measures of force for dealing with threats to peace.[55] The Secretary-General, in 1963, indicated that it had only been resorted to once by the United Nations, namely in the Korean case, and he likened it to war.[56]

By reason of this predominant idea of the meaning of collective measures, it was evidently apprehended that to place operations like UNEF in this Charter category would give a misleading idea of their purpose, would have undesirable psychological consequences, and would, in particular, cause states to be reluctant to contribute troops for fear that they would become engaged in hostilities.[57]

Consequently, operations like UNEF, which were designed for lesser applications of pressure having more similarity to the normal concept of the police function and less to outright war, were taken clear out of the collective measures function, placed in the peaceful settlement category of United Nations functions,[58] and given the sub-designation of "peace-keeping operations." A basic part of the concept is the proposition that such forces can operate only with the consent of the parties to the situations in which they are deployed.[59]

Since the object of the concept is to reassure states that the forces in question are prevented by the Charter itself from engaging in hostilities, there is a corollary rule to the effect that once an operation is placed in this category, its status becomes fixed.[60]

Among several objections herein conceived to exist in respect to the concept in question, the most intangible has to do with the fact that there has been demonstrated on the part of members of the United Nations a certain willingness to accept the risks of participation in collective action for the maintenance of peace. It seems a questionable policy to adopt Charter distinctions designed to encourage participation on the grounds that the participants will not be undertaking risks.

Turning to more concrete considerations, the existence of the kind of risks under consideration, and the practical impossibility of knowing in advance when they will arise, was demonstrated by the experience of the United Nations Force in the Congo, which was and still is regarded as a peace-keeping operation.[61] It seems doubtful that governments ever were inclined to place great reliance upon the Charter

[55] Advisory Opinion on Certain Expenses of the United Nations, [1962] I.C.J. 151, 177.

[56] Address by Secretary-General, June 13, 1963, U.N. Press Release SG/1520, June 12, 1963.

[57] Schachter, *supra* note 53, at 220-22.

[58] Introduction to the Annual Report of the Secretary-General on the Work of the Organization, 16 June 1957—15 June 1958, 13 U.N. GAOR, Supp. 1A, at 2, U.N. Doc. A/3844/Add. 1 (1958).

[59] *Id.*; Advisory Opinion on Certain Expenses of the United Nations, *supra* note 55, at 164; Address by Secretary-General, *supra* note 56.

[60] Report of the Secretary-General on the withdrawal of the United Nations Emergency Force, U.N. Doc. A/6730/Add. 3, 26 June 1967, at 21; 4 U.N. MONTHLY CHRON., No. 7, at 135, 136 (July 1967).

[61] *See* Address by Secretary-General, *supra* note 56.

designation given a United Nations operation, in estimating what might be required of it in a tense international situation; any such inclination must have ended when the Force referred to became engaged in hostilities with troops of the secessionist regime of Katanga Province,[62] and was widely regarded as having suppressed that regime by force.

The inadequacy of the concept of the "peace-keeping operation" was again demonstrated when, in May 1967, the Secretary-General withdrew UNEF upon the demand of the United Arab Republic, explaining that this was a peace-keeping operation and consequently could not operate without the consent of the host state.[63]

There were numerous expressions of dismay at this latter action, including one by the President of the United States.[64] What the protestors appear to have wanted was a force that would have had at least the constitutional power of remaining in the United Arab Republic, notwithstanding the withdrawal of that country's consent. Under the Charter as written, such a force would have had to be a collective measure.

There was, of course, no denial that the United Nations had the right to deploy a force designated as a collective, or enforcement, measure in appropriate situations. However, the rule was de-emphasized and attention focused on UNEF which, it was said, was not intended to be such a force.[65]

The Secretary-General did explain, in addition to the constitutional justification for the withdrawal of the Force, that withdrawal was the only *practical* possibility in the circumstances, when demanded by the United Arab Republic.[66] It would have been equally impractical, after withdrawing UNEF, to have sent it in again properly designated as a collective measure, or to have deployed a new force with that designation, and the possibility of doing so was not mentioned. Also applicable was the rule mentioned above that the designation of a measure as a "peace-keeping operation" is to be regarded as permanent.

As a result of these different considerations, the only reason based on the Charter firmly brought before the people of the world in explanation of the withdrawal of UNEF was that consent of the United Arab Republic was a constitutional prerequisite to the functioning of the Force and that, once this was withdrawn, there was no alternative but to remove the Force. Consequently, the impression must have been conveyed that the rights of the United Nations to deal with the situation were

---

[62] *See, e.g.,* Annual Report of the Secretary-General on the Work of the Organization 16 June 1962— 15 June 1963, 18 U.N. GAOR, Supp. 1, at 8-9, U.N. Doc. A/5501 (1963).

[63] *See* U.N. Doc. A/6669, 18 May 1967, at 9. The rule, as a general rule applicable to all "peace-keeping operations," was rather less strongly emphasized in the Secretary-General's later and definitive memorandum of June 26, 1967, *supra* note 60. However, it seems doubtful that a trend away from the rule was intended. *See* the subsequent Introduction to the Annual Report of the Secretary-General on the Work of the Organization 16 June 1966—15 June 1967, 22 U.N. GAOR, Supp. 1A, at 4, U.N. Doc. A/6701/Add. 1 (1967).

[64] 56 DEP'T STATE BULL. 870 (1967).

[65] *Cf.* references cited note 63 *supra.*

[66] U.N. Doc. A/6730, *supra* note 60, at 17-18; 4 U.N. MONTHLY CHRON., *supra* note 60, at 147-49.

subordinated to a kind of contractual relationship between the Organization and the host state.

It would seem detrimental to the development of law, on a Charter basis, thus to convey the impressions that the United Nations is legally unable to act in some situations in which action is evidently required for the maintenance of peace, and that the right of the Organization to act in some cases is even subordinated to the consent of one or more states concerned in the respective situations. On the basis of the theory being pursued in this discussion, it would be preferable to strive for a comprehensive and generally understood capability corresponding to the Charter definition of collective measures. The mission of a particular operation could then be defined by the competent organ in light of practical circumstances without giving rise to confusion as to what was permitted under the Charter.

The suggested course of recognizing a single, basic, comprehensive collective measures function, with the scope indicated in the relevant language of the Charter, gives rise to the corollary question whether governments and peoples would have adequate confidence in the judgment and responsibility of the competent organs of the United Nations in defining the missions of such forces. It is believed impossible to escape the proposition, clearly recognized by the framers of the Charter, that competent and responsible decision-making organs are essential prerequisites if the Organization is to fulfill its major purpose.[67] This aspect of the over-all task is especially relevant to the necessity of developing confidence in the system.

It is submitted that the concept of the "peace-keeping operation" might be recognized as a sub-category of the collective measures, or police function. In this way its value might be realized to the appropriate extent, while, at the same time, it is placed in proper relationship to the overriding value believed to inhere in developing an appropriate police function.

The United Nations moved in this direction in the Congolese case when, in 1961, in the Matadi incident, the Congolese Government informed the United Nations that it was placing certain restrictions on the operations of the United Nations Force in that country.[68] The Secretary-General, in reply, while recognizing that the operation had been undertaken with the consent of the Congolese Government, insisted that the resulting relationship was not merely a contractual one in which the host state may determine the circumstances under which the United Nations operates. The role of the Force was rather determined by the responsibilities of the Council with respect to the maintenance of peace and security and it was that organ, alone, it was said, which could determine the discontinuance of the operation.[69]

[67] Report of Rapporteur of Committee III/3 to Commission III on Chapter VIII, Section B, Doc. 881, III/3/46, 12 U.N.C.I.O. Docs. 502, 505-506 (1945), reprinted in UNITED NATIONS CONFERENCE ON INTERNATIONAL ORGANIZATIONS: SELECTED DOCUMENTS 761, 763-64 (1946).

[68] Report dated 8 March 1961 . . . , 16 U.N. SCOR, Supp. Jan.-March 1961, at 239, U.N. Doc. S/4761 (1961).

[69] Id. at 262-63.

At least under the Charter as written, a force operating under authority of the United Nations, irrespective of consent of the host state, would have to be a collective measure. UNEF was, in fact, initiated by the General Assembly, and for the Secretary-General to have followed the Matadi precedent in the crisis of May 1967, it would have been necessary to give some recognition to a power on the part of the General Assembly to initiate such measures.

The need for at least a residual power on the part of that organ to apply collective measures is inherent in the thesis of the present discussion, which relates to the necessity of formulating a new and more adequate theory than that originally entertained as to the handling of disputes and situations under the Charter, and the subsidiary view that the Organization should endeavor to develop a comprehensive collective measures function comparable to the normal concept of the police function. The inadequacy of the originally predominant theory in according to the Security Council a monopoly of power with respect to collective measures was recognized in 1950, in connection with the Korean case, and led to the General Assembly's Uniting for Peace Resolution of that year which asserted the right of that organ to initiate measures when the Council was prevented by the unanimity rule from taking action deemed necessary.[70] This resolution can be interpreted as outlining the theory that the Security Council has the primary authority to apply necessary measures for the maintenance of peace and security, and that the Assembly has a residual authority enabling it to act when the Council is prevented from doing so. This line of thought leads to the logical conclusion that the Assembly has a residual power to apply collective measures; however, the interpretation given the resolution by the Secretary-General, and the great majority of members, has stopped short of this last step.

A trend in the direction of recognizing at least a residual power of collective measures on the part of the Assembly would, it is believed, be constructive in terms of the development of law.

It is not intended to suggest that once such a power were recognized, that organ would immediately begin to apply such measures in an effective manner. There are various problems underlying a widespread doubt as to the General Assembly's present capability of participating responsibly in a system of collective security.[71] However, the option of waiting, before dealing with the questions of its power pertaining to collective measures, does not seem to exist. The fact is that the Assembly has already on various occasions initiated measures of tangible pressure, or at least has given the appearance of doing so.[72] At the same time, of course, its power to initiate collective measures has been consistently denied, and the explanations, or lack thereof,

---

[70] G.A. Res. 377, 5 U.N. GAOR, Supp. 20, at 10, U.N. Doc. A/1775 (1950).

[71] See, e.g., Murphy, The Trend Towards Anarchy in the United Nations,·54 A.B.A.J. 267, 269-70 (1968).

[72] In addition to UNEF itself, see particularly G.A. Res. 498, 5 U.N. GAOR, Supp. 20A, at 1, U.N. Doc. A/1775/Add. 1 (1951); also Assembly resolutions cited supra note 33. See generally, J. HALDERMAN, THE UNITED NATIONS AND THE RULE OF LAW 150-51 (1966).

for the measures in question have been such as to contribute to public confusion as to the true powers of the Organization. Proper objectives, in the view of this discussion, are, first, to bring all such actions within a coherent, workable theory and then gradually, through continuous efforts, to translate the theory into actuality. Such efforts, it is believed, can contribute to the development of the Assembly, along with other United Nations organs, as component parts of an effective Organization.

The necessity of such a theory is illustrated by the problem under discussion. The designation given UNEF as a peace-keeping operation proved at least arguably unsatisfactory in the crisis of May 1967. If, in consequence, there should be an important trend of thought toward classifying such operations as collective measures, it would become necessary to consider the power of the General Assembly to initiate such measures. The validity of the particular theory herein advocated is of course arguable. What can be insisted upon is the necessity of some basic rethinking of the Charter to the end of formulating a coherent theory, upon which may be developed a system capable of maintaining peace and security.

SOME LEGAL IMPLICATIONS OF THE 1947 PARTITION RESOLUTION AND THE 1949 ARMISTICE AGREEMENTS

Nabil Elaraby*

I

Plan of Partition with Economic Union

The legal aspects of the 1947 partition resolution may today appear merely academic, outdated events of the past, fit for oblivion and without relevance to the future. The future, however, is determined by the accumulation of past events, and no reasonable concern for the future can possibly exclude a firm grasp of past events.

Discussing the legal aspects of any problem is imperative, if a correct assessment is to be accomplished; more so in the case of Palestine, since the legal considerations were consistently disregarded when the decisions were taken. Even the United Nations, which was created to save succeeding generations from the scourge of war and reaffirm faith in fundamental human rights so that justice could always be maintained, failed to consider the juridical aspects of the Palestine question.

The fate of the Palestinians was decided for them by the United Nations, to their detriment, without reference to the rule of law. No impartial observer could, in all fairness, deny that the United Nations was rushed into far-reaching actions affecting the lives of nearly two million Palestinians without having given careful and thorough examination to the legal implications involved. The legitimate aspirations and the high hopes of the whole Arab nation were consequently shattered when they saw with deep sorrow that the United Nations, the supposed conscience of mankind, had reached biased conclusions that brought grievous damage to the cause of justice and international morality.

In fact, throughout the twenty-year debate on Palestine in the United Nations, the international organization deviated time and again from the path which justice, law, and ethics would dictate. The law of the Charter was sacrificed for the convenience of political expediency.

A comprehensive treatment of the various historical developments is beyond the scope of this presentation. It is only proposed to examine how the United Nations proceeded to decide the fate of Palestine without due regard to the rule of law and the basic requirements of justice.

---

* Mr. Elaraby is First Secretary, Mission of the United Arab Republic to the United Nations. He is a graduate of the Faculty of Law, Cairo University, in 1955, and received the Diploma de Perfezionamento in Diritto e Politica Internazionale after study at the Institute of Political Science at the University of Rome. He is presently studying for a doctorate at New York University School of Law, where he is a candidate for an LL.M. degree in International Law.

Great Britain brought the question of Palestine before the United Nations by letter of April 2, 1947,[1] indicating the wish to relinquish the Mandate which had been conferred upon it by the League of Nations, and suggesting that the United Nations make recommendations for the future government of Palestine.

As stated in the Preamble of the Mandate for Palestine, the United Kingdom undertook "to exercise it on behalf of the League of Nations."[2] The Mandate must be considered in the light of the Covenant. One of the primary responsibilities of the Mandatory Power was to assist the peoples of the territory to achieve full self-government and independence at the earliest possible date. Article 22, paragraph 1 of the Covenant stipulated that "the well-being and development of such peoples form a sacred trust of civilization." Palestine also fell within the scope of Article 22, paragraph 4, of the Covenant, which stipulated that

> Certain communities, formerly belonging to the Turkish Empire, have reached a stage of development where their existence as independent nations can be provisionally recognized, subject to the rendering of administrative advice and assistance by a mandatory power until such time as they are able to stand alone.

The provisions of that paragraph undoubtedly encompassed Palestine, and as a constitutional instrument, the Covenant's stipulations should supersede any previous rule which might contradict it. Likewise, any subsequent agreement regarding the communities formerly constituting the Turkish Empire was preconditioned by the legal status declared in the same paragraph 4, namely, that their existence as independent nations "can be provisionally recognized." Hence, it was originally envisioned that when the stage of rendering administrative advice and assistance had been concluded and the Mandate had come to an end, Palestine would be independent as of that date, since its provisional independence as a nation was legally acknowledged by the Covenant. The only limitation imposed by the League's Covenant upon the sovereignty and full independence of the people of Palestine was a temporary tutelage entrusted to a Mandatory Power. As already stated, this was foreseen as a means of rendering advice and assistance to the Palestinians "until such time as they are able to stand alone." Moreover, the Covenant clearly differentiated between the communities which formerly belonged to the Turkish Empire and other, less advanced, people. Regarding the latter, the Mandatory Power was held responsible for the complete administration of the territory and was not confined to administrative advice and assistance.[3] These distinct arrangements can be interpreted as further recognition by the Covenant of the special status of the former Turkish territories.

Accordingly, the only course of action which the Charter dictated in 1947 was

---

[1] Letter from the United Kingdom delegation, U.N. GAOR, 1st Spec. Sess., Plenary, Annex 1, at 183 (1947).

[2] CMD. No. 1785 (1923), reprinted in Report of the U.N. Special Committee on Palestine [hereinafter cited as UNSCOP Report], 2 U.N. GAOR, Supp. 11, vol. II, at 18, U.N. Doc. A/292 (1947).

[3] Article 22, para. 5, Covenant of the League of Nations.

for the United Nations to ascertain the wishes of the lawful inhabitants of Palestine. International law and justice required that those Jews and Arabs who, by virtue of birth, length or status of residence, could satisfy the general requirements of "nationals," should determine the future government of Palestine. However, it is axiomatic that only legal residents have a legitimate right to participate in any plebiscite. Rules to this effect are embodied in the laws of all countries and are universally accepted.

In 1947, over two-thirds of the Palestinians were Arabs who would unreservedly have opted for independence. Any alteration of their lawful and inalienable right to self-determination would run counter to the principles on which the Charter was founded. Yet, when five Arab states communicated to the Secretary-General their request that the agenda of the General Assembly's special session include an item entitled "the termination of the Mandate over Palestine and the declaration of its independence," the General Committee declined to recommend its inclusion.[4] The argument raised by the Arab delegates, namely, that their item should be included on the agenda, since it sought not to limit debate but to assure that independence was taken into account as a possible solution, was disregarded.

The Arab states, from the outset, demanded the independence of Palestine as the only logical solution to the termination of the Mandate. They based their case on the terms of Mandate and Covenant, mentioned above, and on the fact that all other mandated areas covered by Article 22, paragraph 4 of the Covenant, obtained their independence when the respective Mandates came to an end. The rights of the minorities could have been properly safeguarded in accordance with international law and the United Nations Charter.

This analysis seems to be substantiated by the United Nations Charter, the prime purposes of which, as set forth in Article 1, include, *inter alia*, the development of friendly relations among nations "based on respect for the principle of equal rights and self-determination of peoples."

It might be argued that the Palestine Mandate was, however, conditioned by the international recognition accorded the Balfour Declaration.[5] This pronouncement could not have altered the legitimacy of Palestine's independence. The fate of the Palestinians as a whole, Arabs and Jews alike, was governed by the relevant provisions of the Covenant and, subsequently, the Charter. These fundamental documents, having a much higher legal value, took precedence over any provision incorporated in a mandate or trusteeship agreement.

The General Assembly, having refused to include independence for Palestine as a separate item on its agenda, established a Special Committee on Palestine (UNSCOP) to prepare a report for the second session of the Assembly. Logic

[4] U.N. GAOR, 1st Spec. Sess., General Comm. 81 (1947).
[5] For text, see CMD. No. 5479, at 22 (1937); UNSCOP Report, *supra* note 2.

would have required UNSCOP to confine its investigation solely to the problem of Palestine. The fact that there were destitute and homeless Europeans of Jewish faith outside of Palestine should not have been a factor in deciding the future government in Palestine.

However, it was decided in the General Assembly resolution of May 15, 1947,[6] which established UNSCOP, to give the Committee broad powers. Paragraph 4 of that resolution permits it to conduct its investigations "wherever it may deem useful." The resolution also allowed it to receive and examine testimony not only from the Palestinians, both Arabs and Jews, and the governments concerned, but also "from such organizations and individuals as it may deem necessary." This was considered as giving UNSCOP the right to tackle questions beyond the boundaries of Palestine such as the problem of the displaced persons in Europe. This interpretation was reaffirmed by the broad terms of reference embodied in paragraph 2 of the same resolution which vested UNSCOP with "the widest powers to ascertain and record facts . . . *relevant* to the problem of Palestine."[7] One is inclined to believe that by so broadening the scope of the Special Committee's investigative authority, the United Nations prejudiced the fate of Palestinian Arabs. This course of action could hardly have contributed to the achievement of an impartial and just solution for Palestine.

At any rate, the UNSCOP report to the General Assembly did contain two recommendations relevant to the problem of displaced persons of Jewish faith in Europe. The first (recommendation VI) was adopted unanimously.[8] It requested the Assembly to undertake immediately the necessary measures whereby the problem of the displaced European Jews would be dealt with as a matter of extreme urgency. This was recommended as an important factor in allaying the fears of Arabs in Palestine as well as in other Arab states, so that their countries would not be marked as the sole place of settlement for the Jews of the world. Thus UNSCOP expressly stated that the problem of the displaced European Jews should not be solved at the expense of the Arabs. The second recommendation, approved by a substantial majority, stated that "in the appraisal of the Palestine question, it accepted as incontrovertible that any solution for Palestine can not be considered as a solution of the Jewish problem in general."[9]

It would seem abundantly clear that although the majority of UNSCOP did recommend partition and the creation of a Jewish state in Palestine, it was not suggested that the creation of this state would be the solution for displaced European Jews. Unlimited Jewish immigration was not espoused by the members of UNSCOP. In fact, the essence of recommendation VI entitled "Jewish displaced

---

[6] G.A. Res. 106, U.N. GAOR, 1st Spec. Sess., Resolutions 6, U.N. Doc. A/310 (1947).
[7] Emphasis added.
[8] UNSCOP Report, *supra* note 2, vol. I, at 44.
[9] Recommendation XII, *id*. at 46.

persons,"[10] was that this problem was an international responsibility emanating from the Second World War, and should have been dealt with separately. In other words, immigration to Palestine was clearly ruled out as the only solution to this humanitarian question. It can be inferred from the UNSCOP recommendation that the countries of the new world, whose vastness, and potentialities could easily accommodate hundreds of thousands, should be called upon to open their doors for the displaced Europeans. Even President Roosevelt had accepted this premise in dealing with Mr. Churchill during the Second World War.[11] Alleviating the sufferings of the Nazi victims in a noble humanitarian endeavour was not, however, explored seriously by the General Assembly, which forsook the lofty principles of the Charter and sought, instead, to foster the political objectives of Zionism.

In the committee stage of the second regular session of the General Assembly, the Palestine case was handled by the Ad Hoc Committee on the Palestinian Question, which based its work on the report of UNSCOP. Instead of considering adoption of the Report's unanimous recommendations, and then endeavoring to reconcile the divergent views, the Ad Hoc Committee chose a path which widened the cleavages between proponents of the majority and minority plans.

It seems anomalous that the procedure adopted for the consideration of the report was delegated to two subcommittees of the Ad Hoc Committee, one composed of pro-partition delegates and the other of Arab delegates plus Colombia and Pakistan, which were sympathetic to the Arab cause. It was obvious that those two subcommittees were so unbalanced as to be unable to achieve anything constructive. As was later made evident, the task of reconciling their conflicting recommendations was impossible. In such circumstances, it was not surprising that no serious attention was given to the legitimate aspirations of the Palestinians.

Subcommittee 2 attempted to draw the attention of the Assembly to the legal and constitutional issues involved. It sought to ascertain not only the competence of the General Assembly to deal with the problem, but equally its ability to recommend and enforce any specific solution.

Its report recommended the adoption of three proposals, of which one called for the submission of eight questions to the International Court of Justice for advisory opinions in accordance with Article 96 of the Charter and Chapter 4 of the Statute of the Court. The questions called for interpretations of commitments, obligations, and responsibilities growing out of the administration of Palestine under the League of Nations, and the competence of the United Nations to recommend partition or trusteeship for Palestine without obtaining the consent of the inhabitants. It was proposed specifically that the Court be asked to decide

> Whether the United Nations, or any of its Member States, is competent to enforce or recommend the enforcement of any proposal concerning the constitution and

---

[10] UNSCOP Report, *supra* note 2, vol. I, at 44.

[11] R. STEVENS, AMERICAN ZIONISM AND UNITED STATES FOREIGN POLICY 1942-1947, at 71 (1962).

future government of Palestine, in particular, any plan of partition which is contrary to the wishes, or adopted without the consent of, the inhabitants of Palestine.[12]

The vote on these questions is of considerable significance and indicates that legal aspects were not clear in the minds of a substantial number of states. Seven of the questions were defeated by twenty-five countries voting against while eighteen voted in favor and eleven abstained. The eighth question, quoted above, was defeated by twenty-one votes to twenty, with thirteen abstentions.[13] Doubts which existed continued to persist and remained unanswered. It was obvious that it was extremely difficult for many delegations to pronounce any judgment without further study and reference to the total dimensions of the problem. Yet, the General Assembly rejected all attempts to postpone the voting on the partition resolution[14] and proceeded to vote on partition while member states were unjustifiably denied a reasonable period of time to study the relevant aspects in order to satisfy their conscience. Now, it is not even of academic value to speculate on the outcome of the Assembly's debate, had the legal issues been clarified.

However, no definite plan should have been endorsed by the United Nations without a comprehensive study of the manifold legal problems involved. True, it might have been somewhat difficult to scrutinize the conflicting claims under the confused and chaotic conditions which prevailed in Palestine in 1947. Nevertheless, this fact should not suggest that such scrutiny was too much to expect from the international community.

Partition—at least partition under the above-mentioned circumstances—was not the inevitable solution which the Assembly had no alternative but to recommend. What was and is unacceptable was the recommendation of partition of Palestine without clarifying the sound legal objections raised by the Arabs. What was and is inconceivable was the allocation of forty-two per cent of the total area of Palestine to two-thirds of the population, while the remaining one-third of the population was generously granted over fifty-six per cent.

Today, in retrospect, it might be proper to refrain from passing judgment on the merits of the concept of partition. Yet, it is safe to state that the complete dereliction by the United Nations of its duty toward the legitimate interests of Palestinians is directly responsible for the bloodshed that has distressed the area for over twenty years.

The General Assembly did recommend the partition of Palestine[14a] and that is a historic fact. However, the Assembly's powers according to Articles 10, 11, 12, and 14 of the Charter are only recommendatory and without binding force on Member States. Hence, the Arab states did not contravene their Charter obligations when

---

[12] 2 U.N. GAOR Ad Hoc Comm. on the Palestinian Question, Annex 25, at 300-01, U.N. Doc. A/AC.14/32 and Add. 1 (1947).

[13] Both votes are recorded, *id*. at 203.

[14] *E.g.*, *id*. at 201 (Colombia).

[14a] G.A. Res. 181, 2 U.N. GAOR, Resolutions 131, 132 (1947).

they, responding to the will of the Palestine Arab majority, rejected the Partition Plan.

After this somewhat lengthy, yet inexhaustive review of what may be called "the ancestry of partition," it is now appropriate to make special reference to two of the consequences of the partition resolution which have far-reaching legal implication.

A. The Legal Nature of the Partition Resolution

The first is that Israel considered the General Assembly resolution as the legal basis for its establishment. On May 14, 1948, the following declaration was issued in Tel Aviv:[15]

> We, members of the People's Council, representatives of the Jewish Community of Eretz-Israel and of the Zionist Movement, are here assembled on the day of the termination of the British mandate over Eretz-Israel and, by virtue of our natural and historic right and on the strength of *the resolution of the United Nations General Assembly,* hereby declare the establishment of a Jewish State in Eretz-Israel, to be known as the State of Israel.

I shall refrain from discussing the alleged national and historic rights with roots which are thousands of years old and which are, to say the least, fraught with controversy and ambiguity. Nevertheless, even if established, it is doubtful that these factors could create a legal right which supersedes the right of the Palestinian Arabs. As to the partition resolution itself, it is to be reiterated and clearly understood that the General Assembly could do no more than recommend a solution and that its recommendation was not accepted by an Arab majority in Palestine. Hence, it could not possibly be considered as a valid legal foundation for the 1948 Zionist declaration of statehood. To this should be added the fundamental fact that the General Assembly resolution of November 29, 1947, recommended the partition of Palestine between an Arab and a Jewish state, with an economic union linking them. The Assembly took great care in drawing their respective boundaries. Although as mentioned above the distribution of land was detrimental to the legitimate rights of the overwhelming majority of the Palestinians, namely the Arabs, yet the boundaries allotted to the Jewish state constitutes a categorical limitation on Israel to claim legitimacy beyond them. Every addition to the 1947 boundaries has been accrued by the use of force contrary to the principles of the United Nations Charter and the rules of the contemporary law of nations.

B. Admission of Israel to the United Nations

The second consequence of Partition to be considered was the admission of Israel to the United Nations, which was based, *inter alia,* on the following factors as indicated in the relevant resolution of the General Assembly:[16]

---

[15] [1948] Laws of the State of Israel, vol. I, p. 3.

[16] G.A. Res. 273, 3 U.N. GAOR, pt. II, Resolutions 18, U.N. Doc. 900 (1949).

Noting furthermore the declaration by the State of Israel that it "unreservedly accepts the obligations of the United Nations Charter and undertakes to honour them from the day when it becomes a Member of the United Nations,"

Recalling its resolutions of 29 November 1947 and 11 December 1948 and taking note of the declarations and explanations made by the representative of the Government of Israel before the *ad hoc* Political Committee in respect of the implementation of the said resolution . . . .

Here again, the General Assembly deviated from the law of the Charter by ascribing legal effects to its recommendation of partition.

Since the General Assembly's partition resolution was taken as a legal justification for both Israel's existence as a state and its subsequent admission to the United Nations, the least which might have been expected from Israel was to respect and fully abide by all United Nations resolutions and every obligation which emanates from them. Ironically, this has not been the case.

The General Assembly resolution of December 11, 1948,[17] referred to in the last quoted paragraph, which represents an endeavor by the United Nations to apply certain principles of justice to the Palestine question, also sheds light on the Assembly's decision to admit Israel.

One of the most thorny and outstanding questions was undoubtedly the refugee problem, which was provided for in paragraph 11 of that resolution.[18] The principle of repatriation or compensation is a just one and was worthy of immediate implementation. The Palestine Conciliation Commission, established by the same resolution, was, in fact, engaged in its arduous task of aiding the parties to reach agreement on this and other relevant questions at the time Israel was admitted to membership. Its failure with respect to the refugee question was due to the failure and refusal of Israel to comply with the Assembly's recommendation on the subject.

II

THE ARMISTICE AGREEMENTS

The hostilities which broke out upon the end of the Mandate in May 1948, led to the conclusion in 1949 of separate armistice agreements between Israel and Jordan,[19] Israel and Syria,[20] Israel and Egypt,[21] and Israel and Lebanon.[22] Apart from the United Nations Charter, the armistice agreements represent the only

---

[17] G.A. Res. 194 (III), 3 U.N. GAOR, pt. I, Resolutions 21, U.N. Doc. A/810 (1948).

[18] "*Resolves* that the refugees wishing to return to their homes and live at peace with their neighbors should be permitted to do so at the earliest practicable date, and that compensation should be paid for the property of those choosing not to return and for loss of or damage to property which, under principles of international law or in equity, should be made good by the Governments or authorities responsible;

"*Instructs* the Conciliation Commission to facilitate the repatriation, resettlement and economic and social rehabilitation of the refugees and the payment of compensation . . . ."

[19] 42 U.N.T.S. 303, no. 656; 4 U.N. SCOR, Spec. Supp. 1, U.N. Doc. S/1302/Rev. 1 (1949).

[20] 42 U.N.T.S. 327, no. 657; 4 U.N. SCOR, Spec. Supp. 2, U.N. Doc. S/1353/Rev. 1 (1949).

[21] 42 U.N.T.S. 251, no. 654; 4 U.N. SCOR, Spec. Supp. 3, U.N. Doc. S/1264/Rev. 1 (1949).

[22] 42 U.N.T.S. 287, no. 655; 4 U.N. SCOR, Spec. Supp. 4, U.N. Doc. S/1296/Rev. 1 (1949).

legal instruments which regulate the relationship between Israel and the Arab states. This fact, per se, should add greater weight to the binding force of the agreements. The parties to the four armistice agreements were, according to the preambles, "responding to the Security Council resolution of 16 November 1948" which called upon them "as a further provisional measure under Article 40 of the Charter of the United Nations to seek agreement forthwith."[23] The preambles further state that the parties "decided to enter into negotiations under United Nations chairmanship" concerning the implementation of that resolution. It should be emphasized that the resolutions in question envisaged action under Chapter VII of the U.N. Charter. The reference to Chapter VII is of paramount importance for it implies that the resolution is a decision and not a recommendation; according to Article 25, United Nations members "agree to accept and carry out the decisions of the Security Council."

The armistice agreements contained several basic principles which were subsequently flouted by Israel with impunity. Reference may be made in this connection to Article 1, paragraph 1, of each agreement, which prescribes that "the injunction of the Security Council against resort to military force in the settlement of the Palestine question shall henceforth be scrupulously respected by both parties." This would be relevant when recalling Article 4, paragraph 1, of the Egyptian-Israeli agreement (Article 2, paragraph 1, of the three other agreements), stating that "the principle that no military or political advantage should be gained under the truce ordered by the Security Council is recognized."

Also relevant is Article I, paragraph 2, of each agreement, which stipulates that "No aggressive action by the armed forces—land, sea or air—of either party shall be undertaken . . . ."

However, hardly two weeks after the signing of the agreement with Egypt, on February 24, 1949, Israel launched its long series of violations. Its armed columns advanced on March 10 to the Gulf of Aqaba and occupied the vicinity of Bir Qattar. This illegal occupation was put before the Egyptian-Israeli Mixed Armistice Commission,[24] and the Special Committee[25] decided on March 20, 1950 that, "The advance of Israel forces on 10 March 1949 to the Gulf of Akaba area and the occupation of Bir Qattar is a violation of article IV, paragraphs 1 and 2 of the Egyptian-Israel General Armistice Agreement."[26]

The matter was further examined by the Security Council which took note of

the statement of the Government of Israel that Israel armed forces will evacuate Bir Qattar pursuant to the 20 March 1950 decision of the Special Committee provided for in article X, paragraph 4, of the Egyptian-Israel General Armistice

---

[23] S.C. Res. 62 (1948). The Egyptian-Israel Agreement also refers in this connection to S.C. Res. 61 (1948).

[24] Provided for in Art. X(1) of the Egyptian-Israel Armistice Agreement.

[25] Provided for in Art. X(4) of the Egyptian-Israel Armistice Agreement.

[26] Cf. 5 U.N. SCOR, 522d meeting 2 (1950).

Agreement, and that the Israel armed forces will withdraw to positions authorized by the Armistice Agreement.[27]

The failure and refusal of Israel to withdraw was a flagrant violation of the letter and spirit of the Armistice Agreement.

Another example of Israel's disrespect of the agreements is the fate of the demilitarized zones provided for in the agreements with Egypt and Syria. Long before its 1967 attack on the Arab states, Israel annexed by force parts of the demilitarized zones.[28]

For some time now, Israel has declared that it is no longer bound by the armistice agreements. Mr. Ben Gurion stated in November 1956 after the Suez war that, "[T]he armistice with Egypt is dead, as are the armistice lines, and no wizards or magicians can resurrect these lines."[29]

Thus, Israel claimed for itself the right to repudiate unilaterally an international agreement concluded under the auspices of the Security Council in conformity with Chapter VII powers.

Is Israel's disavowal of these international obligations vindicated under the norms of international law?

A thorough examination of the historical circumstances preceding the conclusion of the armistice and the legal and political consequences derived from its provisions definitely leads to only one conclusion: the armistice agreements could not be revoked by any one party. However, even when there might be mutual consent of the parties concerned, a decision of the competent United Nations organ would be necessary in order to terminate their effects legally.

A careful perusal of the deliberations and resolutions of the Security Council which relate to the armistice agreements clearly reveals that the armistice is a direct ancillary of decisions which fall within the scope of Chapter VII. Arguments

---

[27] S.C. Res. 89 (1950).

[28] The El Auja demilitarized zone was created by Article VIII(1) of the Egyptian-Israel General Armistice Agreement, providing as follows:

"The area comprising the village of El Auja and vicinity, as defined in paragraph 2 of this Article, shall be demilitarized, and both Egyptian and Israeli armed forces shall be totally excluded therefrom. The Chairman of the Mixed Armistice Commission established in Article X of this Agreement and United Nations Observers attached to the Commission shall be responsible for ensuring the full implementation of this provision."

This area has been occupied by Israel since 21 September 1955. See Report of the Secretary General . . . pursuant to the Council's resolution of 4 April 1956 on the Palestine Question, 11 U.N. SCOR, Supp. April-June 1956, at 30, 46-47, U.N. Doc. S/3596 (1956).

Israel claimed sovereignty, disregarding the fact that Article VIII(5) of the agreement in question stated that:

"The movement of armed forces of either Party to this Agreement into any part of the area defined in paragraph 2 of this Article, for any purpose, or failure by either Party to respect or fulfil any of the other provisions of this Article, when confirmed by the United Nations representatives, shall constitute a flagrant violation of this Agreement."

The demilitarized zone established by the Israeli-Syrian Armistice Agreement had been encroached upon by Israel since 1951, as stated in S.C. Res. 93 (1951), which called for withdrawal of Israeli police units which continued to exercise general control over the demilitarized zone.

[29] N.Y. Times, Nov. 8, 1956, at 6, col. 8.

advanced to suggest that either party is at liberty to relinquish obligations which arise under the agreements cannot be legally substantiated. Equally all arguments which purport to suggest that the mutual consent of the parties, without the approval of the Security Council, suffices to terminate the armistice agreements, ought to be discarded as inaccurate. It is submitted that even by mutual consent, the parties concerned cannot terminate the agreements without the endorsement of the Council. This view is fully corroborated by the fact that the Security Council on 16 November 1948 adopted resolution 62,[30] which, in the preamble, reaffirmed that organ's previous resolutions concerning the establishment and implementation of the truce in Palestine, and recalled, particularly, its resolution of July 15, 1948,[31] which determined that the situation in Palestine constituted a threat to the peace within the meaning of Article 39 of the Charter of the United Nations. The operative part of the former resolution is of particular importance and reads as follows:

> 1. *Decides* that, in order to eliminate the threat to the peace in Palestine and to facilitate the transition from the present truce to permanent peace in Palestine, an armistice shall be established in all sectors of Palestine;
>
> 2. *Calls upon* the parties directly involved in the conflict in Palestine, as a further provisional measure under Article 40 of the Charter, to seek agreement forthwith, by negotiations conducted either directly or through the Acting Mediator, with a view to the immediate establishment of the armistice, including:
>
> > (a) The delineation of permanent armistice demarcation lines beyond which the armed forces of the respective parties shall not move; (b) Such withdrawal and reduction of their armed forces as will ensure the maintenance of the armistice during the transition to permanent peace in Palestine.

By considering the situation in Palestine as "a threat to the peace," the Council established for itself an exclusive right of complete supervision of the functioning and the eventual termination of the armistice agreements. These agreements identically stated that each was concluded pursuant to the Security Council resolution of November 16, 1948. In order for the agreements to be terminated, the Security Council, the organ vested with primary responsibility for the maintenance of international peace and security under the Charter, would have to determine that the situation in Palestine had ceased to be a threat to the peace. Unless the Security Council undertakes this determination, thus endorsing the action embarked upon by the parties with their mutual consent, the armistice agreements are legally valid and the parties are bound by their provisions.

The Secretary-General states, in his annual report for 1966-1967, that "there has been no indication either in the General Assembly or in the Security Council that the validity and applicability of the Armistice Agreements have been changed as a result of the recent hostilities or of the war of 1956."[32] He further states that "there

---

[30] S.C. Res. 62 (1948).

[31] S.C. Res. 54 (1948).

[32] Introduction to the Annual Report of the Secretary-General on the Work of the Organization 16 June 1966-15 June 1967, 22 U.N. GAOR Supp. 1A, para. 42, U.N. Doc. No. A/6701/Add. 1 (1967).

is no provision in them for unilateral termination of their application. This has been the United Nations position all along and will continue to be the position until a competent organ decides otherwise."[33]

I submit that there is no innovation in this view. Indeed it has not been challenged even by the Israelis. In 1951, Mr. Rosenne, then Israel's Legal Adviser, stated that the most difficult question is the meaning of the phrase, "that each agreement shall remain in force until a peaceful settlement between the parties is achieved."[34] He answers this point by stating that

> any purported peaceful settlement by the parties would be subject to review by one of the organs of the United Nations. This is particularly appropriate when it is remembered that the Security Council's action which preceded the Armistice negotiations was taken pursuant to provisions contained in Chapter VII.

This I submit seems to be the correct interpretation of the Security Council's position vis-à-vis the termination of the armistice agreements.[35]

To sum up this point, recognition of the supervisory authority of the Security Council in this regard clearly indicates that the parties' mutual consent does not by itself terminate the armistice agreements. Obviously, unilateral repudiation is completely ruled out and could not possibly be sanctioned by the United Nations as stated in no ambiguous terms by the Secretary-General. Moreover, the Israelis themselves did not even allude to this possibility until 1956 when they invaded Egypt. Mr. Eban, then Israel's representative to the United Nations, stated in 1949 at the Security Council that "the effective position, therefore, is that these Agreements have no time limit and can be altered only by agreed amendments."[36]

III

THE LAW OF TREATIES

Certain articles of the International Law Commission's draft on the Law of Treaties have a direct bearing on international agreements in general, and upon the present subject of discussion in particular.

Although the draft articles are still to be adopted, at the United Nations Conference on the Law of Treaties, which will open shortly in Vienna, and it might therefore be argued that the rules contained therein are not yet binding on any state, it may nevertheless be pointed out that they have been amply discussed in the Inter-

---

[33] *Id.*

[34] S. ROSENNE, ISRAEL'S ARMISTICE AGREEMENTS WITH THE ARAB STATES: A JURIDICAL INTERPRETATION 71 (1951).

[35] Although Mr. Rosenne stated later, *id.* at 72, "but it is believed that a more thorough analysis might show that this is not the case and that if the parties should decide themselves that a peaceful settlement is achieved between them, then the Security Council would have no alternative but formally to take note of the parties' decision and draw the proper consequences therefrom," it is submitted that he nevertheless impliedly acknowledged the supervisory authority of the Council towards the armistice agreements.

[36] 4 U.N. SCOR, 433d meeting 13 (1949).

national Law Commission, and in both the Sixth Committee and plenary sessions of the General Assembly. Therefore, they may be considered evidence of the contemporary norms of international law.

To put the matter in the right perspective, it should be recalled that having attacked and subsequently occupied Arab lands, Israel is now striving to consolidate its newest illegitimate *fait accompli*. It now declares its willingness to conclude new agreements with the Arab states using the occupied territories as a lever to extract concessions from the Arabs.

Would the rules of international law legitimize Israel's attempts? A glance at the law of treaties definitely reveals that what Israel seeks could not be sanctioned by the contemporary law of nations. This submission is in conformity with the International Law Commission's draft.[37] In Article 50, it is stipulated that "A treaty is void if it conflicts with a peremptory norm of general international law from which no derogation is permitted."[38] Hence, the Commission considered that treaties would be invalidated if they contradict a rule having the character of *jus cogens*. It is universally recognized that principles enshrined in the United Nations Charter such as sovereign equality and territorial integrity of states are pertinent examples of *jus cogens*.

Article 49 of the International Law Commission's draft stipulates that "A treaty is void, if its conclusion has been procured by the threat or use of force in violation of the principles of the Charter of the United Nations."[39] This article is self-explanatory and the provisions of the two articles would render any treaty concluded between the Arab states and Israel, resting on seizure of territories by force, void and not legally binding.

It is self-evident that the occupation by one state of territories belonging to other states is contrary to the principles of the United Nations and could only be considered as overt coercion upon the other parties which would invalidate any subsequent treaty.

CONCLUSION

In conclusion, it would seem imperative to require strict adherence from all parties to the armistice agreements as a step to establish stability in the Middle East. Justice is never accomplished unless full respect for international agreements is fully maintained. If peace is to be honestly strived for in the Middle East, the key measure undoubtedly lies in applying the rule of law and justice.

---

[37] Chapter 2 of the Report of the International Law Commission on the work of its eighteenth session, Geneva, 4 May-19 July 1966 (in Part II of the Reports of the Commission to the General Assembly, U.N. Doc. A/6309/Rev. 1) (1966), 2 Y.B. INT'L L. COMM'N 173, 177 (1966).

[38] *Id.* at 183.

[39] *Id.*

LEGAL STATUS OF ARAB REFUGEES

GEORGE J. TOMEH[*]

INTRODUCTION

It is a source of special gratification to participate in a symposium on the Middle East Crisis, in which not only is attention focused on the basic legal issues but in which these issues are considered as a test of international law. If in the course of the last fifty or even the last twenty years the underlying legal principles had been observed—respect for the rights of peoples, the duties and responsibilities of states, and the sanctity of international pledges and undertakings—the recent history of the Middle East would not have been the tragic sequence we have witnessed. Now, in this moment of anxiety and concern experienced by the Arab states, it is understandable that the Arabs should plead unremittingly for their usurped rights. They expect to make this plea in an environment of understanding for the great issues of mankind, the issues of war and peace, of equity, of sovereign and human rights—the environment of our world's faltering steps toward international law and under such law.

I

SCOPE OF THE PROBLEM

The problem of the legal status of the Arab refugees involves the issue of their rights, the basis of these rights, how these rights have been affirmed or denied, what recourse is open to the refugees and what recourse is open to those concerned on their behalf, against the denial of their rights.

A. Definition and Number of Refugees

The Palestinian Arab refugees are primarily those victims of the 1947-48 tragedy, resulting in a mass exodus of the Arabs of Palestine, who have been living in exile since then. These are the *old refugees*. They number 1,344,576 registered with the United Nations Relief and Works Agency for Palestine Refugees (UNRWA) according to the last census, with 722,687 in Jordan, 316,776 in Gaza, 160,723 in Lebanon, and 144,390 in Syria.[1] There is a second generation of refugees, children of parents themselves born after May 1948. These and the inhabitants of border villages who lost their property or their livelihood, or both, but did not lose the bare walls of their homes, have been ineligible for UNRWA assistance, despite ex-

[*] M.A. 1944, American University, Beirut; Ph.D. 1951, Georgetown University. Ambassador Extraordinary and Plenipotentiary, Permanent Representative of the Syrian Arab Republic to the United Nations.

[1] Report of the Commissioner-General of the United Nations Relief and Works Agency, 22 U.N. GAOR, Supp. 13, tables 1 and 2, at 59, 60, U.N. Doc. A/6713 (1967).

treme need.[2] UNRWA relief has always been withheld from 282,000 in villages on the Jordan frontier and in the Gaza Strip. Unquestionably, any Palestinian shut out from his homeland and stripped of money and property falls within the category of refugee. Half a million Palestinian Arabs, however, in addition to the numbers above given, have migrated and are self-supporting in the Arab states, the United States, Canada, South America, and other countries.

A second category of *intermediate refugees* includes over 11,000 Arab inhabitants of the Demilitarized Zones between Israel and the neighboring Arab countries and other areas who were made refugees without provision for help from UNRWA because they were expelled by Israel after July 1, 1952, the deadline for eligibility.[3]

The *new Arab refugees* are the victims of the June 5 war. According to the Report of the Commissioner-General of UNRWA submitted to the Twenty-second Session of the U.N. General Assembly, 234,000 Arabs were refugees from Jordan, Syria, and the Sinai Peninsula following the crisis of June 5, 1967, in addition to 100,000 "old" refugees who fled their refugee camps (where they were registered with UNRWA) when these were overrun by the Israeli army.[4] These numbers are on the increase day by day while the Israelis, systematically as in the past, apply terrorist methods to empty the Arab lands of their Arab inhabitants.

II

RIGHTS OF THE REFUGEES

A. Basic Human Rights

Since the events of the June 5 war, which are still fresh in our minds, the rights of the new refugees have been definitely defined. The Security Council on June 14, 1967 adopted Resolution 237,[5] and the General Assembly reaffirmed it by an overwhelming majority on July 4.[6] The Security Council Resolution specifically calls upon the Government of Israel "to ensure the safety, welfare and security of the inhabitants of the areas where military operations have taken place and to facilitate the return of those inhabitants who have fled the areas since the outbreak of hostilities." Both resolutions requested the Secretary-General to follow their effective implementation and to report thereon. The Secretary-General did report on these matters on September 15, 1967, after having sent a Special Representative, Nils Gussing, to the Middle East.[7] As therein reported and subsequently up until the present time, Israel has persistently refused to implement the two resolutions and

---

[2] Report of the Commissioner-General of the United Nations Relief and Works Agency, 20 U.N. GAOR, Supp. 13, at 4-5, U.N. Doc. A/6013 (1965).

[3] *Id.* at 4.

[4] Report of the Commissioner-General, *supra* note 1, at 11.

[5] 22 U.N. SCOR, 1361st meeting 1 (1967).

[6] G.A. Res. 2252, U.N. GAOR, 5th Emer. Spec. Sess., Supp. 1, at 3, U.N. Doc. A/6798 (1967).

[7] U.N. Doc. A/6797, Sept. 15, 1967.

has adopted further illegitimate measures against the civilian population left in the occupied territories.

We submit it is clear that the Palestinian Arab refugees have certain inalienable rights:

1. the right of sovereignty over Palestine
2. the right to nationality—the Palestinian nationality
3. the right to individual property, together with the right to compensation for property arbitrarily expropriated or taken by force
4. the right of return
5. civil and religious rights
6. the right of visitation to the Holy Places
7. the rights of Palestinians inside Palestine

These rights are not mere claims. There are international documents to validate them—treaties, statements, declarations, pledges, and scores of U.N. resolutions. The denial of these rights constitutes, in essence, what is referred to as the Problem of the Palestine Arab Refugees, which has been and will continue to be the powderkeg of the Middle East. The first such transgression of these rights was the Balfour Declaration,[8] which Henry Cattan has denounced in the following words:

> The Balfour Declaration of 1917 which the Zionists have utilized almost as a document of title for the establishment of a national home in Palestine has never possessed any juridical value. Emanating from the British Government which at no moment possessed any right of sovereignty over Palestine the Balfour Declaration could not validly recognize a right of sovereignty in favour of the Jews because a donor can not dispose of what does not belong to him.[9]

Historically, Syria, an integral part of the Arab world, stretched from the Taurus mountains on the north to Egypt on the south, with no intervening linguistic, natural, or racial boundaries of importance, and unbroken, in the nineteenth century, by any national frontier. The sea on the west, the mountains on the north, the desert south and east gave it unity. But by 1922 this area had been carved up in the interests of power politics. Palestine was one of the fragments, created to implement the Balfour Declaration and satisfy World Zionism. The official report of the Shaw Commission, which the British sent to Palestine in 1929, contained the comment: "Viewed in the light of the history of at least the last six centuries, Palestine is an artificial conception."[10]

In spite of these transgressions, pledges came from the Great Powers to safeguard Arab rights. One could cite the safeguard clause of the Balfour Declaration itself: ". . . it being clearly understood that nothing shall be done which may prejudice the

---

[8] The text is officially quoted in CMD. NO. 5479, at 22 (1937).
[9] H. CATTAN, TO WHOM DOES PALESTINE BELONG? 5 (1967).
[10] CMD. NO. 3530 (1930), reprinted in J.M.N. JEFFRIES, PALESTINE, THE REALITY 2 (1939).

civil and religious rights of existing non-Jewish communities in Palestine." The Anglo-French Declaration to the Arabs of (undivided) Syria and Mesopotamia on November 7, 1918 is explicit: "The object aimed at by France and Great Britain . . . is . . . the establishment of National Governments and administrations deriving their authority from the initiative and free choice of the indigenous populations."[11]

The King-Crane Commission, which was dispatched to the area by President Wilson so that he could ascertain the wishes of the population, recommended, in its report issued June 29, 1919, "that the unity of Syria be preserved, in accordance with the earnest petition of the great majority of the people of Syria." In the words of the report:

> The Commissioners began their study of Zionism with minds predisposed in its favour, but the actual facts in Palestine coupled with the force of the general principles proclaimed by the Allies and accepted by the Syrians have driven them to the recommendation here made.
>
> . . . .
>
> . . . For "a national home for the Jewish people" is not equivalent to making Palestine into a Jewish State; nor can the erection of such a Jewish State be accomplished without the gravest trespass upon the "civil and religious rights of existing non-Jewish communities in Palestine . . . ."[12]

Article 22 of the Covenant of the League of Nations signed on June 22, 1919 is of particular importance, because it was the basis of what later came to be known as the "A" Mandates over Palestine, Transjordan, Iraq, Lebanon, and Syria: "there should be applied the principle that the well-being and development of such peoples form a sacred trust of civilization and that securities for the performance of this trust should be embodied in this Covenant."[13]

Remembering the rights of the Palestine Arab refugees claimed above, let us very briefly look into the Palestine Mandate itself. Article 5 stipulated that "The Mandatory shall be responsible for seeing that no Palestine territory shall be ceded or leased to, or in any way placed under control of, the Government of any foreign Power"; article 7 stated that "The Administration of Palestine shall be responsible for enacting a nationality law. There shall be included in this law provisions framed so as to facilitate the acquisition of Palestine citizenship by Jews who take up their permanent residence in Palestine."[14]

Specific attention should be paid to article 7, because of the right of the refugees to Palestinian nationality, which has been referred to above. The article is unequivocal that the nationality is the Palestinian nationality, that the Jews who take up their permanent residence in Palestine may take up this nationality. Now this

---

[11] Joint Anglo-French Declaration, Nov. 7, 1918, reprinted in CMD. No. 5479, at 25 (1937).

[12] [1919] 12 FOREIGN REL. U.S. 745, 792 (1949), reprinted in 2 J. HUREWITZ, DIPLOMACY IN THE MIDDLE EAST—A DOCUMENTARY RECORD 1914-1956, at 66, 69, 70 (1956).

[13] 3 TREATIES, CONVENTIONS, INTERNATIONAL ACTS, PROTOCOLS AND AGREEMENTS BETWEEN THE UNITED STATES AND OTHER POWERS 1910-1923, at 3336, 3342 (Redmond ed. 1923).

[14] CMD. No. 1785 (1922), reprinted in 2 J. HUREWITZ, *supra* note 12, at 106, 108.

same nationality is denied to the people who comprised, when that article was formulated, ninety-eight per cent of the total population of Palestine, namely, the Arabs.

The history of Palestine from the institution of the Mandate until 1939 was the history of an Arab people in almost continuous armed rebellion as they saw themselves gradually subjugated by piecemeal conquest which became full conquest in 1947. They saw their right to self-determination being denied and minority status imposed upon them.

Meanwhile, the British government realized the conflict of interests between Arabs and Jews in Palestine. It would be cumbersome to discuss all the British statements of policy issued during this period affirming, time after time, Arab rights under the Mandate. Only two will be mentioned here. First, the Churchill Memorandum or "White Paper" of 1922, which states:

> Unauthorized statements have been made to the effect that the purpose in view is to create a wholly Jewish Palestine. Phrases have been used such as that Palestine is to become "as Jewish as England is English." His Majesty's Government regard any such expectation as impracticable and have no such aim in view. Nor have they at any time contemplated, as appears to be feared by the Arab Delegation, the disappearance or the subordination of the Arabic population, language or culture in Palestine. They would draw attention to the fact that the terms of the Declaration referred to do not contemplate that Palestine as a whole should be converted into a Jewish National Home, but that such a Home should be founded *in Palestine*.[15]

Second, the British statement of May 1939, known as the MacDonald "White Paper," reaffirmed the obligation under the Mandate "to safeguard the civil and religious rights of all the inhabitants of Palestine," and asserted that "His Majesty's Government believe that the framers of the Mandate in which the Balfour Declaration was embodied could not have intended that Palestine should be converted into a Jewish State against the will of the Arab population of the country."[16]

These documents and pledges are not obsolete—not matters of academic interest only. They are ineradicable facts, to be reckoned with in assessing later events, and the denial to the Arab people of Palestine, by the act of the Great Powers in backing Zionist nationality claims and institutions, of their right to self-determination. That was the "original sin." One has to remember that Syria, Lebanon, Transjordan, and Iraq all became independent states. Palestine alone, of the "A" Mandate countries, did not, and this was not a mere accident of history.

Even fifty years ago, according to the pronouncements of the Great Powers, the indissoluble, immutable character of fundamental human rights and the concept

---

[15] BRITISH POLICY IN PALESTINE, CMD. No. 1700, at 18 (1922), reprinted in 2 J. HUREWITZ, *supra* note 12, at 103, 104.

[16] PALESTINE: STATEMENT OF POLICY, CMD. No. 6019, at 2, 3 (1939), reprinted in 2 J. HUREWITZ, *supra* note 12, at 218, 219, 220.

of right could not be altered by any act of man. If legality and ethics have not been dissipated in the interval, we must observe that the Zionist state of Israel, the aggressor in the June 5 war, had dubious rights to be in Palestine in the first place. Small wonder, then, that in the League of Nations and now in the United Nations the Palestine problem with its derivative disputes has been interminably on their agenda.

B. Rights as Recognized by United Nations

We turn now to the present, to see in what manner Israel has acted while the United Nations attempts, in debate and through processes of law, to adjudicate the derivative disputes.

The birth certificate of the State of Israel was General Assembly Resolution 181 of November 29, 1947,[17] recommending the annexed Plan of Partition with Economic Union.[18] Political forces were then at play to secure a favorable vote on Partition, at any cost and by any means. The Arab delegations requested that legal aspects of the Palestine question be referred to the International Court of Justice,[19] as the recourse provided by article 36 of the U.N. Charter, and by article 26 of the Mandate, which provided:

> The Mandatory agrees that if any dispute whatever should arise between the Mandatory and another Member of the League of Nations relating to the interpretation or the application of the provisions of the mandate, such dispute, if it cannot be settled by negotiation, shall be submitted to the Permanent Court of International Justice . . . .

It should be noted that Egypt and Iraq, which were among the sponsors of this request, had been members of the League of Nations, which made the provision just quoted unequivocal in its application. When the most important of these requests for adjudication was voted on, however, the count was 20 for, 21 against.[20] One vote decided the fate of Palestine.

This same birth certificate outlined the provisions of the declaration of independence of Israel. Article 10 of Part I of the Plan of Partition stipulated that "The Constituent Assembly of each State [*i.e.*, the proposed Jewish and Arab states] shall draft a democratic constitution for its State and choose a provisional government to succeed the Provisional Council of Government appointed by the [U.N. Palestine] Commission." The constitution, according to paragraph (d) of this article, was to guarantee "equal and non-discriminatory rights in civil, political, economic and religious matters and the enjoyment of human rights and fundamental freedoms."

---

[17] 2 U.N. GAOR, Resolutions, at 131 (1947).

[18] *Id.* at 132.

[19] 2 U.N. GAOR, Ad Hoc Comm. on the Palestinian Question 299-300 (1947).

[20] *Id.* at 203.

On May 14, 1948 Count Folke Bernadotte was appointed Mediator[21] pursuant to a resolution of the General Assembly.[22] In his report to the Third Session of the General Assembly, he stated:

> 6. [N]o settlement can be just and complete if recognition is not accorded to the right of the Arab refugee to return to the home from which he has been dislodged by the hazards and strategy of the armed conflict between Arabs and Jews in Palestine. The majority of these refugees have come from territory which, under the Assembly resolution of 29 November, was to be included in the Jewish State. . . . It would be an offence against the principles of elemental justice if these innocent victims of the conflict were denied the right to return to their homes while Jewish immigrants flow into Palestine, and, indeed, at least offer the threat of permanent replacement of the Arab refugees who have been rooted in the land for centuries.[23]

Obviously the Zionists, who wanted a state as Jewish as England is English, could not have kept the Arabs in their state, since they would have constituted a majority in that state. Count Bernadotte goes on to affirm the large-scale looting, pillaging, plundering, and the destruction of villages without apparent military necessity. He states further: "The liability of the Provisional Government of Israel to restore private property to its Arab owners and to indemnify those owners for property wantonly destroyed is clear, irrespective of any indemnities which the Provisional Government may claim from the Arab States."[24]

But Count Bernadotte was assassinated, with one of his aides, in September 1948, in the holy city of Jerusalem, and the Security Council could only express shock at the "cowardly act" of a "criminal group of terrorists."[25] A month later the Security Council noted with concern "that the Provisional Government of Israel has to date submitted no report to the Security Council or to the Acting Mediator regarding the progress of the investigation into the assassinations," and reminded ". . . the Governments and authorities concerned that all the obligations and responsibilities set forth are to be discharged fully and in good faith."[26]

On December 11, 1948 the United Nations General Assembly adopted Resolution 194, paragraph 11 of which

> . . . *resolves* that the refugees wishing to return to their homes and live at peace with their neighbors should be permitted to do so at the earliest practicable date, and that compensation should be paid for the property of those choosing not to return and for loss of or damage to property which, under principles of international law or in equity, should be made good by the governments or authorities responsible.[27]

---

[21] 3 U.N. SCOR, 299th meeting 4 (1948).

[22] G.A. Res. 186, U.N. GAOR, 2d Spec. Sess., Supp. 2, at 5 (1948).

[23] Progress Report of the United Nations Mediator on Palestine, 3 U.N. GAOR, Supp. 11, at 14, U.N. Doc. A/648 (1948).

[24] *Id.*

[25] S.C. Res. 57 (1948).

[26] S.C. Res. 59 (1948).

[27] 3 U.N. GAOR, Resolutions, at 21, 24 (1948).

The same resolution established a Conciliation Commission with the purpose of implementing the above-quoted paragraph.

On May 11, 1949, the General Assembly voted to accept Israel as a member of the United Nations. Paragraph 4 of the preamble to this resolution took note of "the declaration by the State of Israel that it 'unreservedly accepts the obligations of the United Nations Charter and undertakes to honour them from the day when it becomes a Member of the United Nations.' "[28]

On May 12, 1949, under the auspices of the U.N. Conciliation Commission, the Lausanne Protocol was signed.[29] In the text it is stated that

> The United Nations Conciliation Commission for Palestine, anxious to achieve as quickly as possible the objectives of the General Assembly resolution of December 11, 1948, regarding refugees, the respect for their rights and the preservation of their property, as well as territorial and other questions, has proposed to the delegation of Israel and to the delegations of the Arab States that the "working documents" attached hereto be taken as basis for discussion with the Commission.[30]

To this document was annexed a map on which were indicated the boundaries defined in the General Assembly Resolution 181(II) of November 29, 1947, which was taken as the basis of discussion with the Commission.[31]

What took place later is described by the Conciliation Commission in paragraph 23 of the Third Progress Report: "The signing of the Protocol of 12 May 1949 provided both a starting-point and framework for the discussion of territorial questions."[32] The delegation of Israel submitted proposals regarding the territorial questions, demanding that the international frontiers of Mandatory Palestine be considered the frontiers of Israel. When the Arab delegations protested that these proposals constituted a repudiation by Israel of the terms of the Protocol signed on May 12, the Israeli delegation replied that "it could not accept a certain proportionate distribution of territory agreed upon in 1947 as a criterion for a territorial settlement in present circumstances."[33]

When the Israeli army stands where it stands today, in occupied territories of three Arab states, members of the United Nations, and makes the withdrawal of its troops conditional on having "secure and agreed upon borders," one can, ironically, see how history repeats itself.

---

[28] G.A. Res. 273, 3 U.N. GAOR, pt. 2, Resolutions, at 18 (1949). The quoted words are those of the Foreign Minister on behalf of the Israeli State Council. 3 U.N. SCOR, Supp. Dec. 1948, at 118, U.N. Doc. S/1093 (1948).

[29] Third Progress Report of the Palestine Conciliation Commission, 4 U.N. GAOR, Ad Hoc Pol. Comm., Annex, vol. II, at 6, U.N. Doc. A/927 (1949).

[30] Id. at 9.

[31] G.A. Res. 181, supra note 17, at 150.

[32] Third Progress Report of the Palestine Conciliation Commission, supra note 29, at 7.

[33] Id. at 8.

C. Legal Implications of Paragraph 11 of Resolution 194 of December 11, 1948

The provisions of pargraph 11, sub-paragraph 1, of the General Assembly Resolution 194 of December 11, 1948 affirm the right of the refugees to return to their homes and their right to compensation, classified as compensation to refugees *not* choosing to return, and compensation to refugees for loss of or damage to property.[34] These rights, according to paragraph 11, are to be implemented "under principles of international law or in equity." What is involved here?

In a working paper prepared by the Legal Department of the U.N. Secretariat in March 1950 for the guidance of the Conciliation Commission on the implementation of paragraph 11 of Resolution 194,[35] the principles of repatriation and compensation were dealt with at length and many precedents cited, from the periods before and after the Second World War. It points out that in the former Axis and Axis-occupied countries—France, Rumania, Italy, Bulgaria, Czechoslovakia, Holland, and Yugoslavia—various laws were passed between November 1944 and May 1945 for restitution or compensation to the victims of Nazi action. In the United States occupied zone of Germany a General Claims law was passed in 1949 for restitution to those Nazi victims who had "suffered damage to life and limb, health, liberty, possessions, property or economic advancement."

It further points out that during the Second World War the Institute of Jewish Affairs of the World Jewish Congress took up the question of compensation for Jewish refugees and in 1944 published a book, *Indemnities and Reparations*, by Nehemiah Robinson.[36] The thesis was that great injustice would result from following the general rule that states may seek indemnification from foreign nations only on behalf of their own citizens who were also their citizens at the time the injury occurred. Victims of Axis countries who later acquired the citizenship of these states or merely became residents there would be excluded. As to victims who remained in or would be willing to return to their homeland, the author makes a strong case that the United Nations must intervene on their behalf.

The working paper also refers to a refugee problem of comparatively recent date which presents some similarity with the problem of the Palestine refugees:

> The Pakistan and India Governments agreed on the principle that the ownership of refugees' property, movable as well as immovable, should remain vested in the refugees. Custodians were appointed to look after and manage such property on behalf of the owners. Similarly, registrars of claims were appointed and instructed to make records of the property left behind by the evacuees.[37]

---

[34] 3 U.N. GAOR, Resolutions, at 21, 24 (1948).

[35] Historical Survey of Efforts of the United Nations Conciliation Commission for Palestine to Secure Implementation of Paragraph 11 of G.A. Res. 194(III), U.N. Doc. A/AC.25/W81/Rev. 2 (1961).

[36] N. ROBINSON, INDEMNITIES AND REPARATIONS (1944).

[37] Historical Survey of Efforts, *supra* note 35.

In contrast to all this, and the fact that Israeli, Zionist and Jewish organizations and Jewish individuals have had over a billion dollars in reparations from Germany,[38] we find Israeli legislation providing for confiscation of lands of "absentee" Arab owners. In three laws passed in 1948-49 (the Abandoned Areas Ordinance, the Absentee Property Regulations, and the Emergency Cultivation of Waste Lands Regulations) an "absentee" is defined as any person who was, on or after November 29, 1947 (the date of the General Assembly Resolution concerning partition of Palestine)—

(a) a citizen or subject of any of the Arab states
(b) in any of these states, for any length of time
(c) in any part of Palestine outside the Israeli-occupied area
(d) in any place other than his habitual residence, even if such place as well as his habitual abode were within Israeli-occupied territory.[39]

A conquered, surrendered, or deserted area was declared to be abandoned and sold by the Israeli Custodian to a Development Authority.[40]

Enquiry into this matter from the standpoint of the ownership of land in Palestine shows the unbelievable dimensions and grave iniquity of the liquidation of Arab rights and interests. It is established by official statistics of the Mandatory Government of Palestine,[41] submitted to the United Nations in 1947, that Jewish property in Palestine did not exceed a proportion of 5.66 per cent of the total area of the country. The document contains a breakdown of the areas owned in each district. In 1948, in violation of the territorial limits proposed by the U.N. Partition Resolution, and in 1949, in violation of the armistice agreements concluded with the neighboring countries, Israel seized another 1,400 square miles of the territory of Palestine, gaining control over seventy-one per cent of the total area of the country. Under the Israeli legislation referred to, the Israeli authorities have legalized the seizure of Arab refugee property and assets and provided for the subsequent wholesale confiscation of further property belonging to Arabs, whether refugees or not.

For twenty years now the Conciliation Commission has failed to secure legitimate Arab rights. Nineteen resolutions passed from 1949 up till now, affirming and reaffirming those rights, regretting or deploring the non-implementation by Israel of previous resolutions, have been completely disregarded.

As to the rights of the "intermediate" refugees, article V of the General Armistice Agreement with Syria provided for the "return of civilians to villages and settlements in the Demilitarized Zone"[42] and Security Council resolutions have urged

---

[38] Selzer, *The Diplomacy of Atonement: Germany, Israel and the Jews*, ISSUES, Summer 1967, at 23.

[39] Absentees' Property Law, [1950] Laws of the State of Israel, vol. 4, p. 68; reprinted in FUNDAMENTAL LAWS OF THE STATE OF ISRAEL 129 (J. Badi ed. 1961).

[40] See S. HADAWI, PALESTINE, LOSS OF A HERITAGE 52 (1963).

[41] 2 U.N. GAOR, Ad Hoc Comm. on the Palestinian Question, Annex 25, at 270, 292-93; Appendix VI, at 307, U.N. Doc. A/AC.14/32 (1947).

[42] 4 U.N. SCOR, Spec. Supp. 2, at 4 (1949).

on Israel their return forthwith. We get a picture of the situation from the Secretary-
General's Report on the Present Status of the Demilitarized Zone Set Up by the
General Armistice Agreement Between Israel and Syria:

> 16. The part of the central sector of the D/Zone which is on the eastern bank
> of the Jordan River is a narrow strip of land, generally controlled by Syria, while
> the western bank, generally controlled by Israel, is a large area. On the western
> bank Arab villages have been demolished, their inhabitants evacuated. The in-
> habitants of the villages of Baqqara and Ghanname returned following the Security
> Council resolution of 18 May 1951 (S/2517). They were later (on 30 October 1956)
> forced to cross into Syria where they are still living. Their lands on the western
> bank of the river, and Khoury Farm in the same area, are cultivated by Israel
> nationals.[43]

The question duly arises here: Does the rule of force or a political decision
terminate a legal right? Does conquest give the conqueror legal title to an occupied
territory? Philip Marshal Brown has given one answer: "Military occupation by
itself does not confer title or extinguish a nation. . . . [S]o long as a people do not
accept military conquest; so long as they can manifest, in one way or another, their
inalterable will to regain freedom, their sovereignty even though flouted, restricted,
and sent in exile still persists."[44]

III

RESPONSIBILITY FOR INITIATION OF HOSTILITIES

Now, it is widely assumed that the Arabs themselves were responsible for the
misfortunes that befell them, because they were the ones who defied the U.N. Partition Resolution, and that all went peacefully in Palestine from November 29, 1947
until May 14, 1948, when the establishment of Israel was declared, with the Arabs
attacking the new state. It has been concluded that the Arabs brought about the
loss of their own rights through their aggression. Such is not the case. Emphasis
on the real facts of the history of this period is not only relevant but necessary in the
assessment of Arab claims.

To put the matter in perspective, I cite two official communications, one a letter
sent by Brigadier General Patrick J. Hurley, Personal Representative of President
Roosevelt, to the President from Cairo on May 5, 1943:[45]

> For its part, the Zionist organization in Palestine has indicated its commit-
> ment to an enlarged program for (1) a sovereign Jewish State which would
> embrace Palestine and probably Transjordania, (2) an eventual transfer of the Arab
> population from Palestine to Iraq, and (3) Jewish leadership for the whole Middle
> East in the fields of economic development and control.

---

[43] U.N. Doc. S/7573, at 4-5, Nov. 2, 1966.

[44] Brown, *Sovereignty in Exile*, 35 AM. J. INT'L L. 666, 667 (1941).

[45] Letter from Brig. Gen. Patrick Hurley to President Roosevelt, [1943] 4 FOREIGN REL. U.S. 776,
777 (1964).

The other was a telegram sent from Cairo by U.S. Minister Kirk in Egypt to the Secretary of State on January 23, 1943:

> On the Jewish side I have found Zionist officials of the Jewish Agency uncompromisingly outspoken in their determination that Palestine at end of this war shall become not merely a national home for the Jews, but a Jewish state despite any opposition from the 1,000,000 Arabs living there. In various ways main result of many of their efforts seems to be to goad Palestinian Arabs into breaking informal truce that has existed since war began. . . .
>
> It is no secret that the Hagana, their secret Jewish military organization, has plans fully made and is well equipped not only with small arms, but also with tommy-guns and machine guns many of them purchased from Vichy French forces in Syria and smuggled into Palestine during past 2 years.[46]

As to what really happened, rather than the propagandized version, we have the aid of I. F. Stone, American author of *Underground to Palestine* and *This is Israel*, who tells us that he

> first arrived in Palestine on Balfour Day, Nov. 2, 1945, the day the Haganah blew up bridges and watch towers to begin its struggle against the British and immigration restrictions. The following spring I was the first newspaperman to travel with illegal Jewish immigrants from the Polish-Czech border through the British blockade. In 1947 I celebrated Passover in the British detention camps in Cyprus and in 1948 I covered the Arab-Jewish war.[47]

In an article published August 3, 1967 he goes on to say:

> Jewish terrorism, not only by the Irgun, in such savage massacres as Deir Yassin, but in milder form by the Haganah, itself "encouraged" Arabs to leave areas the Jews wished to take over for strategic or demographic reasons. They tried to make as much of Israel as free of Arabs as possible.[48]

He also points out that:

> The myth that the Arab refugees fled because the Arab radios urged them to do so was analyzed by Erskine B. Childers in the London *Spectator* May 12, 1961. An examination of British and U.S. radio monitoring records turned up no such appeals and "even orders to the civilians of Palestine, to stay put."[49]

Irrefutable proof that the Zionists were the first aggressors in the war of 1947-48 is given by Menachem Begin, the alleged perpetrator of the Deir Yassin massacre, in his book *The Revolt*.[50] He tells us how the Haganah, the recognized "defense" force of the Zionist establishment in Palestine, having gone over to the principle of "offensive defense," joined forces with the Irgun, the terrorist group, and of the

---

[46] Letter from Minister Kirk to Secretary of State, [1943] 4 FOREIGN REL. U.S. 747-48 (1964).

[47] I.F. Stone, in review of special issue of *Les Temps Moderne* entitled *Le Conflict Israélo-Arabe*, The New York Review of Books, Aug. 3, 1967, at 12, col. 4.

[48] *Id.* at 10, col. 3.

[49] *Id.* at 10, col. 2.

[50] M. BEGIN, THE REVOLT, STORY OF THE IRGUN (1951).

signing of a secret agreement between the Jewish Agency, as the supreme authority over the Haganah, and the Irgun Zvai Leumi for attack on the Arabs. This was in January 1948, while the duly constituted Commission of the United Nations was still seeking a peaceful implementation of the General Assembly's recommendation. In a chapter entitled "The Conquest of Jaffa" he states:

> In the months preceding the Arab invasion . . . we continued to make sallies into the Arab area. In the early days of 1948, we were explaining to our officers and men, however, that this was not enough. Attacks of this nature carried out by any Jewish forces were indeed of great psychological importance; and their military effect, to the extent that they widened the Arab front and forced the enemies on to the defensive, was not without value. But it was clear to us that even most daring sallies carried out by partisan troops would never be able to decide the issue. Our hope lay in gaining control of territory.
>
> At the end of January, 1948, at a meeting of the Command of the Irgun in which the Planning Section participated, we outlined four strategic objectives: (1) Jerusalem; (2) Jaffa; (3) the Lydda-Ramleh plain; and (4) the Triangle.[51]

(According to the Partition plan, Jerusalem was to be a *corpus separatum*, and Jaffa was definitely to be part of the Arab state.) On April 25, 1948 (three weeks before the alleged Arab initiation of hostilities), Begin addressed his troops, en route to Jaffa: "Men of the Irgun! We are going out to conquer Jaffa. We are going into one of the decisive battles for the independence of Israel."[52] After an account of the battle, he assures us that "The conquest of Jaffa was one of the fateful events in the Hebrew war of independence."[53]

Thus the Palestine refugee problem originated, for Jaffa was practically all Arab in population. Before any Arab soldier set foot on the soil of Palestine, 400,000 Arabs had fled their Palestinian homeland in terror.

Of course, the Zionists had their own view of activities such as this, expressed by a member of the Haganah, Munya M. Mardor (now Director-General of the Israel Weapons Research and Development Authority) in a book entitled *Haganah*.[54] He tells of secret arms purchases in foreign countries: "We were conspirators, outside the law, and yet obeying what to us was a higher law."[55]

In the name of compromise, realism, and *fait accompli*, the Arabs are asked to recognize these achievements "outside the law" and admit the "conspirators" as lawful and legal successors to their land and rights.

CONCLUSION

It must have become clear that the legal imperatives affirming Arab rights in Palestine are firm and unequivocal, but that Israel and World Zionism have been

[51] *Id.* at 348.
[52] *Id.* at 354.
[53] *Id.* at 371.
[54] M. MARDOR, HAGANAH (1957).
[55] *Id.* at 230.

able to flout them and disregard not only all international safeguards and guarantees prior to 1947, but also the scores of U.N. resolutions concerning Arab rights.

The argument has time and again been made that the Arabs should accept the *fait accompli* established by Israel, but between 1947 and today there has been not one but several *fait accompli* to subvert Arab rights.

The Arabs prefer to see not only what is, but what ought to be and what might be, and agree with U.S. Secretary of Labor W. Willard Wirtz when he told the Labor Ministers' Conference in Venezuela: "Change is our ally, and we face squarely those who fight change because the status quo has been good to them. The divine right of the successful is as false a notion as the divine right of kings."[56]

Does a *fait accompli* constitute a norm for international law and behavior—since we are dealing with basic legal considerations? We hold, with the two American legal authorities quoted below, that no *fait accompli* can establish a precedent to be accepted in international law so long as the victims of the *fait accompli* object to it.

In 1954 the Legal Adviser of the State Department, Mr. Herman Phleger, made this statement:

> International law has been defined as those rules for international conduct which have met general acceptance among the community of nations . . . .
> . . . .
> But there is such a thing as international law. It has had a long and honorable, though chequered, career. I predict that it will play an even more important part in world affairs in the future than it has in the past. Indeed, in this rapidly shrinking world, it becomes increasingly evident that our survival may depend upon our success in substituting the rule of law for the rule of force.[57]

From the American Law Institute comes a *Restatement of the Foreign Relations Law of the United States,* which contains the following:

> e. Objection to practice as means of preventing its acceptance as rule of law. The growth of practice into a rule of international law depends on the degree of its acceptance by the international community. If a state initiates a practice for which there is no precedent in international law, the fact that other states do not object to it is significant evidence that they do not regard it as illegal. If this practice becomes more general without objections from other states, the practice may give rise to a rule of international law. Because failure to object to practice may amount to recognition of it, the objection by a state to a practice of another is an important means of preventing or controlling in some degree the development of rules of international law.[58]

The *fait accompli* of Israel, doing away with Arab rights, has been objected to, not only by the Arab states, but by the majority of Members of the United Nations, who throughout twenty years past have affirmed and reaffirmed the rights of Arab

---

[56] N.Y. Times, May 11, 1966, at 18, col. 2.
[57] 1 M. WHITEMAN, DIGEST OF INTERNATIONAL LAW 2 (1963).
[58] RESTATEMENT (SECOND) OF FOREIGN RELATIONS LAW OF THE UNITED STATES § 1, comment *e* (1965).

refugees for return or compensation. The United States Government has voted consistently in favor of those resolutions, while regrettably opposing draft resolutions designed to safeguard Arab property rights.

The most succinct and telling objection to Israel's *fait accompli* that I call to mind is implicit in the words of Secretary-General U Thant, in his Annual Report to the 22nd Session of the General Assembly: "People everywhere, and this certainly applies to the Palestinian refugees, have a natural right to be in their homeland and to have a future."[59]

---

[59] 22 U.N. GAOR, Supp. 1A, at 7, U.N. Doc. A/6701/Add. 1 (1967).

PASSAGE THROUGH THE STRAIT OF TIRAN AND IN THE GULF OF AQABA

Leo Gross*

Introduction

The crisis in the Middle East which opened on May 18, 1967, with the request from the Government of the United Arab Republic to the Secretary-General of the United Nations to withdraw the United Nations Emergency Force (UNEF) "from the territory of the United Arab Republic and Gaza Strip,"[1] and which was decisively aggravated by the announcement of the President of the Republic on May 22, 1967 that "the United Arab Republic had decided to prevent Israeli ships and other ships carrying strategic cargoes to Israel, from passing through the mouth of the Gulf of Aqaba"[2] was brought under control by the unanimous adoption on November 22, 1967 in the Security Council of Resolution 242.[3] This resolution contains at least two principles which are directly relevant to the question here under consideration. According to the first, the Council affirmed that the establishment of a just and lasting peace in the Middle East requires the application of the principle:

> Termination of all claims or states of belligerency and respect for and acknowledgment of the sovereignty, territorial integrity and political independence of every State in the area and their right to live in peace within secure and recognized boundaries free from threats of acts of force.

In the second principle the Council affirmed the necessity "[f]or guaranteeing freedom of navigation through international waterways in the area."

A settlement implementing these two principles will have to include the controversies which were aired once again in the Security Council prior to the outbreak of hostilities on June 5, 1967 and in the Fifth Emergency Special Session which followed their termination. These controversies related to the status in international law of the Gulf of Aqaba, the status of Israel as a coastal state in the Gulf, the right of innocent passage through the Strait of Tiran and, of course, the right claimed by the United Arab Republic to exercise belligerent rights in the Strait and Gulf. These problems will now be considered in that order.

---

* Dr. rer. pol. 1927, University of Vienna; S.J.D. 1931, Harvard University. Professor of International Law and Organization, The Fletcher School of Law and Diplomacy, Tufts University. Member of the Board of Editors and Book Review Editor, *American Journal of International Law*.

[1] Special Report of the Secretary-General, U.N. Doc. A/6669, at 1 (1967).

[2] N.Y. Times, May 23, 1967, at 1, col. 8.

[3] S.C. Res. 242 (1967). *See* full text in Rosenne, in this symposium, pp. 44, 56.

I

STATUS OF GULF OF AQABA IN INTERNATIONAL LAW

Since 1957 the Gulf has been claimed by various governments and writers as an historic gulf or bay under exclusive Arab domination, more precisely the domination of the three Arab coastal states: the United Arab Republic, Jordan and Saudi Arabia. The position was first formulated by Saudi Arabia,[4] and was restated by the representative of the United Arab Republic in the Security Council on May 29, 1967.[5] What is involved is a mixed question of fact and law. By its configuration the Gulf of Aqaba has some similarity to the Gulf of Fonseca, which is usually relied upon as an analogue and precedent. It is about 100 miles long, the width varies from seven to fifteen miles, and it is connected with the Red Sea through the narrow Straits of Tiran, about nine miles wide. In the Fonseca case the Central American Court of Justice established three criteria in support of the historic character of the Gulf: first, immemorial possession, secondly, *animus domini* and thirdly, acquiescence by other nations.[6] The Gulf of Aqaba meets none of these requirements.[7] The Gulf has been said to have been Arab in character from 700 to 1517. It was under Ottoman control from 1517 to 1918, and since then it has been bounded by two littoral states and the British Mandate of Palestine, out of which Jordan and the state of Israel arose.[8] There is no evidence of an *animus domini* on the part of the Ottoman Empire. Even if it is assumed that all four present littoral states succeeded to the Ottoman Empire, they succeeded to no verifiable claim or right.[9]

What evidence there is points in the opposite direction. Up to 1917 the Gulf of Aqaba seems to have been a backwater rather than an historic bay. Since that time British ships began to sail through the Gulf, joined by Scandinavian, German and others; ships of Arab states seem to have been rare users of the Gulf.[10] In view of this, the proposition that "foreign Powers probably were not interested in navigation in the Gulf, since it apparently had no commercial importance to them"[11] seems

---

[4] U.N. Doc. A/3575 (1957).

[5] U.N. Doc. S/PV.1343, at 31-42 (1967).

[6] Judgment of March 9, 1917, The Republic of El Salvador v. The Republic of Nicaragua, 11 AM. J. INT'L L. 674, 705 (1917).

[7] *But see* Hammad, *The Right of Passage in the Gulf of Aqaba*, 15 REVUE EGYPTIENNE DE DROIT INTERNATIONAL 118, 132 (1959), who finds that "in considering the legal status of the Gulf of Aqaba the analogy of the case of the Gulf of Fonseca is reasonable and logical." For a recent study of the subject, see H. SULTAN, LE PROBLEME DU GOLFE D'AKABA (Institut de Récherche et Études Arabologiques, Cairo, 1967).

[8] Selak, *A Consideration of the Legal Status of the Gulf of Aqaba*, 52 AM. J. INT'L L. 660, 692 (1958).

[9] Gross, *The Geneva Conference on the Law of the Sea and the Right of Innocent Passage Through the Gulf of Aqaba*, 53 AM. J. INT'L L. 564, 569 (1959).

[10] Melamid, *Legal Status of the Gulf of Aqaba*, 53 AM. J. INT'L L. 412 (1959). Melamid concludes that his research "supports the view that navigation rights have definitely been established in the Gulf of Aqaba by nations other than the Arab states. Use of the Gulf by Arab states, particularly for pilgrim travel, followed only upon the pioneering efforts of other nations." *Id.* at 413.

[11] Selak, *supra* note 8, at 692.

without foundation. Whatever trade existed was "foreign, rather than local."[12] Similarly, the view that because the Gulf is used for pilgrimages to Mecca it "enjoys a specific character that justifies the claim to be regarded as historical bay"[13] is hardly persuasive. Moreover, some of the pilgrims seem to travel on non-Arab ships, and at least one of them, "the British ship *Anchun*, carrying Jordanian pilgrims from Aqaba to Jidda, was fired on by Egyptian shore batteries as a result of a misunderstanding."[14]

All these facts indicate that no juridical analogy can be drawn between the Gulf of Aqaba and the Gulf of Fonseca; there is no acceptable evidence of immemorial usage, of *animus domini* and of acquiescence. When Saudi Arabia formulated the claim to the historic character of the Gulf, the UNEF was stationed on the Strait of Tiran and Israel and other maritime nations passed freely through the Gulf.

In the debate in the General Assembly in 1957 only India seems to have taken the position that the Gulf was "an inland sea," but without any relevant supporting evidence.[15]

India also supported the claim of the United Arab Republic in 1967. It justified it on several grounds, first that the Republic "is not a party to any agreement recognizing the Gulf of Aqaba as an international waterway or guaranteeing the freedom of passage to Israeli ships."[16] This is obviously correct but the Republic is not a party to any agreement establishing the Gulf as an historic or closed bay.[17] Furthermore, in view of Israel's coastline on the Gulf no such agreement could be arrived at and relied upon vis-à-vis Israel without her consent.[18] The legal status of Israel in this context will be considered later.

The second Indian argument was that "there is no universally recognized rule of international law on freedom of navigation applicable to such bodies of water as Aqaba."[19] This is correct but irrelevant. The principle of freedom of the seas applies to all waters which qualify as high seas or parts thereof. States which desire to exclude parts of the high seas from the regime of customary international law on historical or other grounds have the burden of the proof. As suggested earlier no

---

[12] Melamid, *supra* note 10, at 413.

[13] Hammad, *supra* note 7, at 133.

[14] Selak, *supra* note 8, at 670. Mr. Selak may have confused the facts. As stated in the House of Commons on July 6, 1955, by Mr. Nutting, Minister of State for Foreign Affairs, this ship was on the pilgrim run between Jedda and Aqaba but when fired upon and hit it was returning empty to Aqaba. 543 PARL. DEB., H.C. (5th ser.) 1134 (1955), quoted in 4 M. WHITEMAN, DIGEST OF INTERNATIONAL LAW 478 (1965).

[15] Selak, *supra* note 8, at 674, points out that all the water areas cited by the Indian delegate are "indentations in the territory of one state only."

[16] U.N. Doc. A/PV.1530, at 81 (1967).

[17] The absence of any agreement among the Arab littoral states was noted by Selak, *supra* note 8, at 692.

[18] Gross, *supra* note 9, at 570.

[19] U.N. Doc. A/PV.1530, at 81 (1967).

such evidence has been made available by the governments concerned or writers who support them.[20]

Moreover, there is strong evidence that the Arab coastal states as well as Israel have considered the Gulf to be part of the high seas; all of them proclaimed belts of territorial sea in the Gulf varying from three (Jordan) to six (Saudi Arabia, Egypt and Israel) miles.[21] Claims to territorial sea imply that the Gulf is part of the high sea[22] although there are exceptions on historical grounds as in the case of the Gulf of Fonseca.[23] But no comparable exception has been established in favor of the Gulf of Aqaba before or after the establishment of the state of Israel.

In the debates in the General Assembly in February and March, 1957, a great number of Members have formally gone on record that the Gulf of Aqaba comprehends international waters and that there is a right of free and innocent passage in the Gulf.[24] Similar views were expressed at the 1967 Fifth Emergency Special Session.[25]

The third Indian argument was that the status of the Gulf of Aqaba was "still a matter of controversy," and in support of this, the Indian delegate referred to a recent publication of the State Department,

> the *Digest of International Law*, released by the Department of State in April 1965 (vol. IV, p. 233) containing a letter from the Secretary of State dated 15 January 1963, to the Attorney-General setting forth the views of the Department regarding the extent of territorial waters and the closing width of bays. On Aqaba, the letter states as follows: "The Gulf of Aqaba—the exact status of this body of water is still a matter open to controversy." I am sure there are many international lawyers in this august gathering and I make them a present of this quotation from an authoritative American textbook.[26]

This present, in spite of the generosity of the giver, should be accepted, if at all, with caution. It is true that there is a letter from the Secretary of State on the subject but it ends on page 232. The passage quoted by the Indian delegate is not from this letter but from a Memorandum prepared by Frank Boas, Attorney Adviser, Office of the Legal Adviser, Department of State, dated August 1957.[27]

After the passage quoted by the Indian delegate, Mr. Boas goes on to say that the Department of State in a recent statement published in *The New York Times* on June 24, 1957, declared that:

---

[20] No evidence is to be found in Murti, *The Legal Status of the Gulf of Aqaba*, 7 THE INDIAN JOURNAL OF INTERNATIONAL LAW 201 (1967), who supports the Indian Government's viewpoint. Murti does not consider the arguments developed in my article cited *supra* note 9.

[21] See Selak, *supra* note 8, at 666 for relevant information.

[22] *Id.* at 693.

[23] Gross, *supra* note 9, at 570.

[24] Gross, *supra* note 9, at 576, and Selak, *supra* note 8, at 671-75.

[25] *See, e.g.*, U.N. Docs. A/PV.1531, at 29-30 (1967) (Belgium); A/PV.1541, at 13-15 (1967) (Peru); A/PV.1542, at 41 (1967) (Australia); *id.* at 58-60 (Costa Rica).

[26] U.N. Doc. A/PV.1530, at 81 (1967).

[27] *See* 4 M. WHITEMAN, *supra* note 14, at 239.

The United States position is that the Gulf of Aqaba comprehends international waters. That no nation has the right to prevent free and innocent passage in the Gulf and through the Straits giving access thereto. A denial of those waters to vessels of United States registry should be reported to the nearest United States diplomatic or consular offices.[28]

Still, it is true to say that a controversy exists although it is probably not sustained by any serious doubts as to the applicable law. The Arab claims, as one Egyptian writer put it, might not have arisen "except for the fact of Arab hostility toward Israel."[29]

II

STATUS OF ISRAEL AS A COASTAL STATE IN THE GULF OF AQABA

It is part and parcel of the position of some governments and writers that Israel is not entitled to a stretch of the coast of the Gulf, that its presence there lacks legitimacy or is tainted with illegality. Thus the delegate of the United Arab Republic charged in the Security Council on May 29, 1967, that Israel's "presence lacks legitimate foundation."[30] After referring to the resolutions of the Security Council adopted on July 15, 1948 and August 19, 1948, the same delegate declared: "In view of these specific orders, Israel's possession of the coastal strip does not entitle it to any claim to sovereignty. This is in conformity with the well-etablished doctrine in international law that belligerent occupation cannot legally be converted into sovereignty over the occupied territory."[31]

These arguments suffer from a common but fatal defect. They confuse the deployment of military forces which may or may not be compatible with various resolutions of the Security Council or provisions in the relevant Armistice Agreements with exercise of sovereignty over territory. There may be armistice demarcation lines but there are also frontiers in the usual sense of the word, and while the territory of Israel may be determined by such lines it does not mean that the territory itself or parts of it are "armistice territories." No armistice lines were drawn along the coasts of Israel on the Mediterranean and the Gulf of Aqaba. Insofar as the coastline on the Gulf is concerned, it was provided in the 1947 Partition Plan Resolution of the General Assembly that the territory of the new state should extend to and include a stretch of coast which corresponded to the territory of the Mandate for Palestine. The Armistice Agreements with Egypt and Jordan define only the western and eastern demarcation lines or frontiers of this part of the state of Israel.

---

[28] *Id.* at 233. For material on the Gulf of Aqaba and Strait of Tiran, see *id.* at 465. *See also* "The United States Reply to the Arab States Representations Concerning the Suez Canal and the Gulf of Aqaba: Statement Delivered to the Heads of Mission of the Arab States at Washington, June 27, 1957," in STAFF OF SENATE COMM. ON FOREIGN RELATIONS, 90TH CONG., 1ST SESS., A SELECT CHRONOLOGY AND BACKGROUND DOCUMENTS RELATING TO THE MIDDLE EAST 112-15 (Comm. Print 1967).

[29] Hammad, *supra* note 7, at 137.

[30] U.N. Doc. S/PV.1343, at 31 (1967).

[31] *Id.* at 33-35.

Thus the General Armistice Agreement of February 24, 1949 between Egypt and Israel provides in article II, paragraph 2: "No element of the land, sea or air military . . . forces . . . shall advance beyond or pass over for any purpose whatsoever the *Armistice Demarcation Line* set forth in Article VI of this Agreement . . . and elsewhere shall not violate the *international frontier*. . . ."[32]

Article VI, paragraph 1, of this Agreement also refers to "the Egyptian frontier" and article VIII, paragraph 2, refers three times to the Egypt-Palestine frontier. Article VII establishes in "certain sectors of the total area involved" a western and eastern front. This relates to the southern part of the territory of Israel, the western front being governed by the Armistice Agreement with Egypt whereas the eastern front comes under the regime of the Agreement with the "third party," namely, Jordan. Annex II to the Egyptian-Israel Armistice Agreement defines the demarcation between the two fronts. The eastern front is defined as "The area east of the line described in paragraph *a* above, and from point 402 down to the southernmost tip of Palestine, by a straight line marking half the distance between the Egypt-Palestine and Transjordan-Palestine frontiers."[33]

Moreover, the Armistice Agreement explicitly recognizes Israeli possession of the territory by providing in article VII, paragraph 4 as follows: "In the area of the western front under Israeli control, Israeli defensive forces only, *which shall be based on the settlement,* may be maintained. All other Israeli forces shall be withdrawn from this area. . . ."[34] Clearly, a distinction is made between deployment of forces and control. Control remains even if forces are to be withdrawn.

The Jordan-Israel Armistice Agreement of April 3, 1949 follows to some extent the earlier Agreement between Egypt and Israel. The demarcation lines are indicated on maps annexed to the Agreement and it is to be noted that there is no demarcation line along the coast on the Gulf of Aqaba. In the area concerned the lines run from north to south and not from east to west. Thus article V, paragraph 1(d), provides: "In the sector from a point on the Dead Sea . . . to the southernmost tip of Palestine, the Armistice Demarcation Line shall be determined by existing military positions . . . and shall run from north to south as delineated on map 1 in annex I to this Agreement."[35]

Furthermore, and quite explicitly, article VII stipulates: "The military forces of the Parties to this Agreement shall be limited to defensive forces only in the areas extending ten kilometres from each side of the Armistice Demarcation Lines, except where geographical considerations make this impractical, as at the southernmost tip of Palestine and the *coastal strip*."[36]

This coastal strip cannot be any other than that of Palestine under Israel control

---

[32] 4 U.N. SCOR, Spec. Supp. 3, at 2, U.N. Doc. S/1264/Rev.1 (1949). (Emphasis added.)
[33] *Id*. at 11.
[34] *Id*. at 5. (Emphasis added.)
[35] 4 U.N. SCOR, Spec. Supp. 1, at 3-4, U.N. Doc. S/1302/Rev.1 (1949).
[36] *Id*. at 5. (Emphasis added.)

and part of its territory. Finally, mention may be made of Annex II which in paragraph II, section 4, defines the defensive forces in the "Sector Engeddi to Eylat" as three battalions each and various vehicles.[37]

A distinction between Armistice Demarcation Lines and international frontiers was made several times by the Secretary-General of the United Nations in his Special Report of May 18, 1967. Thus, he noted, "UNEF has been deployed in Gaza and Sinai for more than ten years for the purpose of maintaining quiet along the Armistice Demarcation Line and the International Frontier," and "All UNEF Observation Posts along the Armistice Demarcation Line and International Frontier were manned as usual."[38]

The state of Israel is not and was not an "armistice state" but a state with a territory delineated partly by armistice lines and partly by international frontiers. Certainly its maritime boundaries belong to the latter category. Thus there can be no question of the legitimacy in international law of its presence and its port on the Gulf of Aqaba. It certainly is not foreign territory conquered in violation of the Briand-Kellogg Pact or other treaties to which the doctrine of non-recognition may be applicable.

More specifically the delegate of the United Arab Republic referred to Security Council Resolution 89 (1950) as proof of the "illegal occupation" of the port of Elath on the Gulf of Aqaba. In that resolution the Council took note of the declaration of the government of Israel "that Israel armed forces will evacuate Bir Qattar pursuant to the 20 March 1950 decision of the Special Committee provided for in article X, paragraph 4, of the Egyptian-Israel General Armistice Agreement . . . ."[39] The delegate went on "to clarify that the reference to Bir Qattar includes the vicinity of Om Rashrash which the Israelis called 'Elath' after their illegal occupation of the territory."[40]

Apart from the confusion between "occupation" and military deployment this clarification is somewhat misleading. The locality "Om Rashrash" on the Armistice map is on the Israeli side of the demarcation line of the Palestine-Transjordan frontier. There can be no question, therefore, of any "illegal occupation of the territory." Furthermore, the locality is in that sector of the area which has been called "eastern front" and is, therefore, within the legal scope of the Jordan-Israel Armistice Agreement. The distance between Bir Qattar and Om Rashrash may be close enough to permit the delegate to say that the former is in the vicinity of the latter, but this can be only geographic and not juridical vicinity. Inasmuch as the Security Council referred to the Egyptian-Israel General Armistice Agreement, therefore, juridically as well as geographically, Bir Qattar must be in the "western

---

[37] *Id.* at 10.

[38] U.N. Doc. A/6669, at 3 (1967). Further references will be found in *id.* at 7, 9.

[39] U.N. Doc. S/PV.1343, at 32 (1967).

[40] *Id.*

front" area. This Security Council Resolution cannot support any inference whatsoever with respect to Om Rashrash, which the Israelis called Elath.

The delegate of the United Arab Republic also charged that

> The Israeli armed forces on 10 March 1949 usurped and occupied the village
> of Om Rashrash, along with a stretch of about five miles overlooking the Gulf of
> Aqaba . . . . This illegal act was perpetrated two weeks after the signing of the
> Egyptian-Israeli General Armistice Agreement on 24 February 1949. This action
> completely and drastically violated the letter and spirit of the Agreement . . . .[41]

This incident is the trump card in the reasoning designed to show that legally
speaking Israel's territory does not comprise the coastal strip on the Gulf.[42] It formed
the subject of an investigation by the Truce Supervisory Organization and of a
Report from the Acting Mediator of Palestine to the Secretary-General of the
United Nations of March 22, 1949. This report deals with complaints made by
Transjordan. It confirms that an Israel force reached "Umm Reshresh" and that
"the eastern front, pending the conclusion of an armistice agreement with Transjordan, remains fully subject to the existing truce."[43] The Acting Mediator, referring
to the Aqaba area, stated: "It is clear on the evidence available to me as a result of
the investigation by United Nations observers since 7 March that Israeli forces have
effectively occupied this area since that date."[44]

Referring to a couple of incidents, he reported: "I am quite convinced that, other
than those at Aqaba, any positions established in this area either by Transjordan
or by Israeli forces have all been established since the existing truce came into effect
on 18 July 1948 . . . and have, therefore, been established contrary to the terms of
that truce."[45]

However, this incident occurred prior to the signing of the Jordan-Israeli
Armistice Agreement on April 3, 1949 and in an area covered by it. The charge of
the delegate of the United Arab Republic that the deployment of the Israeli troops
in the area of Om Rashrash was contrary to the Egyptian-Israeli General Armistice
Agreement is without foundation. As the Acting Mediator pointed out, "Umm
Reshresh" is in the eastern front area, therefore outside that Agreement. Moreover,
it will be recalled, by virtue of the Jordan-Israeli Armistice Agreement that area along
with the coastal strip fell within the territory of Israel.[46] The demarcation line

---

[41] *Id*. He referred also to paragraphs 1 and 2 of Article IV of the Agreement.

[42] After recounting the above incident, Hammad concludes: "In view of these prohibitions it is clear
that Israel's possession of the coastal strip, gained by the employment of the military instrument, is in
the nature of a military occupation only, without lawful claim to sovereignty." Hammad, *supra* note 7,
at 146.

[43] 4 U.N. SCOR, Supp. March 1949, at 46-47, U.N. Doc. S/1295 & Corr. 1 (1949).

[44] *Id*. at 47.

[45] *Id*. at 47-48.

[46] According to Selak, "in terms of the Armistice Agreements, a strong argument can be made for
Israel's right to possession of its coastline on the Gulf of Aqaba. Just what is the legal nature of this
possession, however, is somewhat unclear." Selak, *supra* note 8, at 681.

follows the old frontier between the Palestine Mandate and Transjordan, and ends on the shores of the Gulf. There would seem to be, therefore, juridically no reason to doubt Israel's right to this part of its territory. True enough, the Armistice Agreements did not pretend to draw political boundaries. But apart from the fact that they did not delineate all the boundaries of Israel—the coastlines being one exception[47]— and even if it is admitted that the armistice lines are normally provisional and subject to confirmation or revision in a peace settlement, Israel was admitted to the United Nations as a state with a territory. The coastline has been, with or without military deployment, part of its territory. As long as this continues to be so it will be legally one of the four riparian states on the Gulf of Aqaba and entitled to the use of its waters as well as ingress and egress through the Strait of Tiran.[48]

III

STATE OF WAR AND RIGHTS OF BELLIGERENCY

No passage in a textbook or treatise on international law has been more often cited in the Middle East crisis over the past few years than that in Oppenheim-Lauterpacht that an armistice does not end the juridical state of war.[49] Predictably it was quoted by the delegate of the United Arab Republic. After emphasizing the essentially military nature of the 1949 General Armistice Agreement, the continued violations thereof "which culminated in the cowardly attack on Sinai in 1956," he contended that "a state of overt war has been existing. Hence my Government has the legitimate right, in accordance with international law, to impose restrictions on navigation in the Strait of Tiran with respect to shipping to an enemy."[50]

If there was nothing more to worry about than the question whether the imposition of the blockade was or was not in accordance with Oppenheim's views on armistices, there would not be much of a problem. However, the delegate claimed that the restrictions were "in accordance with international law," which is another matter. To begin with, if one takes Oppenheim's statement as authoritative then one would be bound to accept also as authoritative his statement that according

---

[47] Selak thinks it unlikely that the coastline on the Gulf is of a different legal nature than the land frontier without, however, elaborating the reasons for his doubts. *Id.* at 697.

[48] A line of reasoning that has not been explored and that cannot be explored here is whether the United Arab Republic and Jordan, which on May 15, 1948, illegally prevented the execution of the Partition Plan, can derive any advantages from their own action. Under the Plan the Jewish state was to comprise territory including the strip of the coast of the Gulf of Aqaba which has been under its sovereignty since 1948.

[49] The full text is as follows: "Armistices or truces, in the wider sense of the term, are all agreements between belligerent forces for a temporary cessation of hostilities. They are in no wise to be compared with peace, and ought not to be called temporary peace, because the condition of war remains between the belligerents themselves, and between the belligerents and neutrals on all points, beyond the mere cessation of hostilities. In spite of such cessation the right of visit and search over neutral merchantmen therefore remains intact, as does likewise the right to capture neutral vessels attempting to break a blockade, and the right to seize contraband of war." 2 L. OPPENHEIM, INTERNATIONAL LAW 546-47 (H. Lauterpacht ed. 1952).

[50] U.N. Doc. S/PV.1343, at 36-37 (1967).

to article 40 of the Hague Regulations respecting the Laws and Customs of War on Land of 1899 and 1907:

> Any serious violation of the armistice by one of the parties gives the other party the right of denouncing it, and even, in cases of urgency, of recommencing hostilities . . . .[51]
>
> Since the terms "serious violation" and "urgency" lack precise definition, the course to be taken is in practice left to the discretion of the injured party.[52]

Consequently, the war of June 1967 would be a lawful war for the same reason as the restrictions imposed by the United Arab Republic were claimed to be lawful. However, this was not the view taken by the Republic at the time and since. In fact, it would seem that the Republic abandoned Oppenheim's international law on armistices which he formulated in the second edition published in 1912, that is, even before World War I,[53] and placed its case on the basis of the Charter of the United Nations, that is, the new international law. The armistice agreements must then be construed and applied in the framework of the Charter. This was done by the Security Council in its resolution of September 1, 1951, and its competence to interpret and apply the armistice agreements cannot be doubted.[54] This resolution declared generally that "since the armistice regime . . . is of a permanent character, neither party can reasonably assert that it is actively a belligerent or required to exercise the right of visit, search, and seizure for any legitimate purpose of self-defence. . . ."[55] The Council made some additional findings of a general character and addressing itself to the specific complaint of Israel regarding Egypt's restrictions in the Suez Canal, called upon Egypt

> to terminate the restrictions on the passage of international commercial shipping and goods through the Suez Canal wherever bound and to cease all interference with such shipping beyond that essential to the safety of shipping in the Canal itself and to the observance of the international conventions in force.[56]

Egypt's non-compliance with this resolution is a matter of record. When Israel on January 28, 1954, complained to the Security Council about illegitimate interference with shipping passing to and from Israel through the Gulf of Aqaba, it was

---

[51] THE HAGUE CONVENTION AND DECLARATIONS OF 1899 AND 1907, at 122 (J. Scott. ed. 1915).

[52] 2 L. OPPENHEIM, INTERNATIONAL LAW 556 (H. Lauterpacht ed. 1952).

[53] 2 L. OPPENHEIM, INTERNATIONAL LAW 290 (2d ed. 1912). Mr. Selak mistakenly attributes Oppenheim's statement on armistices to "the British jurist, Sir Hersch Lauterpacht." Selak, *supra* note 8, at 681.

[54] *See* Gross, *Passage Through the Suez Canal of Israel-bound Cargo and Israel Ships*, 51 AM. J. INT'L L. 530, 545 (1957). Professor R. R. Baxter is of the opinion that this resolution can be regarded "as a legislative or law-creating act, rather than a judicial or law-declaring one," but "its burden is that the Armistice has placed special obligations upon the parties." R. BAXTER, THE LAW OF INTERNATIONAL WATERWAYS 230, 235 (1964).

[55] S.C. Res. 95, para. 5.

[56] *Id.*, para. 10.

not contested by Egypt that the 1951 resolution applied to that waterway as well.[57] Egypt on that occasion rejected again the 1951 resolution as well as the proposed resolution on the Israeli complaint, which in any event failed of adoption as a permanent member of the Council, the Soviet Union, voted against it.

On May 30, 1967, replying to the representative of the United States, who described the first above-quoted passage from the 1951 Security Council resolution[58] as "a fundamental principle,"[59] the delegate of the United Arab Republic recalled that "two highly important factors affected the resolution":

> First, four of the nine States that voted for the adoption of the resolution were parties to the dispute, and according to Article 27, paragraph 3, of the Charter, "a party to a dispute shall abstain from voting." It follows that, according to the provisions of the Charter, the resolution should not have been adopted. . . .
>
> Secondly, the resolution was based on the assumption that for two and a half years no fighting had occurred between Egypt and the Israeli authorities. Again, for political aims, those members of the Council at that time flagrantly disregarded the numerous aggressive acts committed by the Israelis during those two and a half years, in spite of the fact that they were presented to the Council in detail by the representative of Egypt. However, even the assumption on which the resolution was based must have been completely invalidated by the treacherous Israeli attack on Sinai in 1956.[60]

The second argument is incorrect. The Council did not assume that for two and a half years no fighting had occurred, but stated merely as a factual proposition that the armistice regime "has been in existence" for that period of time, which is undeniable. As long as the armistice regime is in force, the conclusions of the Council rest on a firm juridical foundation. It would be open to the United Arab Republic to argue that the hostilities including those of 1956 had destroyed the armistice regime but this it did not do.

The first argument raises a matter of the internal procedure of the Council. In this case the objections of Egypt were heard by the members and not accepted. The Council is master of its own procedure and the September 1, 1951 resolution was declared adopted by the President. Of course, it is open to members to follow their own interpretation of the constitutional law of the United Nations but they do so at their own risk and peril. Certainly one member cannot impose its auto-interpretation on another member or on the Security Council.

The General Assembly in establishing UNEF and directing its deployment has neither explicitly rejected the Egyptian contentions regarding belligerency and incidental rights of visit, search and seizure nor has it explicitly adopted the opposite Israeli contentions. However, the stationing of UNEF along the Armistice Demarcation Line and in the Sharm El Sheikh area gave substantial satisfaction to the Israeli

---

[57] Gross, *supra* note 54, at 559-61; R. BAXTER, *supra* note 54, at 211-12.
[58] See text accompanying note 55 *supra*.
[59] U.N. Doc. S/PV.1344, at 57 (1967).
[60] U.N. Doc. S/PV.1345, at 53-55, 56 (1967).

request that there should be no interference with innocent passage and no assertion of belligerent rights in the Strait of Tiran. The General Assembly and the Secretary-General could do no less without violating the letter and spirit of the Security Council resolution of September 1, 1951.

In this connection it is interesting to note that the withrawal of UNEF from the Strait of Tiran and the imposition of the blockade on May 22, 1967, were presented by the United Arab Republic as "a return to the conditions prevailing prior to 1956."[61] The delegate of Pakistan, speaking at the Fifth Emergency Special Session of the General Assembly on June 22, 1967, stated the point more precisely as follows:

> The action of the United Arab Republic did not create an entirely new situation; it merely restored the *status quo ante* and sought to liquidate a consequence of Israel's aggression in 1956. Israel had enjoyed no right of passage through the Strait of Tiran before 1956, and this position had not aroused opposition on the part of most maritime Powers.[62]

The representative of the United Arab Republic, speaking in the Security Council on May 29, 1967, referred to several statements made in connection with the 1957 discussion in the General Assembly and argued: "The 1956 aggression did not change the legal status of the Gulf of Aqaba and consequently did not affect the United Arab Republic's rights over its territorial waters."[63]

The factual situation which obtained in the Strait and the Gulf prior to the stationing of the UNEF at Sharm El Sheikh must, of course, be distinguished from the juridical situation. The latter was expressed by most of the maritime powers in 1957 and the above mentioned 1951 resolution of the Security Council. The juridical point of view was also formulated by the United States authoritatively and formally with respect to both the pre-1956 conditions and the effect of the Security Council resolution as follows:

> The attitude of the United States with respect to the right of free and innocent passage has not been altered by the events of last October and November. Those rights previously existed and are in no way based on the results of military action. It is, of course, clear that the enjoyment of rights of free and innocent passage is inconsistent with aggression. Thus, in the United States view Israel's right to free and innocent passage was dependent upon withdrawal of its forces behind the armistice lines in accordance with the United Nations resolutions. Once the situation envisaged by the General Armistice Agreements was restored, the principles of international law regarding free and innocent passage again became applicable to Israeli traffic in the Gulf of Aqaba. The Security Council resolution of September 1, 1951, set forth the principle that a party to the armistice agreements could not assert that it was actively a belligerent.[64]

[61] Report by the Secretary-General, U.N. Doc. S/7906, at 3 (1967).
[62] U.N. Doc. A/PV.1531, at 47 (1967).
[63] U.N. Doc. S/PV.1343, at 37 (1967).
[64] The United States Reply to the Arab States Representations Concerning the Suez Canal and the

The establishment in 1957 of the right of free passage through the Strait and Gulf was correctly described as follows: "The legal situation which prevailed constituted a re-establishment of the régime which was established *de jure* by the resolution of the Security Council of September 1, 1951, but not hitherto implemented."[65]

The United Arab Republic by re-imposing the closure of the Strait of Tiran and the Gulf of Aqaba, far from restoring the *status juris quo ante*, has reverted to the *status injuriae*.

The liquidation of UNEF operations and the resumption of belligerent practices by the United Arab Republic in May 1967 thus revived the old problem. The Secretary-General was obviously concerned about the revival of tensions in the area and recognized that "the situation in the Strait of Tiran represents a very serious potential threat to peace." He also urged all the parties to "forego belligerence."[66] The keynote which was echoed by several Members in the discussions in the Security Council and the Assembly was formulated by President Lyndon B. Johnson on May 23, 1967, when he declared:

> The purported closing of the Gulf of Aqaba to Israeli shipping has brought a new and very grave dimension to the crisis. The United States considers the Gulf to be an international waterway and feels that a blockade of Israeli shipping is illegal and potentially disastrous to the cause of peace. The right of free, innocent passage of the international waterway is a vital interest of the entire international community.[67]

The President formulated this as one of the five principles for peace on June 19, 1967: "The right of innocent maritime passage must be preserved for all nations."[68]

The representative of the United States elaborated the President's statements in the Security Council. On May 24, 1967, he stated that the "conditions in the area have taken a still more menacing turn because of a threat to customary international rights which have been exercised for many years in the Gulf of Aqaba."[69] On May 29, 1967, referring to the Secretary-General's report he said, "forgoing belligerence must mean forgoing any blockade of the Gulf of Aqaba," and "surely, stopping, searching and preventing the passage of ships through the Strait would clearly fall within the category of acts against which this [the Secretary-General's] appeal is directed."[70]

Gulf of Aqaba: Statement Delivered to the Heads of Mission of the Arab States at Washington, June 27, 1957. STAFF OF THE SENATE COMM. ON FOREIGN RELATIONS, 90TH CONG., 1ST SESS., A SELECT CHRONOLOGY AND BACKGROUND DOCUMENTS RELATING TO THE MIDDLE EAST 113 (Comm. Print 1967).

[65] R. Baxter, *supra* note 54, at 215.

[66] Report of the Secretary-General, U.N. Doc. S/7906, at 4-5 (1967).

[67] 56 DEP'T STATE BULL. 870-71 (1967).

[68] 57 DEP'T STATE BULL. 33 (1967).

[69] U.N. Doc. S/PV.1342, at 6 (1967).

[70] U.N. Doc. S/PV.1343, at 16, 18-20 (1967). A request for compliance with the Secretary-General's appeal was included in the United States draft resolution introduced on May 31, 1967. *See* U.N. Doc. S/PV.1345, at 22 (1967).

It is interesting to note that these statements do not refer to the Egyptian-Israeli General Armistice Agreement but seem to be based on broader grounds. The President simply considered the blockade "illegal," that is, presumably, contrary to international law. The representative of the United States considered "stopping, searching and preventing passage" as belligerent acts and presumably contrary to international law or the law of the Charter of the United Nations. The Security Council, in its resolution of September 1, 1951, squarely based itself on the Armistice Agreement and the Constantinople Convention but not on the law of the United Nations.[71] And yet it would have been logical and advantageous for the Security Council to adopt the latter position and to declare the Egyptian belligerent practices to be contrary not merely to the Armistice Agreement but above all contrary to the Charter of the United Nations.[72]

While Members of the United Nations do not appear to have expressed themselves on the subject of the compatibility of an active state of war, that is, of the exercise of belligerent acts, with the Charter, it is all the more remarkable that the resolution adopted by the Security Council on November 22, 1967, and referred to earlier in this paper, proceeds from the point of view of the Charter. It does so in the third preambular paragraph which reads: "Emphasizing further that all Member States in their acceptance of the *Charter* of the United Nations have undertaken a commitment to act in accordance with Article 2 of the *Charter*."[73] Article 2 of the Charter includes the twin principles of refraining from the threat of or use of force and of settling international disputes "by peaceful means in such a manner that international peace and security, and justice are not endangered."

Furthermore, in operative paragraph 1, the Security Council "[a]ffirms that the fulfillment of *Charter* principles requires the establishment of a just and lasting peace in the Middle East which shall include the application of both the following principles."[74] While the first principle relates to the "withdrawal of Israeli armed forces from territories occupied in the recent conflict" without any reference to the Armistice Agreements which figured prominently in the General Assembly resolutions with respect to the 1956 Middle East conflict,[75] the second principle states: "Termination of all claims or states of belligerency . . . ."[76] The law of the Charter is the law common to all parties in the conflict and it was high time for the Security Council to declare that the state of belligerency which was claimed by the United Arab Republic to exist, and against which Israel always objected, must be terminated because of incompatibility with Charter principles. Whatever may be the outcome

---

[71] *See* Gross, *supra* note 54, at 564-68.

[72] *See also* N. FEINBERG, THE LEGALITY OF A "STATE OF WAR" AFTER THE CESSATION OF HOSTILITIES UNDER THE CHARTER OF THE NATIONS AND THE COVENANT OF THE LEAGUE OF NATIONS (Jerusalem, 1961).

[73] S.C. Res. 242 (1967); 4 U.N. MONTHLY CHRON. 19 (Dec. 1967). (Emphasis added.)

[74] *Id.* (Emphasis added.)

[75] Resolutions adopted by the General Assembly during its First Emergency Special Session from November 1 to 10, 1956, U.N. GAOR (Emer. Spec. Sess. I), Supp. 1, U.N. Doc. A/3354 (1956).

[76] S.C. Res. 242, *supra* note 73.

of negotiations between the parties, this declaration in itself is a substantial gain for the United Nations.[77]

IV

FREEDOM OF PASSAGE THROUGH THE STRAIT OF TIRAN AND IN THE GULF OF AQABA

It has been shown that the claim to exclusive control of the Gulf of Aqaba on historic or other grounds was without merit. It has also been demonstrated that the territory of Israel includes a coast on the Gulf. There remains to be considered the question of passage through the Strait and the Gulf.

One problem can be eliminated. No government has contested the proposition that the entrance to the Gulf "is situated in the joint territorial waters of Saudi Arabia and the United Arab Republic. Due to navigational hazards the only navigable route to the Gulf runs less than one mile from the Sinai Peninsula. Hence it crosses our undisputed territorial waters."[78] These are undisputed facts. As regards passage through the Strait of Tiran, it might be well to begin with the position of Egypt. On February 11, 1957, the Secretary of State of the United States handed the Israeli Ambassador an aide mémoire in which he stated: "[T]he United States believes that the Gulf comprehends international waters and that no nation has the right to prevent free and innocent passage in the Gulf and through the Straits giving access thereto."[79] He went on to say:

> The United States recalls that on January 28, 1950, the Egyptian Ministry of Foreign Affairs informed the United States that the Egyptian occupation of the two islands of Tiran and Senafir at the entrance of the Gulf of Aqaba was only to protect the islands themselves against possible damage or violation and that "this occupation being in no way conceived in a spirit of obstructing in any way innocent passage through the stretch of water separating these two islands from the Egyptian coast of Sinai, it follows that this passage, the only practicable one, will remain free as in the past, in conformity with international practice and recognized principles of the law of nations."[80]

Thus by its own admission, Egypt considered the Strait of Tiran as open to passage and consequently recognized the right of passage in the Gulf. Clearly, were Egypt or now the United Arab Republic or Saudi Arabia actively involved in a war, they could deny passage to the ships of their opponent. But apart from this, there is no right to deny or obstruct passage. When the Government of Egypt in 1955 issued instructions requiring prior notice from ships, the United States Government maintained its position that "no nation has the right to prevent free

---

[77] It may be noted that none of the three draft resolutions before the Security Council in November 1967 referred to the armistice agreements or armistice lines. 4 U.N. MONTHLY CHRON. 8-9 (Dec. 1967).

[78] Mr. El Kony (U.A.R.), U.N. Doc. S/PV.1343, at 31 (1967). Mr. El Kony gives the length of the Gulf as being about 96 miles and its widest breadth as less than 15 miles.

[79] 4 M. WHITEMAN, *supra* note 14, at 466.

[80] *Id.*

and innocent passage in the Gulf and through the Straits giving access thereto."[81] The
British Government in 1955 "never recognized the legality of the Egyptian blockade
either of the Canal [Suez] or other waters, such as the Gulf of Aqaba, leading to
Israeli ports,"[82] and made no formal agreement with Egypt "about shipping proceeding to the Gulf of Aqaba," but rather it "adopted a *de facto* arrangement"
while maintaining its legal position.[83]

At that period only the alleged existence of a state of war with Israel seemed
to motivate Egypt to deny passage through the Strait.

In connection with the liquidation of the Middle East crisis in 1956-57, a good
deal of attention in the General Assembly was focused on Israel's grievances with
respect to the passage through the Strait of Tiran and in the Gulf of Aqaba. Fourteen Members, including those with the greatest interests in maritime freedom,
expressed themselves in one form or another in favor of freedom of innocent passage
through the Strait and in the Gulf.[84] As indicated earlier, the deployment of UNEF
in the area of the Strait was designed to and in fact did, ensure freedom of passage as
long as it lasted but the General Assembly did not adopt a formal resolution on the
subject.

However, shortly thereafter at the 1958 Geneva Conference on the Law of the
Sea, the question was formally settled.[85] The claim to exclusive control of the
Gulf of Aqaba by the three littoral Arab states which was reiterated at the
Conference found no support. On the contrary, it was generally taken for granted
that there were four littoral states, including Israel. Nor was there any concern
with the allegation that Israel had no legal right to its share of the coast. Whatever
the status of the Gulf may have been prior to the establishment of Israel, it could
not be regarded as a historic bay after establishment of the new state.[86]

The Conference boldly tackled the issues raised by the conflict between Egypt,
Israel and the rest of the maritime community, which so far the International Law
Commission and the General Assembly have avoided. In full awareness of these
issues the Conference by a vote of 65 for, 1 against and 1 abstention,[87] adopted article
16 of the Convention on the Territorial Sea and the Contiguous Zone.[88] The first

---

[81] *Id.* at 469.

[82] 543 PARL. DEB., H.L. (5th ser.) 1135 (1955), quoted in 4 M. WHITEMAN, *supra* note 14, at 478.

[83] 546 PARL. DEB., H.C. (5th ser.) 2288 (1955), quoted in 4 M. WHITEMAN, *supra* note 14, at 480.

[84] Gross, *supra* note 9, at 576-78.

[85] "The seeming general consensus indicated by this debate [in the General Assembly] in favor of
preserving a right of access to straits free of the arbitrary competence of the coastal state nevertheless
found impressive confirmation shortly in the outcome of the 1958 Conference on the Law of the Sea."
M. McDOUGAL & W. BURKE, THE PUBLIC ORDER OF THE OCEANS 210-11 (1962).

[86] "It would no doubt be argued . . . that even if the claim to historic rights were justified the
emergence of a new state bordering on the gulf altered the scope of authority normally associated with
historic waters." *Id.* at 444. A similar change occurred in the Black Sea when Russia established itself
on its shores. *See* Selak, *supra* note 8, at 693.

[87] U.N. Conference on the Law of the Sea, Official Records, Vol. II, Plenary Meetings, at 65, para. 3
(1958).

[88] U.N. Doc. A/Conf.13/L.52 (1958).

paragraph of this article accords to the coastal state the right to "take the necessary steps in its territorial sea to prevent passage which is not innocent," the second paragraph deals with control over ships proceeding to internal waters, the third paragraph permits temporary suspension of innocent passage "if such suspension is essential for the protection of its security," and finally paragraph four, which may be called the Aqaba article, reads as follows: "There shall be no suspension of the innocent passage of foreign ships through straits which are used for international navigation between one part of the high seas and another part of the high seas or the territorial sea of a foreign State."

In addition this Convention, which entered into force on September 10, 1964, and had been ratified by more than thirty states, including the United States, the United Kingdom, the Soviet Union, and France, lays down rules concerning innocent passage (articles 14 and 15) and the permissible laws and regulations applicable to foreign ships exercising the right of innocent passage. Such law and regulations must conform to the articles of the Convention and "other rules of international law" (article 17).[89]

The Conference made some changes in the relevant draft articles of the International Law Commission and "all the changes . . . were clearly in the direction of promoting more inclusive use of straits and of restricting the authority of coastal states."[90] The Conference deleted the word "normally"—the deletion was proposed by the United States—from the Commission's draft,[91] on the ground that the word was not used by the International Court of Justice in its Judgment in the *Corfu Channel* case.[92] The effect of the deletion is "to assure passage through straits which were actually used and to avoid friction over the concept of normal use."[93]

The other important change related to the Commission's words "between two parts of the high seas" which qualified the word "straits." This was of particular importance with respect to the Gulf of Aqaba. Although in the view of some governments, notably of the United States, the Gulf was considered to comprehend international waters, this could be contested by others, and the argument became a casualty when Egypt and Saudi Arabia extended their territorial sea from six to twelve miles. The greatest width of the Gulf being between fifteen and seventeen miles, there is no room left for international waters. The point was made by several governments at the Conference that the essential aspect of the traditional principle of freedom of navigation was for ships to enter the port of destination and to have

---

[89] Concerning these provisions, *see* Gross, *supra* note 9, at 580-92, and M. McDougal & W. Burke, *supra* note 85, at 174-304.

[90] M. McDougal & W. Burke, *supra* note 85, at 211.

[91] This draft was as follows: "There must be no suspension of the innocent passage of foreign vessels through straits normally used for international navigation between two parts of the high seas." 10 U.N. GAOR, Supp. 9, at 20, U.N. Doc. A/2934 (1955).

[92] [1949] I.C.J. 4. *See also* Gross, *supra* note 9, at 586.

[93] M. McDougal & W. Burke, *supra* note 85, at 212.

the right, for this purpose, to pass through the territorial sea.[94] This point was met by changing the words in the Commission's draft to read "between one part of the high seas and another part of the high seas or the territorial sea of another State." In this manner passage in the Gulf of Aqaba was secured. The principle of freedom of navigation was spelled out and placed on a more secure basis. By prohibiting suspension of innocent passage through straits, the Conference rejected decisively the competence of the coastal state "to control the strait as a means of projecting its influence for purposes of special national policy, not necessarily reflecting common interest."[95]

The relevance of article 16, paragraph 4, of the 1958 Convention on the Territorial Sea for the controversy over the Strait of Tiran and the Gulf of Aqaba was contested in the Security Council and in the General Assembly in the debates in 1967.

In arguing the illegality of the blockade measures announced by the United Arab Republic, the representative of the United States referred to article 16, para. 4, of the 1958 Convention as evidence of international law. He described the *status quo* which existed from 1957 to 1967 as being "in accordance with international law." "Such law, indeed," he said, "has been expressed in the 1958 Convention on the Territorial Sea and the Contiguous Zone, to which many nations are parties."[96]

The representative of the United Arab Republic did not deny that the rule laid down in article 16, paragraph 4, was declaratory of customary international law but contended that the Convention was inapplicable "to our case" because it lacked any reference "to the consequences of armed conflict." He supported his view by quoting from the report of the International Law Commission the sentence: "The draft regulates the law of the sea in time of peace only.[97]

This is, of course, correct but the relevant point is that the 1958 Conference did not adopt the Commission's proposal. Thus, quite deliberately, the Convention was intended to apply generally without reference to states of war and peace. But, as has been pointed out, the Convention, within limits, respects the security interests of the coastal states and in case of actual armed conflict the necessary consequences would have to be drawn. In this case, however, the existence of a state of war which would justify appropriate measures by the coastal state has not been recognized and its seems unnecessary to go over the same ground again.

Another argument against article 16, paragraph 4, is that it is a "new rule."[98] The

---

[94] Gross, *supra* note 9, at 587-89.

[95] M. McDougal & W. Burke, *supra* note 85, at 189. These authors also note that "[i]t is evident that there has been a fairly strong tendency over the past century to restrict the competence of coastal states over straits." *Id.* at 213.

[96] U.N. Doc. S/PV.1343, at 16-17 (1967).

[97] U.N. Doc. S/PV.1344, at 47 (1967).

[98] *See* the speech of the representative of the Sudan, U.N. Doc. A/PV.1530, at 28 (1967); Murti, *supra* note 20, at 203. Concerning the pro-Arab position of the Indian Government, *cf.* Kozicki, *Indian Policy Toward the Middle East*, 11 Orbis 786 (1967).

source of this is an article on the 1958 Conference by Arthur H. Dean, who was head of the American delegation, in which he said with reference to this clause: "The Geneva Conference thus, in a politically charged area, achieved agreement sufficient to write a new and beneficent rule into international law."[99]

There is room for argument whether article 16, paragraph 4, creates a new rule which would be binding on the contracting states only or whether it merely specifies or particularizes a rule which is deemed implicit in customary international law, that is, the general principle of freedom of the seas and navigation. At the Conference itself there was substantial evidence that some delegates merely desired to make explicit the right of ships to sail from port to port through international waterways, this right being implicit in the general principle.[100] In this sense there is nothing new in article 16, paragraph 4.

What is undeniably true, however, is that the rule is new in the sense that it differs in important respects, as indicated earlier, from the draft submitted by the International Law Commission. This is indeed the interpretation of Mr. Dean as appears from this clarification:

> In making this statement I was thinking mainly in terms of fact that the question of innocent passage through straits between one part of the high seas and the territorial sea of a foreign state had not been covered by the decision of the International Court in the *Corfu Channel* case or in the draft articles prepared by the International Law Commission. I did not intend to pass upon the question of whether or not this rule represented a codification of customary international law.[101]

In the present submission the rule does represent a codification of customary international law although it could also be argued that it contains an element of progressive development of the law. The very substantial vote in favor of the rule at the Conference must also be considered as an expression of the Conference in favor of free and innocent passage through international waterways. That the Conference was also aware that in article 16, paragraph 4, it "adopted a rule which clearly applied to the Israeli-Arab controversy" is undeniable.[102] More than that, for in Mr. Dean's view, "it specifically *determines* the heated controversy between Israel and Arab states as to the right of Israeli shipping to pass through the Strait of Tiran to the Gulf of Aqaba."[103]

Obviously, the rule could not achieve this purpose if it depended upon ratification of Arab states involved in that controversy.

---

[99] Dean, *The Geneva Conference on the Law of the Sea: What Was Accomplished*, 52 AM. J. INT'L L. 607, 623 (1958).

[100] Gross, *supra* note 9, at 587-89, 592-94.

[101] Letter from Arthur H. Dean to Leo Gross, Feb. 29, 1968.

[102] Dean, *supra* note 99, at 623.

[103] *Id.* at 621. (Emphasis added.)

V

CONCLUSIONS

There is no need to summarize the results of this analysis of the controversy over the right of free and innocent passage through the Gulf. In the present submission none of the propositions advanced by the United Arab Republic and its supporters can be accepted as juridically persuasive: neither the claim that the Gulf of Aqaba has been from time immemorial an historic gulf, a discovery which at least on the juridical plane was made only in 1957, nor the claim that Israel's territory does not comprise a stretch of the coast of the Gulf, neither the existence of belligerent rights and of a continuing state of war, nor the claim that the Strait of Tiran is not an international waterway.

Apart from the specific issues relating to the conflict, there emerged in the 1958 Geneva Conference and in the 1967 debates in the Security Council and the General Assembly a concern for ensuring free and innocent passage through international waterways for all states. For if it is admitted that a coastal state is entitled to use waterways as an instrument of national policy no state would contemplate the future with equanimity. While many delegations addressed themselves, in the 1967 debates, to the concrete issue of innocent passage through the Suez Canal and the Strait of Tiran and in the Gulf of Aqaba, the delegate of Italy formulated the problem in comprehensive terms when he said:

> There are, moreover, questions which affect the more general interests of the international community. I have in mind the problems of international waterways, the freedom of which is guaranteed by international law and is a matter of primary interest for the whole world and particularly for those countries which, like Italy, are separated from the oceans by canals and straits.[104]

The issue is of transcendent importance for the welfare of all nations, the developed and the developing ones.

At the 1958 Geneva Conference the proposal had already been made to include in article 16, paragraph 4, the words "straits or other sea-lanes," on the ground that "[t]he term 'straits' was much too narrow, because there were sea-lanes used for international navigation elsewhere than in straits."[105]

---

[104] U.N. Doc. A/PV.1530, at 66 (1967). In this connection mention may be made of the statement of the British representative:

"In addition, there is one most urgent and most dangerous issue of all: the question of the right of passage for shipping of all nationalities through the Strait of Tiran. The maintenance of the provisions of the Geneva Convention on the Territorial Sea dealing with international navigation between the high seas and territorial waters is of the gravest concern to my Government, as it must be to all engaged in international trade."

U.N. Doc. S/PV.1342, at 18-20 (1967). *See also* statements by the delegations indicated in U.N. Docs. A/PV.1531, 22 June 1967, at 29-30 (Belgium); A/PV.1537, 27 June 1967, at 46 (Nigeria); A/PV.1541, 29 June 1967, at 13-15 (Peru); A/PV.1542, 29 June 1967, at 41 (Australia); and *id*. at 58-60 (Costa Rica).

[105] The words are those of the delegate of the Netherlands, U.N. Conf. on the Law of the Sea, Off. Rec., vol. III, 1st Comm. 94, U.N. Doc. A/Conf.13/39 (1958). *See* Gross, *supra* note 9, at 588.

The inclusion of the word "sea-lanes" would have had the same justification as the deletion of the word "normally," that is, avoidance of technical controversies over meanings of "strait" or "canal" and concentration on the use as a highway for international navigation.

In view of this precedent and the concern for freedom of navigation on the high seas, it was probably no mere accident that the resolution of the Security Council adopted on November 22, 1967, used the comprehensive term "international waterways" when it affirmed the necessity "[f]or guaranteeing freedom of navigation through international waterways in the area."[106]

It may also have been a matter of intent rather than mere choice of words that the resolution expresses the concern of the Security Council for guaranteeing freedom of navigation through international waterways "in the area." For while the conflict between Israel and its Arab neighbors in the past has related, insofar as freedom of navigation was involved, to the Suez Canal, the Strait of Tiran, and the Gulf of Aqaba, there are "in the area" other international waterways such as the Straits of Bab El Mandeb.

These straits have a vital function in the area for they "join the high seas of the Gulf of Aden to those of the Red Sea and form part of the international route from the Mediterranean to the Far East."[107] Four states border on these Straits: Ethiopia and French Somaliland on the African side, and Yemen and the Republic of South Yemen, the former British Aden Protectorate, on the Arabian side. Perim Island itself was formerly part of the British Colony of Aden and has become part of the Republic of South Yemen.

As concerns freedom of passage through these straits, one would assume that in the contemplation of the United States they would be covered by article 16, paragraph 4, of the 1958 Convention. This would follow from the traditional policy of the United States in favor of freedom of transit through international waterways including international straits.

Insofar as the United Kingdom and the new Republic of South Yemen are concerned, the following statement by the British Foreign Secretary, Mr. George Brown, in the House of Commons on November 29, 1967 may be quoted:

> There is as yet no new Government, but the delegation from the N.L.F., in the course of discussions in Geneva, as the communiqué shows, had agreed to accept

---

[106] S.C. Res. 242 (1967), *supra* note 73. It is worth noting that all three draft resolutions before the Council—a three-power (India, Mali, and Nigeria) draft, a United States draft and a Soviet Union draft—emphasized in one way or another freedom of navigation or innocent passage. *See* 4 U.N. MONTHLY CHRON. 9 (Dec. 1967). The resolution which was unanimously adopted issued from a United Kingdom draft. *Id.* at 15, 17.

[107] Kennedy, *A Brief Geographical and Hydrographical Study of Straits Which Constitute Routes for International Traffic*, 1 United Nations Conference on the Law of the Sea, Official Records, U.N. Doc. A/Conf.13/6, at 115 (1958). The length of the Straits is 50 miles, the Large Strait between Perim Island and the African coast is about 9¼ miles wide, and the Small Strait between Perim Island and Arabia is about 1½ miles wide. *Id.*

the international obligations which we have extended to Aden, and one of those is the Geneva Convention which seeks to ensure free passage through international waterways. One of these is the waterway of the Straits of Perim.[108]

The situation appears then to be adequately covered by the devolution or inheritance agreement between the United Kingdom and the Republic of South Yemen, although it is not clear from the statement whether the agreement is a formal one or sufficiently formal to be registered with the United Nations.

Conflict among nations has often contributed to the strengthening and revitalization of international law and organization. One has to remind himself of the major wars in the modern era which promoted the growth of law and organization: the Napoleonic Wars contributed through the Congress of Vienna to the development of international river law and gave birth to the Concert system; the First World War gave birth to the League of Nations and the Permanent Court of International Justice; the Second World War created the United Nations; the Indus River conflict between India and Pakistan contributed powerfully to the study and development of the law of river basins. Examples could be multiplied. Problem-solving has been a constructive experience for nations. It may then be legitimate to expect that the solution of the conflict in the Middle East will hasten the establishment of the law governing international waterways on a firm foundation by the application of the principle that such waterways shall not be used as an instrument of national policy but for the benefit of all nations. In the long run an increasingly interdependent world cannot settle for less.

---

[108] PARL. DEB., H.C. (5th ser.) 438 (1967). Concerning the politics of the area, see Klieman, *Bab Al-Mandab: The Red Sea in Transition*, 11 ORBIS 758 (1967).

CLOSURE OF THE SUEZ CANAL TO ISRAELI SHIPPING

MAJID KHADDURI*

INTRODUCTION

The Arab-Israeli war of June 1967 has again raised the question as to whether Egypt can lawfully close the Suez Canal to Israeli shipping. Israel, since its establishment, has repeatedly demanded the same right of free passage accorded to other nations, but Egypt has insisted on denying her such a right despite resolutions of the United Nations Security Council calling on Egypt to terminate the restrictions imposed on the passage of Israeli shipping and goods through the Suez Canal.[1] The six-day war gave Israel the opportunity to demand again the opening of the Canal to her shipping;[2] but President Nasir, in his speech on November 24, 1967, two days after the Security Council's resolution 242 had been adopted, calling for withdrawal from occupied territory and termination of belligerency, declared in no uncertain terms that "we shall never allow Israeli ships, whatever the cost, to pass through the Suez Canal."[3] Israel's demand and Nasir's rejection call for a reconsideration of the question in the light of the new circumstances brought about by the June war and the Security Council's resolution of November 22, 1967. It is not my purpose to review the arguments of the two parties relative to the conditions preceding the June war, except in so far as they relate to the conditions after the war, since they have been thoroughly scrutinized by a number of scholars from the two opposing viewpoints.[4] In order to examine the legal aspect of the closure of the Canal specifically to Israeli shipping, I propose to deal with the question under three headings: (1) the fundamental principles governing the present legal status of the Suez Canal; (2) Israel's claim to the right of free passage; (3) Egypt's right to control of the Canal.

* B.A. 1932, American University, Beirut; Ph.D. 1938, University of Chicago. Director of the Center for Middle East Studies, and Professor, The School of Advanced International Studies, The Johns Hopkins University. Author, INDEPENDENT IRAQ (1951); WAR AND PEACE IN THE LAW OF ISLAM (1955); ISLAMIC JURISPRUDENCE (1961); MODERN LIBYA (1963).

[1] The most important resolution was, of course, S.C. Res. 95 (1951). It cited S.C. Res. 73 (1949) and other resolutions and acts calling for the cessation of hostile acts and the resolution of outstanding issues between the parties.

[2] See Abba Eban's speech at the Emergency Session of the General Assembly of the United Nations on June 19, 1967, U.N. Doc. A/PV.1526 (1967) and subsequent declarations.

[3] For full text of the speech, see *al-Ahram*, Cairo, Nov. 25, 1967. See also N.Y. Times, Nov. 24, 1967, at 13, col. 1.

[4] Two books might be cited which deal with the divergent views in detail: B. AVRAM, THE EVOLUTION OF THE SUEZ CANAL STATUS FROM 1869 UP TO 1956 (1958), and J. OBIETA, THE INTERNATIONAL STATUS OF THE SUEZ CANAL (1960).

I

FUNDAMENTAL PRINCIPLES GOVERNING THE LEGAL STATUS OF THE SUEZ CANAL

When the Suez Canal was opened in 1869, Egypt had not yet attained independence. Its territory was part of the Ottoman Empire. The Khedive of Egypt, one of the Sultan's principal governors, had no power to act in entering into agreements relating to foreign affairs without the approval of the Sultan. Thus, the acts of concession issued by the Khedive in 1854, 1856, and 1866, granting the right to connect the Mediterranean and the Red Seas by a canal and to operate it, had to be ratified by the Sultan's firman (decree), issued on March 19, 1866, in order to be valid under the Ottoman law in force in Egypt.[5] However, no rights were derived from the concession by any third party nor was any surrender of the Sultan's sovereignty over the Canal ever intended. On the contrary, the acts of concession stressed Egypt's right to supervise the Canal, to enforce law and public order, and to occupy any point on the borders of the Canal whenever this was deemed necessary for the defense of the country, as a manifestation of sovereignty over the territory of the Canal. But the intent of throwing open the Canal to the free navigation of all nations without distinction of flag was made abundantly clear.

Nor was the Sultan's sovereignty over the Canal's territory restricted by the provisions of the Convention regulating the use of the Canal signed in Constantinople on October 29, 1888. The Convention of 1888 aimed at confirming the practices that had developed concerning free navigation for all nations, but no surrender of any sovereign rights was ever contemplated. For if the Sultan had given away any of his sovereign rights, he would have committed an act of servitude in derogation of his sovereignty over Egypt. The first principle governing the present status of the Suez Canal is, therefore, the principle of territorial sovereignty which was recognized by the signatories of the Convention of 1888. But to the manner in which the rights of sovereignty were to be exercised, we shall return later.

Next to the principle of territorial sovereignty is the principle that the Suez Canal is an "international waterway." This "internationality" was the product of a voluntary act on the part of the Ottoman Sultan in an effort to extend the benefits of free passage through the Canal to all nations without qualifying his sovereign rights. Even before the construction of the Canal was completed, the intent was, both in

---

[5] The concession, concluded with a private company, did not imply an international obligation on Egypt's behalf and could have been signed by the Khedive without the approval of the Sultan in accordance with the firman of appointment of the Khedive of 1841. But since the concession contained an obligation assumed by the two parties toward each other affecting third parties in their undertaking that they would not discriminate against other parties, and Article 14 of the 1866 concession provided that the canal and its ports would always be open as a neutral passage, the Sultan's approval became necessary. In the concession of 1866, it was stipulated that the Sultan's ratification was necessary. For texts of the acts of concession and the firmans of ratification, see U.S. DEP'T OF STATE, PUB. No. 6392, THE SUEZ CANAL PROBLEM: A DOCUMENTARY PUBLICATION 1-16 (1956); B. BOUTROS-GHALI, LE CANAL DE SUEZ, 1854-1957: CHRONOLOGIE DOCUMENT 10 (1958); 1 J. HUREWITZ, DIPLOMACY IN THE NEAR AND MIDDLE EAST 146-49 (1956).

the acts of concession as well as in unilateral declarations, to grant the right of free navigation to all nations. Article 14 of the Concession of 1856 reads:

> We solemnly declare, for ourselves and our successors, subject to ratification by His Imperial Majesty the Sultan, that the great maritime canal from Suez to Pelusium and the ports belonging to it shall be open forever, as neutral passages, to every merchant vessel crossing from one sea to the other, without any distinction, exclusion, or preference with respect to persons or nationalities, in consideration of the payment of the fees, and compliance with the regulations established by the universal company, the concession-holder, for the use of the said canal and its appurtenances.[6]

In this, as well as in other relevant declarations of unilateral nature, the purpose was to assure the company and all nations that the canal would always be open to free navigation. Notwithstanding these declarations, as one Israeli writer stated, "[t]he passage of ships was not a right but a privilege granted by the Ottoman Empire to other nations."[7] It is also questionable that a right was established by the Sultan's declaration made at a conference held in Constantinople, in 1873, to deal with technical matters, in which he said:

> It is understood that no modification, for the future, of the conditions for the passage through the Canal shall be permitted, whether in regard to the navigation toll or the dues for towage, anchorage, pilotage, etc., except with the consent of the Sublime Porte, which will not take any decision on the subject without previously coming to an understanding with the principal Powers interested therein.[8]

Some writers have argued, on the analogy of the *Eastern Greenland Case,* that the unilateral declaration of a Foreign Minister on behalf of his country, would be "binding upon the country to which the Minister belongs."[9] Such a declaration was, in that case, held by the Permanent Court of International Justice to be binding on the country making it. The so-called "Ihlen doctrine" may or may not be accepted, but it is of no great significance to our discussion, since an internationally binding act had been accepted by the Ottoman Porte in 1888 which established beyond any doubt the international character of the Suez Canal.

In the preamble of the Constantinople Convention[10] (October 29, 1888), the nine signatory Powers[11] stated that their intention was to establish "a definitive system intended to guarantee, at all times and to all the Powers, the free use of the Suez Maritime Canal, and thus to complete the system under which the navigation of

---

[6] THE SUEZ CANAL PROBLEM, *supra* note 5, at 7; B. BOUTROS-GHALI, *supra* note 5, at 6; and 1 J. HUREWITZ, *supra* note 5, at 148.

[7] B. AVRAM, *supra* note 4, at 31.

[8] Great Britain, *Parliamentary Papers*, Commercial 19, C. 1075, at 319.

[9] [1933] P.C.I.J., ser. A/B, No. 53, at 21, 71.

[10] For English text of the Convention, *see* Great Britain, *Parliamentary Papers*, Commercial, No. 2, Suez Canal, C. 5623 (1889); THE SUEZ CANAL PROBLEM, *supra* note 5, at 16-20; B. BOUTROS-GHALI, *supra* note 5, at 16; 1 J. HUREWITZ, *supra* note 5, at 202-05.

[11] They were Great Britain, Austria-Hungary, France, Germany, Italy, The Netherlands, Russia, Spain, and Turkey.

this Canal had been placed by the Firman of His Imperial Majesty the Sultan, dated February 22, 1866 . . . ."

Moreover, the preamble indicates the principle of "internationality" as having evolved from the inception of the Canal and that the Convention was to "complete" the legal status envisioned in early declarations. As a legal obligation, however, it is Article 1, specifying free navigation to all nations, which established the principle of internationality to include freedom of passage in time of war and peace. Article 1 reads: "The Suez Maritime Canal shall always be free and open, in time of war as in time of peace, to every vessel of commerce or of war, without distinction of flag. Consequently, the High Contracting Parties agree not in any way to interfere with the free use of the canal, in time of war as in time of peace."

In order to insure "free navigation," it was realized that a "guarantee," as stated in the preamble, was necessary. To achieve such a guarantee, the signatories provided, under Article 2, that: "They undertake not to interfere in any way with security of that Canal and its branches, the working of which shall not be the object of any attempt at obstruction."

This "security" of the Canal was to be guaranteed by the acceptance of another principle, already stated in earlier declarations, that the Canal would be neutral, although the term *neutrality* is not used in the text of the Convention. Article 4 reads:

> The Maritime Canal remaining open in time of war as a free passage . . . , no right of war, act of hostility or act having for its purpose to interfere with the free navigation of the Canal, shall be committed in the Canal and its ports . . . even though the Ottoman Empire should be one of the belligerent Powers.

All other acts on the part of belligerent Powers were forbidden in the Canal and its ports. Moreover, the Canal, as Article 1 further states, "shall never be submitted to the exercise of the right of blockade." The legal consequence of these stipulations is that the Canal, in time of war, shall be excluded from the area of warfare.[12] Thus, the neutrality of the Suez Canal, even if the Ottoman Empire were one of the belligerent Powers, is the third principle governing the present legal status of the Canal. Various terms have been used to characterize this neutral regime, from "inviolability" to "neutralization," but this should be distinguished from the neutralization of states.[13]

The three principles of territorial sovereignty, internationality, and neutrality

---

[12] This means that the neutral zone should be excluded from the region where war can lawfully be prepared or waged.

[13] *See* J. OBIETA, *supra* note 4, at 68-69. Colombos, however, held a different point of view on the Canal's neutrality. He said: ". . . the Suez Canal is not neutralized in the proper sense of the term, since neutrality does not admit the passage of belligerent forces across a territory . . . . It is only subject to a particular regime for the purpose of withdrawing it from all acts of hostility within its waters and protecting it from any damage or any attempt to close it to the detriment of the World's navigation." C. COLOMBOS, THE INTERNATIONAL LAW OF THE SEA 175 (4th ed. 1961).

have been assessed differently by various writers. Some, stressing internationality and neutrality, have maintained that sovereignty was restricted by the Convention of 1888 which imposed a "perpetual servitude" over Egypt in the area of the Suez Canal.[14] Others, rejecting the imposition of an international servitude, stressed the overriding principle of territorial sovereignty and recognize neither an international character for the Canal nor an implied neutrality in its zone.[15] The latter position has been maintained by writers who either tried to defend Egypt's position on the closure of the Canal against Israel or pushed to the extreme the doctrine of territorial sovereignty in the relationship among states. On the other hand, the writers who argued the case of Israel's claim to free passage have stressed Egypt's international obligations under the Convention of 1888 without qualifications. A third position, however, may be maintained in which Egypt's contractual obligations may be respected without compromising the doctrine of sovereignty. This is the position taken in this paper.

II

ISRAEL'S CLAIM TO THE RIGHT OF FREE PASSAGE
THROUGH THE SUEZ CANAL

Since its establishment more than two decades ago, Israel has repeatedly demanded the same right of free passage through the Suez Canal enjoyed by other nations, and has claimed that Egypt's closure of the Canal to its shipping had been done in violation of the general principles of international law, of the Convention of 1888, and of the Armistice Agreement of 1949. Let us examine Israel's complaints from these three legal angles.

Under the general principles of international law, according to Israel, all nations possess the right to navigate freely on the high seas, through international waterways that connect high seas, and through international rivers. This right, according to Israel, is "a cornerstone" of international law, and, therefore, cannot be denied to her as one of the members of the international community.

In the specific case of the Suez Canal, the right of free passage, clearly stated in the Constantinople Convention of 1888, was, in this area, to be enjoyed by all nations without distinction of flag. Israel, as one of the nations presumably included under the general term "without distinction of flag," was therefore entitled to enjoy the same right as other nations, but Egypt is alleged to have denied Israel such right in violation of the general principle of international law and of her obligations under the Convention of 1888.

Moreover, Egypt's restrictive measures, according to Israel, constitute an act of war in the Canal waters contrary to Articles 1 and 4 of the Convention of 1888, on

---

[14] See B. AVRAM, *supra* note 4, at 48-50.

[15] See Huang, *Some International and Legal Aspects of the Suez Canal Question*, 51 AM. J. INT'L L. 300-03 (1957).

the ground that Egypt possessed no right to take defensive measures in the Canal Zone.[16] Egypt proceeded to act on the assumption that she was at war with Israel, but this assumption was not justified, according to Israel, because no state—other than the Arab states—recognized such a state of war to have existed. On the contrary, the United Nations had on more than one occasion called on Egypt to open the Suez Canal presumably on the assumption that Egypt and Israel, as peace-loving members of that Organization, can no longer remain at war with one another. If they had ever been at war, as the Arab states held, such a state of war must be superseded by membership in the United Nations.[17]

Finally, the Armistice Agreement between Egypt and Israel (February 24, 1949)[18] has prohibited hostile acts. According to Israel, not only war in the military sense, but also the state of war between her and Egypt had been terminated. As stated by an Israeli jurist, the Agreement was intended to achieve four aims:

1. To facilitate the transition from the present truce to permanent peace and bring all hostilities to an end.

2. To fulfill the obligation of the Security Council to act with respect to threats to the peace, breaches of the peace and acts of aggression.

3. To delineate permanent demarcation lines beyond which the armed forces of the respective parties should not move.

4. To provide for the withdrawal and reduction of armed forces in order to insure the maintenance of the armistice during the transition to permanent peace.[19]

These aims, intended to establish eventual peace between Egypt and Israel, have been endorsed by the United Nations resolutions of 1949 and of 1951, which explicitly called upon Egypt to open the Suez Canal. Egypt's refusal to open the Canal, according to Israel, was a violation of both the Armistice Agreement and the United Nations Security Council resolutions of 1949 and 1951.[20]

Egypt, however, has refused to accept the charge that she has denied Israel's right of free passage in violation of international law. Israel has put forth a claim to free passage under international law on the ground that the Suez Canal—like any other strait—is an international waterway and, therefore, according to her, should be open to free navigation. But should the Suez Canal, even if regarded as an international waterway, be treated as other waterways, like straits, and, therefore, as subject to the same rules of international law? Straits, as "natural" waterways provided

---

[16] 9 U.N. SCOR, 658th meeting 1-25 (1954). *See also* B. AVRAM, *supra* note 4, at 119-21.

[17] This viewpoint is based on the assumption that members of the United Nations are peace-loving members and therefore no one can be at war with another member without violating the Charter of this organization. *See* H. KELSEN, THE LAW AND THE UNITED NATIONS 69 (1950); AND L.M. BLOOMFIELD, EGYPT, ISRAEL AND THE GULF OF AQABA IN INTERNATIONAL LAW 164 (1957).

[18] 42 U.N.T.S. 251, no. 654. *See also* 2 J. HUREWITZ, *supra* note 5, at 299-304.

[19] S. ROSENNE, ISRAEL'S ARMISTICE AGREEMENTS WITH THE ARAB STATES 33 (1951).

[20] *See* note 1 *supra*. For an interpretation of these views, *see* Gross, *Passage Through the Suez Canal of Israel-Bound Cargo and Israel Ships,* 51 AM. J. INT'L L. 530-68 (1957).

by nature, have existed from time immemorial and, therefore, the free passage enjoyed by all nations must be distinguished from free passage through canals which have been artificially constructed. Before a canal is opened, its territory must be under the control of some state sovereignty. Canals must, therefore, fall in a different category from straits, because they are artificial waterways opened by the express or tacit approval of the sovereign power and, *ipso jure*, the consent of the sovereign power must be first obtained. If the sovereign grants free passage by an express declaration or by an obligation under a treaty or an international agreement, it is the legal obligation undertaken by the sovereign which entitles other nations to enjoy free passage, rather than the geographical analogy with natural waterways.[21]

In the case of the Suez Canal, it was the Convention of 1888 rather than the general principles of international law that granted the right of free passage to other nations. If Israel possesses any right to enjoy free passage through the canal, such right must be derived from the aggregate right granted to other nations and not by an analogy with natural waterways which nations ordinarily enjoy under international law.

The Convention of 1888 merely confirmed the right of free passage already recognized by the Ottoman Porte before 1888 and the powers that signed this convention acquired such rights both in time of peace and war. At the time of signature, other nations were invited to adhere to the Convention, but failed to do so. With regard to non-signatory states, the question whether the Convention is obligatory on them is an open one. Israel may be said to fall in a different category of non-signatory states. As a successor state, would she not, like Egypt, be entitled to special rights?

There is no question that Egypt, already mentioned in the Convention, was granted special rights as the country immediately connected with the canal, and certain obligations were imposed on her.[22] Egypt, according to the general principles of international law, must also accept the obligations already undertaken on her behalf by the former sovereign power. Moreover, Egypt has formally declared its acceptance of the obligations under the Convention of 1888 after independence on more than one occasion.[23]

---

[21] "Unlike international rivers and straits, which are natural waterways, international canals are artificially constructed. This essentially differentiating factor has been overlooked by a number of writers who, misled by the similarity of regimes to which both international canals as well as rivers and straits are subject, have tried to find, by an analogy to the latter, a geographical or physical criterion which would serve to define an international canal."
J. OBIETA, *supra* note 4, at 24.

[22] *See* Articles 8, 9, 10, and 14 of the Convention of 1888. *Cf. supra* note 11.

[23] From 1938 in formal statements concerning the Canal following the declaration of independence to 1954, the year of signature of the treaty with Britain for evacuation of the Canal Zone. *See, e.g.,* letter from Mustafa al Sadik Bey to Lord Perth, April 16, 1938, 195 L.N.T.S. 108 (1939); Agreement between . . . Egypt and the . . . United Kingdom, October 19, 1954, 210 U.N.T.S. 1 (1955); Letter from the Minister for Foreign Affairs to Egypt to the Secretary-General . . . 24 April 1957, 12 U.N. SCOR, Supp. April-June 1957, at 8, 9, U.N. Doc. S/3818/Add. 1 (1957); statement by Egyptian Representative in Security Council, 2 U.N. SCOR 1756 (1947).

Unlike Egypt, however, Israel falls in a special category. First, she has not adhered to the Convention of 1888, which has an accession clause, and therefore may enjoy the right of free passage in time of peace like other non-signatory states to whom the right of free passage was granted before 1888, but not the right of free passage in time of war which was granted under the Convention of that year. Second, if Israel may be considered to have adhered tacitly, she must have acquired not only the right to enjoy the right of free passage, but also the obligations of the Convention. Such obligations, for instance, require that the Canal must remain neutral and not involved in the area in which war is lawfully waged, and that the Canal should not be subject to blockade. Obviously Israel has neither declared her acceptance of such obligations nor, since she carried her military operations to its very eastern bank, has she respected the neutralization of the Suez Canal.[24] Third, Egypt's territory has become the subject of an Israeli attack in 1967, which raises the question of Egypt's right to take defensive measures irrespective of whether Israel possesses the right of free passage or not. This latter point, so significantly affecting the status of the Canal, deserves to be treated separately in the following section, concerned with Egypt's right to control the Canal.

It follows from our foregoing argument that if Israel were not involved in a war with Egypt—a war in which Egypt closed the Canal as a defensive measure—Israel would be entitled to the right of free passage. There can be no doubt that Israel's attack on Egyptian territory on June 5, 1967, presumably to settle a dispute by force rather than by peaceful methods as provided by the Charter of the United Nations, was an act of war which justified Egypt's position concerning the security of the Suez Canal, since, as noted above, Israel was not entitled to enjoy the same rights and obligations as a signatory of the Convention of 1888. As a third party beneficiary, a right concerning which jurists are not all in agreement,[25] Israel might claim to enjoy certain rights to use the Canal. But in a war which Israel initiated, and in which it attacked the territorial Zone of the Canal, Egypt would be empowered to close the Canal in self-defense, no less by general law than by the very provisions of the Convention of 1888 which obligate Egypt to take measures to prohibit any state from conducting war in the Canal Zone.[26]

A controversy has raged among several writers as to whether a state of war existed between Egypt and Israel before June 5, 1967. Those who defend Israel's right to free passage through the Canal hold that belligerency between the two states created by the Palestine war of 1948-49 was terminated by the Armistice

---

[24] Although Israel did not reach the Canal Zone in the invasion of Sinai in 1956, in the June war she reached and asserted control over the eastern bank of the Canal in violation of Articles 1 and 4 of the Convention. See notes 11 and 12 *supra*.

[25] *See* LORD McNAIR, LAW OF TREATIES 309-21 (1961); HARVARD RESEARCH IN INTERNATIONAL LAW: LAW OF TREATIES 924 (J. Garner ed. 1935).

[26] In practice this seems to have been the position maintained by the Ottoman Porte and later Egypt since 1888. See J. OBIETA, *supra* note 4, at 79-87.

Agreement of February 28, 1949.[27] Moreover, the Security Council resolution of September 1, 1951, calling upon Egypt to open the Canal to Israeli shipping on the ground that hostilities had been terminated by the armistice of 1949, was asserted by some to be binding on Egypt. Egypt, according to those who supported this viewpoint, has violated the Convention of 1888 and ignored the resolution of the Security Council.[28] Those who hold an opposing viewpoint argue that the Armistice Agreement of 1949 did not terminate the state of war, since an armistice puts an end to fighting but does not establish peace. Only a peace treaty can terminate the state of war and establish peace.[29] Moreover, the Security Council resolution, based on the assumption that the intent of the Armistice Agreement was to establish peace, cannot be regarded as binding on Egypt without her consent, because the resolution was recommendatory and not mandatory in nature.[30]

The controversy between these opposing viewpoints is deemed outside the scope of this paper, which deals with the problem of the closure of the Suez Canal in the circumstances created by the war of 1967. Even if a state of war had not existed before June 5, 1967, Egypt's decision to keep the Canal closed to Israeli shipping after the June war would be justified by the measures necessary for self-defense against sudden attack on the ground that the closure of the Canal against a non-signatory to the Convention falls within Egypt's sovereign rights.

Finally, it may be asked to what extent Egypt's obligations under the Convention of 1888 have restricted her sovereign rights over the Canal? This raises the question of Egypt's right to control the Canal, which falls under the third heading of our discussion.

III

EGYPT'S RIGHT TO CONTROL OF THE CANAL

The control of the Suez Canal raises the question of the relevance of territorial sovereignty to the status of the Canal and to what extent it was restricted by an international agreement. As already stated, the internationality of the Canal may be regarded as a balancing principle between the doctrine of sovereignty and the binding obligations of an international agreement. It is in the light of this balance that Egypt's right of the control of the Canal should be assessed.

---

[27] See S. ROSENNE, supra note 19, at 82.

[28] See B. AVRAM, supra note 4, at 119.

[29] For a summary of the Egyptian point of view, see id. at 122-27.

[30] For a discussion on the nature of the U.N. resolution, see Halderman, Some International Constitutional Aspects of the Palestine Case, in this symposium, p. 78. Colonel Howard S. Levie makes the following remarks on the Security Council resolution of 1951:

"It is considered more likely that the Security Council's action was based upon a desire to bring to an end a situation fraught with potential danger to peace than that it was attempting to change a long established rule of international law. By now it has surely become fairly obvious that the Israeli-Arab General Armistice Agreements did not create even a de facto termination of the war between those states."

Levie, The Nature and Scope of the Armistice Agreement, 50 AM. J. INT'L L. 880, 886 (1956). See 2 L. OPPENHEIM, INTERNATIONAL LAW 546-51 (7th ed. H. Lauterpacht 1952).

Admitting her obligations under the Convention of 1888, Egypt has held that she has not violated Article 1 concerning "free passage" through the Canal, because the measures taken in time of war were "reasonable and necessary measures" for defense purposes, as the Egyptian Prize Court of Alexandria states.[31] It might be argued that even "reasonable" and "necessary" measures might be restricted by the Convention of 1888, since Articles 10 and 11 prohibited Egypt from actions, even for the defense of her territory, because they might interfere with the free use of the Canal. It is also argued that, as held by the World Court in the *Wimbledon* case,[32] the Canal should remain permanently free as an international waterway.

Egypt's insistence on her right to close the Canal against Israeli shipping in time of war has naturally raised the question as to whether she can close the Canal during war against any other nations including signatory powers. This seems to be different from closing the Canal against a country that had attacked Egyptian territory, including the Canal Zone. It was in the exercise of her inherent right of self-defense that Egypt denied free passage to Israel.[33] Such a situation seems either to have been taken for granted by the Convention of 1888, because it falls within the rights of sovereignty, or left undecided. Egypt's actions might, however, be justified even if the Convention is held binding upon it to grant free passage to all nations, including Israel, on the ground of the internationality of the Canal. Any such obligation would necessarily entail the reciprocal obligation on the part of Israel to respect the neutrality of the Canal and the territorial sovereignty of Egypt. It cannot be claimed that Egypt is bound by the Convention *in toto* regardless of whether Israel accepts the obligations imposed on the nine signatory powers. Such a rule would clearly be imposing an international servitude over Egypt in order to grant to Israel the right of free passage in time of peace and war and denying Egypt the right of self-defense in case of an attack on her territory. If we take this position, the purposes of the Convention would be inconsistent with the general principles of international law which recognize Egypt's right to repudiate restrictive measures on her sovereignty imposed without her consent. Nor would the Ottoman Porte have agreed to sign the Convention and acquiesce in such a servitude, because it had consistently declared before 1888 that its control over the Canal was not to be restricted by throwing the Canal's doors open to other nations.[34]

A balancing view of the principle of internationality seems to restrict Egypt's right to close the Canal in time of peace against any nation including Israel if Egypt's security were not involved. So long as Israel insists on a right of free passage under the Convention of 1888 by threatening Egypt's security, Israel seems to pursue a

---

[31] The Flying Trader, [1950] Ann. Dig. 440, 446-47 (No. 149) (Prize Court of Alexandria), 7 REV. EGYPTIENNE DE DROIT INTERNATIONAL 127 (1951).

[32] [1923] P.C.I.J., ser. A, No. 1.

[33] See Baxter, *Passage of Ships Through International Waterways in Time of War*, 31 BRIT. YB. INT'L L. 208 (1954).

[34] See J. OBIETA, *supra* note 4, at 78-87.

contradictory legal position by invoking one article of the Convention (Article 1) while denying Egypt's right to invoke another (Article 10).[35]

In 1956, when Egypt nationalized the Suez Canal, the Security Council passed a six-point resolution on October 13, 1956, in which it was affirmed that any settlement of the Suez Canal question should, *inter alia*, meet the following requirements: (1) free and open transit through the Canal, and (2) respect for Egypt's sovereignty.[36]

This resolution seems to embody the balancing principle of internationality by proposing to grant freedom of navigation without compromising Egypt's sovereignty. Thus, the balancing principle of internationality must be considered with due respect to Egypt's sovereignty. The principle of internationality would cease to be a balancing principle if Egypt were to be denied the right to close the Canal, as a measure of self-defense, in case of an attack. Israel can claim the right to be a beneficiary of the principle of internationality if she ceases to present a threat to Egypt's security, one of her sovereign rights.

CONCLUSION

From the time of the nationalization of the Canal, Egypt has not only reiterated her affirmation of the binding obligations of the Convention of 1888 and her respect of the principle of free navigation, but also declared that any dispute or disagreements which may arise in respect of that Convention would be settled in accordance with the Charter of the United Nations, and that any differences that may arise concerning the interpretation of that Convention would be referred to the International Court of Justice. In a letter dated July 18, 1957, addressed to the Secretary-General of the United Nations, Egypt accepted the compulsory jurisdiction of the International Court in all legal disputes that may arise from the application of the Convention of 1888.[37] Since Egypt has accepted the compulsory jurisdiction of the International Court on all legal disputes relating to the Suez Canal, Israel's claim to the right of free passage through the Canal might well be an appropriate case to be brought to the International Court for adjudication and might be regarded as an example for solving other Arab-Israeli issues on the basis of law and justice rather than force or diplomatic pressures.[38]

---

[35] Article 10, paragraph 1, of the Convention of 1888 provides:
"Similarly, the provisions of Articles IV, V, VII, and VIII shall not stand in the way of any measures which His Majesty the Sultan and His Highness the Khedive in the name of His Imperial Majesty, and within the limits of the Firmans granted, might find it necessary to take to assure by their own forces the defence of Egypt and the maintenance of public order."
Supra note 11.
[36] S.C. Res. 118.
[37] [1956-1957] I.C.J.Y.B. 213-14, 241. *Cf.* U.N. Doc. S/3818/Add. 1, *supra* note 23.
[38] One of the states which supported Security Council resolution 95 (1951), calling on Egypt to open the Suez to Israeli shipping, might either voluntarily or upon Israel's request refer the Suez Canal dispute to the International Court of Justice in accordance with article 36, para. 1, of the statute of that Court. Article 36, paragraph 1, provides: "The jurisdiction of the Court comprises all cases which the parties refer to it and all matters specially provided for in the Charter of the United Nations or in treaties and conventions in force."

LEGAL ASPECTS OF INTERNATIONALIZATION OF INTEROCEANIC CANALS

Luke T. Lee*

Twice in the last twelve years the Suez Canal has fallen victim to the Middle East crisis. Today, the Canal remains blocked, with no sign as to when it may be reopened to traffic. Pursuant to the Security Council resolution unanimously adopted on November 22, 1967,[1] Dr. Gunnar Jarring, Special Representative of the Secretary-General, has been dispatched to the Middle East to help bring about a peaceful settlement[2] based upon principles which include the guarantee of "freedom of navigation through international waterways."[3] It may be noted that the free navigation principle was contained also in the draft resolutions submitted to the Security Council by the Soviet Union,[4] the United States[5] and one jointly by Mali, Nigeria and India[6] as well as one submitted to the General Assembly co-sponsored by twenty Latin American states, including Panama.[7] The invariable inclusion of this principle in all these proposals underscores the universal concern for a permanent and sound arrangement whereby international waterways could be converted into instruments of peace and progress, instead of being sources of war and destruction.

Halfway around the globe from Suez is the Panama Canal, itself, just a few years ago a scene of disorder and violence resulting in the severance of diplomatic relations between the United States and Panama.[8] Though the relations appear normal

---

* A.B. 1944, St. John's University (Shanghai); M.A. 1947, Columbia University; Ph.D. 1954, Fletcher School of Law and Diplomacy, Tufts University; Certificate 1959, Hague Academy of International Law, Center for Study and Research in International Law and Relations; LL.B. 1963, University of Michigan. Director, New York Office, Rule of Law Research Center, Duke University; Lecturer in Law, New York University School of Law.

[1] S.C. Res. 242. This resolution was originally proposed by the United Kingdom delegation on Nov. 16, 1967. See U.N. Doc. S/PV.1379, Nov. 16, 1967, at 2-8.

[2] For reports on Dr. Jarring's latest activities, see N.Y. Times, July 5, 1968, at 1, col. 8

[3] S.C. Res. 242, para. 2(a). For full text, see Rosenne, in this symposium, pp. 44, 56.

[4] U.N. Doc. S/8253; proposed on Nov. 20, 1967, U.N. Doc. S/PV.1381, Nov. 20, 1967, at 6-15.

[5] U.N. Doc. S/8229, based upon President Johnson's address of June 19, 1967 (57 DEP'T STATE BULL. 31 (1967)) and proposed by Ambassador Goldberg on Nov. 9, 1967, U.N. Doc. S/PV.1373, at 121-31.

[6] U.N. Doc. S/8227. See statements by the Indian and Nigerian delegations, Nov. 9, 1967, U.N. Doc. S/PV.1373, at 66-95.

[7] U.N. Doc. A/L.523/Rev. 1.

[8] Twenty-four persons were killed and several hundred wounded during a mob violence touched off by a flag incident. The incident occurred when American students hoisted only the American flag at the Balboa High School in the Canal Zone on January 9, 1964, in defiance of a 1963 agreement for Panamanian flags to be flown alongside those of the United States. See N.Y. Times, Jan. 13, 1964, at 1, col. 6; id., Jan. 22, 1964, at 1, col. 2; id., Feb. 17, 1964, at 1, col. 5. See also INTERNATIONAL COMMISSION OF JURISTS, REPORTS ON THE EVENTS IN PANAMA, JANUARY 9-12, 1964 (1964), submitted by the Investigating Committee of the Commission.

For earlier unrests and anti-American sentiments in Panama, see N.Y. Times, Aug. 30, 1956, at 1, col. 7; id., Sept. 16, 1956, at 24, col. 3; id., Sept. 22, 1960, at 14, col. 6; The Times (London), Dec. 24, 1957, at 5, col. 3; America's Troubled Canal, FORTUNE, Feb. 1957, at 129.

today, it would be self-deceiving to regard them as anything but a temporary calm before another storm, unless advantage could be taken of the present opportunity to seek a mutually satisfactory solution. And yet negotiation for a new canal treaty between the two countries is reportedly stalled because of disagreement over the composition of the membership of a proposed joint canal commission, with the United States insisting on five Americans and four Panamanians, and Panama demanding equal representation—five each—with the eleventh member to be appointed by the Secretary-General of the United Nations as his Special Representative.

How to get out of these canal quagmires remains a central problem of today. Since time does not permit a discussion of the legal and historical backgrounds of all the canals, the ensuing space will be devoted to a search for possible solutions on a long-term basis.

It would be useful to define the terms of reference at the outset for this paper. The term "internationalization" is open to many meanings: from mere advice or supervision by an international body to complete control and operation of a canal by an international authority. During the 1956 London Conferences on Suez, for example, no less than three versions of "internationalization" were given at different times. In the order of their presentation, they were: the "International Authority for the Suez Canal,"[9] which would assume operation of the Canal; the "Suez Canal Board,"[10] in which Egypt would participate; and the "Suez Canal Users Association,"[11] a consultative organ of the Canal's users and a possible instrument for limiting the financial powers of the new Egyptian authority operating the Canal. At a symposium on "International Control of the Suez Canal," given at the annual meeting of the American Bar Association in Hawaii in August 1967, both the speakers, John Laylin and Richard Young, discussed "internationalization" in terms of complete control and operation of the Canal by an international authority.[12] For the purpose of this paper, "internationalization" means *international supervision over national control or operation of interoceanic canals, pursuant to an international canals convention to be adopted by a United Nations diplomatic conference*. This paper starts from the premise that interoceanic canals, by virtue of their forming integral parts of the territories of the states through which they flow, are in principle under the jurisdiction and control of the territorial states.[13] Exception may be made, but

---

[9] Tripartite Proposal for the Establishment of an International Authority for the Suez Canal, Aug. 5, 1956, U.S. DEP'T OF STATE PUB. NO. 6392, THE SUEZ CANAL PROBLEM, JULY 26-SEPTEMBER 22, 1956, at 44 (1956).

[10] Attachment to the Aide Mémoire Delivered by the Suez Committee at Meeting with President Nasser, Sept. 3, 1956, *id*. at 306-09.

[11] Declaration Providing for the Establishment of a Suez Canal Users Association, Sept. 21, 1956, *id*. at 365-66.

[12] Laylin, *The Case for International Control*, 2 INT'L LAWYER 33 (1967); Young, *The Case for National Control*, *id*. at 39.

[13] General agreement obtains on the principle that, in point of law, a canal situated entirely within

only with the express consent of the territorial state, as in the case of the Panama Canal. At the same time, however, national control is not incompatible with international supervision because of international obligations inherent in an interoceanic canal. This paper is not concerned with the nature of the agency operating the canal, be it a private, public, or a joint enterprise.

Legal bases for transit rights through interoceanic canals are in many respects similar to those over land, sea and air. All seek to harmonize territorial sovereignty with the needs, interests and interdependence of the world community. Indeed, more than three hundred years ago, Grotius already maintained:

> lands, rivers, and any part of the sea that has become subject to the ownership of a people, ought to be open to those who, for legitimate reasons, have need to cross over them; as, for instance, if a people . . . desires to carry on commerce with a distant people . . . it is altogether possible that ownership was introduced with the reservation of such a use, which is of advantage to the one people, and involves no detriment to the other. Consequently, it must be held that the originators of private property had such a reservation in view.[14]

In upholding this universal right of transit, Grotius was supported to varying extents by such other founders of international law as Pufendorf[15] and Vattel.[16] It may be of interest to note that in persuading Great Britain to accept the Clayton-Bulwer Treaty of 1850, U.S. Minister to France William C. Rives was instructed to assure Lord Palmerston "that the United States would not, if they could, obtain any exclusive right of privilege in a great highway *which naturally belonged to all mankind*."[17] Again in 1858, when consideration was given to the possible construction of an interoceanic canal through Nicaragua, Secretary of State Lewis Cass was represented by Lord Napier, British Ambassador in Washington, as saying that international law was "not a stationary law," and that a kind of natural right existed for all nations to avail themselves of the interoceanic passage.[18]

That the right of transit is imbued with a natural law quality has been not

the territory of a state is in no way different from the land territory or the national rivers of that state. See 1 L. OPPENHEIM, INTERNATIONAL LAW 480, 484 (8th ed., H. Lauterpacht, 1955) (definition of "national waters"); W. HALL, A TREATISE ON INTERNATIONAL LAW 176 (8th ed., A. Higgins, 1924); J. BRIERLY, THE LAW OF NATIONS 233 (6th ed., H. Waldock, 1963); O. SVARLIEN, AN INTRODUCTION TO THE LAW OF NATIONS 157 (1955); Young, *The Case for National Control*, 2 INT'L LAWYER 39-40 (1967).

[14] 2 DE JURE BELLI AC PACIS LIBRI TRES ch. 2, § 13 (1646), translated in CLASSICS OF INTERNATIONAL LAW 196-97 (J.B. Scott ed. 1925).

[15] 2 DE JURE NATURAE ET GENTIUM LIBRI OCTO ch. 3, §§ 5-7 (1688), translated in CLASSICS OF INTERNATIONAL LAW 354-61 (J.B. Scott ed. 1934).

[16] LE DROIT DES GENS, OU PRINCIPES DE LA LOI NATURELLE, APPLIQUÉS À LA CONDUITE AUX AFFAIRES DES NATIONS ET DES SOUVERAINS § 123 (1758), translated in CLASSICS OF INTERNATIONAL LAW 150-51 (J.B. Scott ed. 1916).

[17] SENATE COMM. ON FOREIGN RELATIONS, THE PROPOSED INTEROCEANIC CANAL, S. DOC. No. 268, 56th Cong., 1st Sess. 2 (1900). (Emphasis added.)

Commenting on the Clayton-Bulwer Treaty, C. Davis of the Senate Foreign Relations Committee said: "In no instance has the Government of the United States intimated an objection to this treaty on account of the features of neutrality and its equal and impartial use by all other nations." *Id.* at 3.

[18] Fontes Juris Gentium, Ser. B, I, at 420 (1932).

only advocated by many publicists, but also implied in the *Corfu Channel Case.* In this case Albania contended *inter alia* that the Corfu Channel was not an international highway since it was only of secondary importance and not even a necessary route between two parts of the high seas. The International Court of Justice rejected that argument and said:

> the decisive criterion is rather its [the strait's] geographical situation as connecting two parts of the high seas and the fact of its being used for international navigation. Nor can it be decisive that this Strait is not a necessary route between two parts of the high seas, but only an alternative passage between the Aegean and the Adriatic Seas. It has nevertheless been a useful route for maritime traffic.[19]

In light of all the above, E. Lauterpacht was moved to suggest that the right of transit existed when (a) states claiming the right can justify it by reference to considerations of necessity or convenience, and (b) the exercise of the right will cause no harm or prejudice to the transit state.[20]   It finds its counterparts in the municipal law sphere in such doctrines as the "right of way" and "way of necessity."

Despite its natural right quality, the right of transit remains what Mr. Lauterpacht would call an "imperfect right"—distinguishable from "perfect right" in the want of enforceability.[21]   What is needed as an intermediate step is the conclusion of treaties to govern the exercise of that right. Since an "imperfect right" is nevertheless a legal right, states do not have an absolute freedom *not* to conclude such treaties. Uniform treaty provisions may in turn become a source of customary international law.[22]

But whether one traces the right of transit to natural law or customary international law origin, its codification on a world-wide basis is consistent with the modern development of international law. Article 23(e) of the Covenant of the League of Nations specifically obligated members "to make provision to secure and maintain freedom of communications and of transit and equitable treatment for the commerce of all Members of the League." Pursuant to this provision, a number of important treaties were concluded between the two world wars.[23]   Since the establishment of the United Nations, the process of crystallizing customary international law into conventional international law has been quickened under Article 13(1)(a) of the Charter.[24]   On the subject of freedom of transit, the Geneva Conventions on the Law of the Sea not only confirmed the right of innocent passage over the territorial sea

---

[19] [1949] I.C.J. 28.

[20] Lauterpacht, *Freedom of Transit in International Law*, 44 TRANSACT. GROT. SOC'Y 332 (1958-59).

[21] *Id.* at 347.

[22] See LORD MCNAIR, LAW OF THE AIR 9 (3d ed., M. Kerr & A. Evans, 1964), in which he discussed the relationship between uniform rules in a series of international air navigation conventions and customary international law (international air law).

[23] *E.g.*, the two Barcelona Conventions of 1921 relating to Waterways of International Concern (1 M. HUDSON, INTERNATIONAL LEGISLATION 638 (1931)) and Freedom of Transit on Land (*id.* at 625); and the 1923 Conventions Relating to the International Regime of Railways (2 *id.* at 1130), and the Transmission in Transit of Elecrtic Power (*id.* at 1173).

[24] See Lee, *The International Law Commission Re-examined*, 59 AM. J. INT'L L. 545, 567 (1965).

and straits,[25] but also called for agreement between land-locked states and coastal states with a view to ensuring the former the right of free access to the sea.[26] The right was subsequently amplified and systematized by the 1965 Convention on Transit Trade of Land-locked States.[27]

With the completion of the codification of transit rights of land-locked states and, earlier, those over the territorial sea and air, the logical next step would be codification of the law of interoceanic canals for reasons set forth below.

In his excellent treatise, *The Law of International Waterways*, Professor Baxter outlined four premises upon which rights of passage through interoceanic canals have been based:[28] The first is the doctrine of "international servitude," which Professor Baxter regards as occupying "at best a questionable position in international law." He explained that even though *The S.S. Wimbledon*[29] offered an opportunity for the Permanent Court of International Justice to decide the question of free passage on that doctrine, the Court expressly declined to do so.

The second is the doctrine of third-party beneficiaries: States not parties to a treaty conferring rights upon them may in their own right assert the rights so conferred. This doctrine has been used to justify third states' rights to the many interoceanic canals treaties, in particular, the Constantinople Convention of 1888,[30] the Hay-Pauncefote Convention of 1901[31] and the Hay-Varilla Convention of 1903.[32] However, not only is there a serious doctrinal dispute over the validity of third states' rights, but the Permanent Court itself did not apply the doctrine with consistency.[33] Even if such rights exist, they may be terminated or modified by the original parties to the treaty. Although the Draft Articles of the Law of Treaties adopted by the International Law Commission in 1966 recognize the validity of third states' rights,[34]

---

[25] See Convention on the Territorial Sea and the Contiguous Zone, April 29, 1958, section 3, Right of Innocent Passage, 516 U.N.T.S. 205, 52 AM. J. INT'L L. 834, 837 (1958).

[26] Convention on the High Seas, April 29, 1958, art. 3, 450 U.N.T.S. 82; [1962] 13 U.S.T. 2312; T.I.A.S. No. 5200.

[27] U.N. Doc. TD/TRANSIT/9, July 9, 1965. This Convention came into force on June 9, 1967. See MULTILATERAL TREATIES IN RESPECT OF WHICH THE SECRETARY-GENERAL PERFORMS DEPOSITARY FUNCTIONS: LIST OF SIGNATURES, RATIFICATIONS, ACCESSORIES ETC., AS OF 31 DECEMBER 1967, at 182 (1968).

[28] The following passages are, unless otherwise noted, summarized from R. BAXTER, THE LAW OF INTERNATIONAL WATERWAYS 177-84 (1964).

[29] [1923] P.C.I.J., ser. A, No. I, at 24.

[30] 15 G. MARTENS, NOUVEAU RECUEIL GÉNÉRAL DE TRAITÉS (2d ser.) 414 (1885-86); 76 BRITISH AND FOREIGN STATE PAPERS 4 (1884-85).

[31] Treaty with Great Britain to Facilitate the Construction of a Ship Canal, 32 Stat. 1903 (1901); T.S. No. 401.

[32] Convention with the Republic of Panama for the Construction of a Ship Canal to Connect the Waters of the Atlantic and Pacific Oceans, 33 Stat. 2234 (1903); T.S. No. 431.

[33] *Compare* the court's decision in Case Concerning Certain German Interests in Polish Upper Silesia, [1926] P.C.I.J., ser. A, No. 7, at 28-29, and the Chorzow Factory Case, [1928] P.C.I.J., ser. A, No. 17, at 45, *with* that in the Case of the Free Zones of Upper Savoy and the District of Gex, [1929] P.C.I.J., ser. A, No. 22, at 20.

[34] See International Law Commission, art. 32, Draft Articles on the Law of Treaties, U.N. Doc. A/CN.4/190, July 22, 1966; 21 U.N. GAOR, Supp. 9 (A/6309/Rev. 1); [1966] 2 Y.B. INT'L L. COMM'N 181.

as well as limit the original parties' freedom to revoke or modify the treaty creating such rights,[35] they remain to be adopted by diplomatic conferences scheduled for 1968 and 1969.[36]

The third view is that "treaties which open rivers and canals to general or limited use by the vessels of states other than the parties to the instrument in question are dispositive in nature," hence creating "real rights which are attached to a territory and are therefore not dependent upon the treaty creating them." These real rights are said to exist independently of international servitudes. Again, this view is open to the same criticism as that directed against third states' rights. In addition, it is not clear whether this doctrine can satisfactorily account for legal privileges which may be claimed by states not parties to the dispositive treaty nor successors to the original parties.

The fourth theory is that dedication of a waterway by a state to international use, if relied upon, creates legally enforceable rights in favor of the shipping of the international community. Such dedication may take the form of a treaty, a unilateral declaration, or perhaps even a concession. This dedication-reliance theory is preferred by Professor Baxter, who improved upon the Permanent Court of International Justice's decision in *The S.S. Wimbledon*,[37] wherein the Court spoke of Kiel as "an artificial waterway connecting two open seas . . . permanently dedicated to the use of the whole world." According to Profesor Baxter, "Justice does not demand that third states acquire any rights until there has been actual international use of the waterway." Such rights should not be gained by third states "unless the dedication has induced them to make some measurable use of the canal or of the river and to make it one of their shipping routes."[38]

While this theory is of much jurisprudential interest, it may at best justify the rights of nonsignatories to the use of the existing major canals, which have already been so "dedicated." It would not, however, justify third states' rights to the use of any new canal, *e.g.*, the proposed sea-level canal in Central America, if the canal builder or the territorial state refuses to give similar dedication. In the absence of such a dedication, may third states' shipping or cargoes be barred or discriminated against? To answer affirmatively would surely violate the natural right of transit or customary international law governing canals usage.

A better solution would be for the United Nations to convene a diplomatic conference which would synthesize customary international law on canals into conventional international law; standardize the various rules and regulations pertaining to navigation, neutralization, jurisdiction over vessels in transit, tolls and other administrative matters; and, in general, harmonize the interests of the users with those

---

[35] International Law Commission, *supra* note 34, art. 33.

[36] See G.A. Res. 2166(XXI) of Dec. 5, 1966, 21 U.N. GAOR, Supp. 16, at 95 (A/6316).

[37] See note 29 *supra*.

[38] Baxter, *supra* note 28, at 183.

of the proprietors or operators of the canals. As has been stated earlier, customary international law has increasingly been crystallized into conventional international law,[39] which means relations between states are more and more governed by treaties to which they are signatories. This emphasis on treaty as the basis for rights and duties of signatories is reflected in the increasing number of multilateral treaties concluded by diplomatic conferences under the United Nations auspices, the most recent of which are the Vienna Conventions on Diplomatic and Consular Relations.[40] The proposed United Nations conference on interoceanic canals and the resultant convention would merely follow this codification trend, while simultaneously filling a most important gap which has given rise to innumerable disputes and conflicts. At the same time, since the convention must be signed and ratified by both the territorial and user states, it would be based on the sovereign equality of states, free of the "unequal treaty" stigma associated with some of the earlier canals treaties. This treaty approach would also avoid the difficulties inherent in the four theories which have been used to justify the free navigation of the interoceanic canals by all nations. In addition, it would constitute, especially to the naturalists, the requisite intermediate step to transform a hitherto "imperfect right" of transit to a "perfect right."[41]

More specifically, with respect to the Panama Canal, both the United States and Panama could stand to gain by the internationalization of the existing as well as the projected sea-level canals. For the United States, its agreement to internationalization would not impair its real interests in the operation and security of the Canal.[42] Such an agreement would be consistent with its advocacy of the internationalization of the Suez Canal proposed during the London Con-

---

[39] See note 23 *supra.*

[40] For the background and significance of these Conventions, see LUKE T. LEE, THE VIENNA CONVENTION ON CONSULAR RELATIONS (1966); Cahier & Lee, *Vienna Conventions on Diplomatic and Consular Immunities,* INT'L CONC. No. 571 (forthcoming in January 1969).

[41] See text accompanying notes 21 and 22 *supra.*

[42] In their elucidating article, *Control of the Panama Canal: An Obsolete Shibboleth?*, 37 FOREIGN AFFAIRS 417-18 (1959), Professors Martin B. Travis and James T. Watkins wrote:

"Internationalization would leave unimpaired the real interests of the United States, namely, the preservation of the Canal and access to it, good service at low cost, and a voice in the operation of the Canal. The security of the Canal would be, if anything, enhanced. Already hopelessly vulnerable, an internationalized Canal might seem to a potential aggressor a less attractive target than one under the exclusive jurisdiction of the United States. In any case, the United States would be entitled to come to the defense of the Canal, if defense were feasible, by acting within the United Nations under Article 51 of the Charter or the 'Uniting for Peace' procedures. Such action in defense of an international agency would enjoy moral and practical support which the defense of an exclusive interest claimed by the United States could not evoke. . . .

"Good service at a reasonable cost could also be expected from an international agency. Indeed, from a strictly economic standpoint internationalization would offer every hope of bringing an improvement. Less exposed to special-interest pressures than is the United States Congress, a Panama Canal Commission [under the United Nations] could more readily determine an optimum toll schedule for facilitating the flow of traffic and yet building up reserves for needed improvements. And, finally, participation in the operation of the Canal would be ensured as long as the United States remained one of the principal users."

ference on Suez[43] in view of the fundamental legal analogies between Suez and Panama.[44] Internationalization might also take the sharp edge off the latent anti-American sentiment associated with the United States policy in the Canal zone.[45] It would help insulate the canal from the domestic politics of any country. Furthermore, regularization of the canal regime through a multilateral convention would avoid a potentially embarrassing situation posed by Panama's claim of a twelve-mile territorial sea in 1958,[46] in light of the fact that the Hay-Varilla Convention specifically limits the Canal Zone to a three-mile water in either direction.[47]

As for Panama, impacts of modern nationalism have prompted an increasing sentiment for the return or joint administration of the Canal Zone.[48] Pending the final outcome, internationalization would at least serve as a cushion to soften whatever impact a direct relationship with the colossal North might produce. That the disproportionate strength of the United States in such a direct relationship has been a source of serious concern for Panama is reflected in the disagreement over the composition of membership in the proposed joint canal commission described at the beginning of this paper.

With respect to Suez, in addition to long-term benefits which the proposed canals convention could bring, internationalization would go a long way towards fulfilling the relevant portion of the Security Council resolution adopted on November 22, 1967. Agreement by the United Arab Republic to accept international supervision of its operation and control of the Suez Canal pursuant to an international canals convention containing a compulsory arbitration clause, applicable to all interoceanic canals alike, might conceivably remove a major obstacle to the resumption of the Suez Canal traffic. Indeed, politics being so filled with imponderables, there might even be room for hope that such an agreement to conclude a specific agreement in the future (*pactum de contrahendo*) might yet constitute a significant step forward to an overall Middle East peace settlement.

If a diplomatic conference on the law of interoceanic canals were to be held, which, if any, of the past conventions could best lend itself as a model for a waterway treaty? In this regard, serious consideration should be given to the 1965 Convention on Transit Trade of Land-locked States[49] as a possible model. As the latest convention dealing with transit rights, it has benefited from past experiences and

---

[43] The United States joined with seventeen other countries in proposing the internationalization of the Suez Canal during the Second Suez Conference at London, September 19-21, 1956. U.S. DEP'T OF STATE PUB. No. 6392, THE SUEZ CANAL PROBLEM, JULY 26-SEPTEMBER 22, 1956, at 366, 308 (1956).

[44] R. BAXTER, *supra* note 28, at 44, 307.

[45] See note 8 *supra*.

[46] Law No. 58, *Gaceta Oficial*, No. 13.720 (Dec. 24, 1958).

[47] See Art. II of the Convention, *supra* note 32.

[48] Nationalization of the Panama Canal, for example, was demanded in a manifesto issued by the Panama students' federation. See The Times (London), Dec. 24, 1957, at 5, col. 3. Former Deputy Foreign Minister Castillero likened the geographical position of the Canal to such natural assets as Venezuela's oil, thus justifying an equal sharing of the gross revenues. *Id*.

[49] U.N. Doc. TD/TRANSIT/9, July 9, 1965.

mistakes. It has sought a balance of interests between land-locked states and transit states. But above all, it contains a compulsory arbitration clause as an integral part of the convention. Because of the importance of this convention, its major provisions may be briefly summarized.

Article 2 (freedom of transit) obligates contracting states to "facilitate traffic in transit without discrimination as to the place of origin, departure, entry, exit or destination or in any circumstances relating to the ownership of the goods or the ownership, place of registration or flag of vessels." The Contracting States agree to "apply administrative and customs measures permitting the carrying out of free, uninterrupted and continuous traffic in transit,"[50] as well as to charge reasonable rates for the use of transit facilities so as to "facilitate traffic in transit as much as possible."[51] In case of an emergency[52] or war[53] or on grounds of public health and security,[54] exceptions may be made to the above provisions. The danger of abuse of these exceptions is, however, minimized by Article 16, which provides for compulsory arbitration in the event that a dispute arising from the interpretation or application of the provisions of the Convention (including those concerning security and emergency measures) could not be settled by direct negotiation or other peaceful means within a period of nine months. An arbitration commission would be created to consist of three members: one to be appointed by each of the disputing parties, with the third to be mutually agreed upon between the parties, or, failing an agreement within three months, to be appointed by the President of the International Court of Justice. If any of the parties fail to make an appointment within three months, the President of the International Court of Justice shall fill the remaining vacancy or vacancies.[55] Unlike the Geneva Conventions on the Law of the Sea and most

---

[50] Id., Art. 5.

[51] Id., Art. 4.

[52] Id., Art. 12.

[53] Id., Art. 13.

[54] Id., Art. 11.

[55] This provision was designed as a safeguard against the exigency in which one of the parties might refuse to appoint its own representative to an arbitration commission, thus throwing a monkey wrench into the arbitral process. It may be recalled that in the peace treaties concluded in Paris in 1947, Bulgaria, Hungary and Rumania agreed that all persons within their jurisdiction would be entitled to basic human rights and fundamental freedoms. Provisions were made for disputes concerning the interpretation or execution of the treaties to be settled by certain procedures which included arbitration by a treaty commission. The commission would be composed of one representative of each party and a third member, selected by mutual agreement of the two parties from nationals of a third country. Should the two parties fail to agree within a period of one month upon the appointment of the third member, the Secretary-General of the United Nations may be requested by either party to make the appointment.

Failure of these countries to appoint their representatives to the treaty commissions following charges of their violations of human rights prompted the General Assembly to request advisory opinions from the International Court of Justice in October 1949. Among the questions were whether the three states were obligated to appoint their representatives to the treaty commissions and, if so, whether the Secretary-General would be authorized to appoint the third member of the commission upon the request of one party in the event the other party failed to appoint its representative. The Court, while holding that the obligation of the three states to appoint their representatives to the treaty commissions existed, interpreted the terms of the treaties restrictively to preclude the possibility of the Secretary-General's

of the other recent multilateral conventions which resort to compulsory judicial settlement by the International Court of Justice under optional protocols, the 1965 Convention, by including the disputes clause in the text itself, has the merit of leaving no potential dispute incapable of resolution while at the same time avoiding the cumbersome machinery of the International Court of Justice, whose impartiality and efficacy have been much questioned anyway, especially by developing countries, since the *South-West Africa* case.[56]

The question concerning the desirability of including a permanent machinery in a United Nations-sponsored convention for the purpose of supervising the implementation of its provisions has not been answered with uniformity. On the one hand, there are, for instance, the International Civil Aviation Organization, a specialized agency,[57] charged with the functions of implementing the provisions of the Convention on International Civil Aviation,[58] and the Commission on Narcotic Drugs, the responsible arm of the various instruments of narcotics control.[59] On the other hand, central supervisory organs are lacking in such treaties as the Geneva Conventions on the Law of the Sea and the Convention on Transit Trade of Landlocked States.

In choosing between these precedents, consideration should be given to whether the nature of the subject matter is such as to lend itself to centralized supervision and whether such supervision is warranted in the light of the present situation. Applying these tests to the canals, it would appear that a central supervisory organ ought to be established with a balanced representation among transit states, major users and third states. The reasons for such an organ, say an International Canals Commission, may be briefly explained.

In the first place, the number of interoceanic canals, both actual and potential, is small, which in itself would facilitate supervision. Since interoceanic canals share many similar characteristics and problems, a regular exchange of information and experiences through the proposed commission would be of mutual benefit. Indeed, the commission might even render technical assistance to improve existing canal facilities or help develop new canals.

---

appointment of the third member unless both parties to the dispute had appointed their representatives to the commission. See Advisory Opinion on Interpretation of Peace Treaties with Bulgaria, Hungary and Rumania, in [1950] I.C.J. 77, 226-30.

[56] South West Africa, Second Phase, Judgment, [1966] I.C.J. 6

[57] See Agreement between the United Nations and the ICAO, which came into force on May 13, 1947; text in YEARBOOK OF THE UNITED NATIONS 1946-47, at 741-45.

[58] The Convention was signed in Chicago on December 7, 1944, text in *id*. at 728-40.

[59] The Single Convention on Narcotic Drugs of 1961 came into force on December 13, 1964, to replace gradually the nine former international narcotics instruments adopted between 1912 and 1953. While the Economic and Social Council remains the chief policy-making body in the international narcotics control systems, the responsible arm is the Commission on Narcotic Drugs assisted by the International Narcotics Control Board, which came into existence in March 1968. YEARBOOK OF THE UNITED NATIONS, 1964, at 339-44; U.N. OFFICE OF PUBLIC INFORMATION, INTERNATIONAL CONTROL OF NARCOTIC DRUGS (1965); and annual reports of the Commission on Narcotic Drugs.

Shipping concerns throughout the world are constantly affected by changes of canal tolls, transit facilities, sanitary and customs regulations, pilotage, jurisdiction over vessels in transit, and emergency measures. Among the functions of the proposed commission might well be the collection and periodic publication of such information as well as traffic statistics.

Where a dispute has arisen over the interpretation or application of the provisions of the proposed convention, the commission might perform the services of fact-finding, mediation, or bringing the arbitral machinery into play. Upon the settlement of the disputes, the commission should publicize the nature and fact of the dispute as well as the terms of the settlement, thereby building up a useful body of case law.

But, above all, the establishment of an international canals commission linked to the United Nations could not fail to have a certain stabilizing influence over the tension-ridden canals of the world.

Will the United Nations, having assisted in the Suez clearance operation in 1957[60] and the stabilization of the military front since 1967, be prepared to take the next forward step toward a long-term settlement of the world's canal problems by calling a diplomatic conference on interoceanic canals and cooperating in the implementation of the ensuing convention?

---

[60] The initial costs for clearing the Suez Canal, which amounted to about $8,200,000, were borne by the United Nations. See Clearance of the Suez Canal, Report of the Secretary-General 12-13 (A/3719) (1957). Reimbursement was secured through a 3% surcharge on Canal tolls beginning in September 1958 over a two and one-half year period. G.A. Res. 1212(XII), 12 U.N. GAOR, Supp. 18, at 59 (A/3805); Reimbursement of the Cost of Clearing the Suez Canal, Report by the Secretary-General, Aug. 1, 1958 (A/3862); Financial Report and Accounts for the Year Ended 31 December 1961 and Report of the Board of Auditors, 17 U.N. GAOR, Supp. 6, at 7-8 (A/5206).

THE STATUS OF JERUSALEM:
SOME NATIONAL AND INTERNATIONAL ASPECTS

S. SHEPARD JONES[*]

I

SCOPE AND PURPOSE

If a genuine Arab-Israeli peace settlement is to be achieved as an aftermath to the 1967 war and the subsequent diplomatic efforts of the United Nations in 1967 and 1968, some understanding must be reached on the future status of Jerusalem. Of course, this is only one of many troublesome questions that evoke political malaise. The purpose of this short essay is to put the problem of Jerusalem in perspective by drawing attention to some of the background considerations that shed light on the present situation. These considerations are as much political as legal; they are both national and international, religious and secular. While the purpose is primarily to provide perspective, not to argue for a particular resolution of the future status of Jerusalem, this article does conclude with an indication of the direction and spirit within which a settlement might be sought, if the interests of all the parties are to be protected. These interests are complex and varied, and it is assumed that the cause of international peace and justice demands respect for the interests of all concerned and therefore not the complete triumph of the purposes of any one nation or religious community. The multiple interests in Jerusalem suggest the wisdom of redefining national purposes to the higher good.

II

THE NATURE OF "THE QUESTION OF JERUSALEM, 1967-68"

The more restricted "problem of Jerusalem" in its present context arises out of the suddenly upset military balance and the emotional shock produced by the lightning-like war of June 1967. A part of that reality—but not its beginning[1]—was the attack by Jordanian forces on Israel on June 5, following the outbreak of war on the Egyptian-Israeli front earlier the same day. After hard fighting there followed, on June 7, the capture of Arab Jerusalem, governed by Jordan since 1948, and Israel's announcement of June 28[2] that "the law, jurisdiction and administration of the

---

[*] A.B. 1930, Georgetown College; A.M. 1931, University of Kentucky; Ph.D. (Rhodes Scholar) 1936, Oxford University. Burton Craige Professor of Political Science, University of North Carolina. Author, THE SCANDINAVIAN STATES AND THE LEAGUE OF NATIONS (1939); co-editor [with D. P. Myers], DOCUMENTS ON AMERICAN FOREIGN RELATIONS (vols. I-III (1939, 1940, 1941); AMERICA'S ROLE IN THE MIDDLE EAST (1958).

[1] M. HOWARD & R. HUNTER, ISRAEL AND THE ARAB WORLD: THE CRISIS OF 1967 (Adelphi Papers, no. 41, October 1967); Yost, *The Arab-Israeli War: How It Began*, 46 FOREIGN AFF. 304-06 (1968).

[2] Under ordinance of the preceding day. Summaries at p. 8 of the Report of the Secretary-General under General Assembly resolution 2254(ES-I), U.N. Doc. A/6793, Sept. 12, 1967. Also issued as U.N. Doc. S/8146.

State of Israel" were being applied to the Old City and to an enlarged East Jerusalem, as Arab Jerusalem is now designated.

Bitter protest came from Jordan[3] and other Arab states and from non-Arab states including the United States,[4] and allegations that international law had been violated by Israel. Israel asserted that Jordan was responsible for initiating the attack on Jerusalem and must accept the consequences.[5]

The United Nations General Assembly adopted two resolutions without opposition on July 4 and 14, 1967 (the latter by a vote of one hundred to zero, with eighteen abstentions, including that of the United States[6]), declaring Israel's action "invalid," and calling upon Israel "to rescind all measures already taken and desist forthwith from taking any action which would alter the status of Jerusalem."[7] Israel refused to comply, contending that "no international or other interest would be served by the institution of divisions and barriers which would only sharpen tension and generate discrimination." The claim was made that Israel was responding to "the intrinsic necessity of ensuring equal rights and opportunities to all the city's residents."[8] This answer did not meet the major issue at stake, as the General Assembly debate made clear.[9]

Looking ahead, the Israeli Government stated that its policy of integrating all of Jerusalem "does not foreclose the final settlement of certain important aspects of the Jerusalem situation which lie at the origin of the international interest in the city." Reference was made to "the need to secure appropriate expression of the special interest of the three great religions in Jerusalem." But this statement seemed to acknowledge the concerns and interests of others as something to be considered in the future, since the Foreign Minister added: "I am confident that in an atmosphere of international tranquility substantial progress could be made toward this aim, which has hitherto had no concrete fulfillment."[10] Reference was here made,

---

[3] *See, e.g.,* remarks of King Hussein, U.N. Doc. A/PV. 1536, June 26, 1967, at 11.

[4] *See, e.g.,* remarks of U.S. Delegation, U.N. Doc. A/PV. 1546, July 3, 1967, at 8-10.

[5] The Israeli Foreign Minister stated to the General Assembly on June 19, 1967:

"While fighting raged on the Egyptian-Israel frontier and on the Syrian front, we still hoped to contain the conflict. Jordan was given every chance to remain outside the struggle. Even after Jordan had bombarded and bombed Israel territory at several points, we still proposed to the Jordanian monarch that he abstain from any continuing hostilities . . . .

". . . Jordan's responsibility for the second phase of the concerted aggression is established beyond doubt. Surely this responsibility cannot fail to have its consequences in the peace settlement. As death and injury rained on the city, Jordan had become the source and origin of Jerusalem's fierce ordeal. The inhabitants of that city can never forget this fact, or fail to draw its conclusions." U.N. Doc. A/PV. 1526, June 19, at 50-51.

[6] U.N. Doc. A/PV. 1554, at 41.

[7] G.A. Resolutions 2253 and 2254, U.N. GAOR, 5th Emer. Spec. Sess., Supp. 1, at 4, U.N. Doc. A/6798 (1967).

[8] Exchange of letters between the Secretary-General of the U.N. and the Israeli Foreign Minister, July 15, 1967, and Sept. 11, 1967, published in U.N. Doc. A/6793, *supra* note 2, at 29, 30.

[9] *See, e.g.,* Docs. A/6743, July 3, 1967, and A/6774, July 25, 1967. *See also* remarks of Iraqi Delegation, U.N. Doc. A/PV. 1559, Sept. 18, 1967, at 6-16.

[10] U.N. Doc. A/6793, *supra* note 2, at 30.

apparently, to deprivation of access to Holy Places in the Old City of almost all citizens of Israel from 1949 to 1967, for instance to the Wailing Wall, and to acts of desecration of Jewish cemeteries.[11]

This reply should be viewed in the light of the conclusion of the United Nations Secretary-General, based on information supplied by his Personal Representative in Jerusalem,[12] that it has been "made clear beyond any doubt that Israel was taking every step to place under its sovereignty those parts of the city" not previously controlled by Israel.[13] Ambassador Thalmann reported that "The Israel authorities stated unequivocally that the process of integration was irreversible and not negotiable."[14]

The Personal Representative reported that he was told that "the Arabs recognize a military occupation régime as such and were ready to co-operate with such a régime in dealing with current questions of administration and public welfare. However, they were opposed to civil incorporation into the Israel State System," which action they regarded "as a violation of the acknowledged rule of international law which prohibited an occupying Power from changing the legal and administrative structure in the occupied territory." The population of East Jerusalem "was given no opportunity to state for itself whether it was willing to live in the Israel State community." It was claimed that the right of self-determination, in accordance with the United Nations Charter and the Universal Declaration of Human Rights, had therefore been violated.[15]

The report of the Secretary-General dated September 12, 1967 indicates that "most of the Arabs interviewed" by the Personal Representative—Arab notables in Jerusalem, both governmental and religious—stated that the Muslim population "was shocked by Israel acts which violated the sanctity of Muslim Shrines."[16]

Muslim leaders informed the Personal Representative that statements by Israeli officials and Jewish personalities "concerning Jewish claims and plans in the Temple area had had an alarming effect" on Muslim opinion.[17] The dynamiting and bull-dozing of 135 houses in the Maghrabi quarter (in front of the Wailing Wall) had also aroused strong feelings. This action involved "the expulsion of 650 poor and pious Muslims from their homes in the immediate vicinity of the Mosque of Omar and the Aksa Mosque."[18]

In a letter of July 24, 1967 the Israeli Military Governor for the West Bank was

---

[11] See U.N. Docs. A/7064 and A/7064/Add. 1, March 6, 1968, a distribution of a pictorial document entitled "Desecration," issued by the Israeli Ministry of Foreign Affairs, Information Division, Jerusalem, November 1967 and transmitted to the Secretary-General of the U.N., March 5, 1968.

[12] Ambassador Thalmann, a Swiss national. He arrived in Jerusalem on August 21, 1967, and departed on September 3, 1967.

[13] U.N. Doc. A/6793, supra note 2, at 7.

[14] Id.

[15] Id. at 24.

[16] Id. at 21.

[17] Id.

[18] Id.

informed that the twenty-four signatories of the letter "had constituted themselves as the Muslim body in charge of Muslim affairs on the West Bank, including Jerusalem."[19] "This 'Higher Muslim Council,' as it is also called, designated four Arab personalities to carry out the responsibilities of public administration . . . on the West Bank, including East Jerusalem, in accordance with the applicable Jordanian law." But the decisions of the "Higher Muslim Council" were not recognized by the Israeli authorities, although publicized to the Arab population through Amman radio.[20]

The Secretary-General's Personal Representative in Jerusalem also reported the text of the statement issued June 27, 1967 by the Prime Minister of Israel concerning access to the Holy Places of Jerusalem and their administration.[21] Also reported was the "Protection of the Holy Places Law," passed by the Knesset the same day,[22] as well as the Prime Minister's statement of June 7, 1967 to spiritual leaders of all communities.[23] The statement of June 27 indicated that the Holy Places in Jerusalem "are now open to all who wish to worship at them—members of all faiths, without discrimination. The Government of Israel has made it a cardinal principle of its policy to preserve the Holy Places, to ensure their religious and universal character, and to guarantee free access." It was indicated that the policy would be carried out in consultation with representatives of the religious communities. The statutory measures provided for protection of the Holy Places from desecration and other violations.

The Personal Representative reported that these measures "were very favorably received," although some took a "wait and see" attitude.[24] The Muslim reaction has been indicated above. The Catholic Church was reported as having essentially a divergent attitude to various other Christian denominations. The Holy See remained convinced that "the only solution which offers a sufficient guarantee for the protection of Jerusalem and of its Holy Places is to place that city and its vicinity under an international régime in the form of a *corpus separatum*."[25]

III

THE UNITED STATES AND THE QUESTION OF JERUSALEM, 1967-68

On June 19, 1967 the President of the United States said there must be "adequate recognition of the special interest of three great religions in the holy places of Jerusalem."[26] On June 27, 1967 the Israeli Parliament approved legislation authorizing the Government to extend Israel's laws, jurisdiction and administration over addi-

---

[19] *Id.* at 44, 46.
[20] *Id.* at 22-23.
[21] *Id.* at 26.
[22] No. 5727-1967. Text printed in English, *id.*
[23] *Id.* at 25-26.
[24] *Id.* at 27.
[25] *Id.*
[26] 57 DEP'T STATE BULL. 33 (1967).

tional territory of *Eretz* Israel ("the Land of Israel"). On June 28 the Government of Israel defined the Old City of Jerusalem and certain other territory of the former mandate of Palestine which had been under the control of Jordan since 1948 as territory to be incorporated into an enlarged city of Jerusalem.[27] On June 28 the White House indicated that the President "assumes" that "before any unilateral action is taken on the status of Jerusalem there will be appropriate consultation with religious leaders and others who are deeply concerned" and that "the world must find an answer that is fair and recognized to be fair."[28] On June 28, the Government of Israel took administrative action under the new legislation to extend its municipal services and controls over the entire city of Jerusalem.[29] Later on that day a State Department press release[30] read:

> The hasty administrative action taken [by Israel] today cannot be regarded as determining the future of the holy places or the status of Jerusalem in relation to them.
>
> The United States has never recognized such unilateral actions by any of the states in the area as governing the international status of Jerusalem . . . .

On July 3, the United States Representative to the General Assembly said that "the safeguarding of the Holy Places, and freedom of access to them for all, should be internationally guaranteed."[31]

On July 7, 1967 the Executive Committee of the National Council of Churches of Christ in the United States of America adopted a resolution[32] which, in part, read:

> With due consideration for the right of nations to defend themselves, the National Council of Churches cannot condone by silence territorial expansion by armed force. Israel's unilateral retention of the lands she has occupied since June 5 will only deepen the divisions and antagonisms which separate her from those neighbors in the midst of whom she must dwell.
>
> The territorial frontiers of the states of the Middle East should now be definitely established by negotiation in treaties of peace and the integrity of such frontiers should be assured by international protection.

More specifically, on the issue of Jerusalem, the resolution of the National Council of Churches states:

> We support the *establishment of an international presence* in the hitherto divided city of Jerusalem which will preserve the peace and integrity of the city, foster the welfare of its inhabitants, and protect its holy shrines with full rights of

---

[27] Measures summarized in U.N. Doc. A/6793, *supra* note 2, at 8.

[28] 57 DEP'T STATE BULL. 60 (1967).

[29] *See* note 27 *supra*.

[30] 57 DEP'T STATE BULL. 60 (1967).

[31] U.N. Doc. A/PV. 1546, July 3, 1967, at 3-5.

[32] Memorandum entitled "Resolution on the Crisis in the Middle East." *See* N.Y. Times, July 15, 1967, at 28, col. 1.

access to all. We encourage the earliest possible advancement of U.N. proposals to make such arrangements practicable.

We cannot approve Israel's unilateral annexation of the Jordanian portions of Jerusalem. This historic city is sacred not only to Judaism but also to Christianity and Islam.

On July 14, Ambassador Goldberg, speaking for the United States Delegation to the Fifth Emergency Special Session of the U.N. General Assembly, reiterated that "the United States does not accept or recognize . . . as altering the status of Jerusalem" the measures taken by the Israeli government on June 28. He said further that the United States did not recognize that these measures

> can be regarded as the last word on the matter, and we regret that they were taken. We insist that the measures taken cannot be considered as other than interim and provisional, and not as prejudging the final and permanent status of Jerusalem.
> Unfortunately, and regrettably, the statements of the Government of Israel on this matter have thus far, in our view, not adequately dealt with this situation.[33]

Nevertheless, the United States abstained from voting on General Assembly resolution A/2254,[34] the resolution not fully corresponding to United States government views, particularly since, even as revised

> it appears to accept, by its call for rescission of measures, that the administrative measures which were taken constitute annexation of Jerusalem by Israel, and because we do not believe that the problem of Jerusalem can realistically be solved apart from the other related aspects of the Middle Eastern situation.

There are, it was said, important practical issues in addition to "transcendent spiritual interests" that must be resolved. The United States representative implied that the Assembly should have gone no further than to declare itself against any unilateral change in the status of Jerusalem.[35]

Following reports in January 1968 of Israeli plans for development of certain areas of the occupied sector of Jerusalem—being between Mt. Scopus and the former armistice line—a State Department spokesman reiterated that the United States does not recognize "any unilateral actions affecting the status of Jerusalem."[36] The United States position is that Arab territories now administered by Israel as a result of the six-day war should be administered under the law of occupation as recognized by international law, not under a right of conquest. The Department of State apparently regards the Hague Convention of 1907 as applicable to the existing situation.[37]

---

[33] U.N. Doc. A/PV. 1554, July 14, 1967, at 48.
[34] Note 6 *supra* and accompanying text.
[35] U.N. Doc. A/PV. 1554, *supra* note 33, at 48, 51.
[36] N.Y. Times, Jan. 16, 1968, at 16, col. 6.
[37] For some recent statements as to rules considered applicable, see 1 M. WHITEMAN, DIGEST OF INTERNATIONAL LAW 946-52 (1963).

IV

SOME LEGAL AND POLITICAL QUESTIONS

A question has been raised as to whether acquisition of territory by conquest is valid in the light of the United Nations Charter obligations accepted by both sides. Press reports frequently refer to "territory conquered," but the Israeli government has apparently avoided making a claim on that basis. Does the integration of Arab Jerusalem by Israel hurt the prospects for an agreed settlement of larger aspects of the Arab-Israeli confrontation? What is the legal meaning and the political effect of Israel's contention that the future of Arab Jerusalem is not negotiable? Have Israel's leaders concluded that the prospects for a settlement with the Arab states are so unlikely, because of Arab intransigence; that the integration or annexation of Jerusalem does not actually endanger prospects for a peace settlement, because the prospects for the foreseeable future, despite efforts of the Secretary-General's Special Representative, Dr. Gunnar Jarring, are hopelessly dim?

It may be useful to divide the Jerusalem question into three major aspects: (1) *who* will govern Jerusalem—*i.e.*, whose "law, jurisdiction and administration" will prevail in the future? Will the city remain unified as it was prior to 1948 and in 1967-68 or again be divided? Or will it be managed in a third way? And will the determination be made by unilateral action or by agreement? (2) What arrangements can be made to assure "adequate recognition of the special interest of three great religions in the holy places of Jerusalem," *i.e.*, to guarantee the protection of the Holy Places within and outside Jerusalem and for assurance of access thereto? (3) Should an *international presence* be maintained in Jerusalem with functions broader than that of protecting the holy places? What practical proposals can be agreed to and maintained in the face of diverging interests? These are difficult political questions which confront or may confront the interested governments. The answers can best be found through the process of negotiation. Recognizing that such negotiations must inevitably be affected by other questions lying beyond the scope of this paper, let us consider certain background facts that help put the present situation in perspective.

A. Political

How does the experience of history relate to these questions? A quick look may give a distorted image, but hopefully may suggest essential reality if only approximate. Who has governed Jerusalem and how was title gained? In the past 3500 years the city has changed hands more than twenty-five times.[38] We can begin with David who about 1000 B.C. captured the old Jebusite Town and claimed it as the City of David. Later it was conquered by one empire after another—Babylonian,

---

[38] S. PEROWNE, THE ONE REMAINS 11 (1954). *See also* REPORT OF THE COMMISSION APPOINTED BY HIS MAJESTY'S GOVERNMENT . . . TO DETERMINE THE RIGHTS AND CLAIMS . . . IN CONNECTION WITH THE WESTERN OR WAILING WALL AT JERUSALEM: DECEMBER 1930, at 9-15 (1931). Distributed as U.N. Docs. A/7057/Add. 1 and S/8427/Add. 1, Feb. 23, 1968.

Persian, Macedonian, Ptolemy, Selucid, and Roman. In 638 A.D. the Caliph Omar captured Jerusalem for Islam. Later it was held by Seljuk Turks, by Christian Crusaders, and by Egyptian Mameluks. From 1517 to 1917 Jerusalem was ruled by the Ottoman Turks, who then gave way to General Allenby of Great Britain. Following World War I, the Principal Allied Powers decided that Palestine should be a League of Nations mandate assigned to Great Britain. On July 24, 1922 the Council of the League of Nations confirmed and defined the terms of the Mandate for Palestine, with Great Britain as the Mandatory Power. The Palestine Mandate went into effect September 29, 1923.[39] When it terminated on May 15, 1948 Arabs and Jews of Palestine, and Arab armies from without, fought for possession of Jerusalem and of Palestine. The outcome confirmed the reality of what actually had already become a divided city, now occupied by Israeli and Jordan authorities,[40] with a set of conflicting claims, which, in turn, conflicted with plans and proposals of the United Nations to establish Jerusalem as a *corpus separatum* under an international régime. This proposal was part of the Plan of Partition with Economic Union, which was recommended by the General Assembly on November 29, 1947[41] in an effort to provide for the future government of Palestine, upon the termination of the British Mandate. This Plan was never fully implemented.[42]

At no time did the international community acting through the United Nations recommend that the City of Jerusalem or a portion of it be assigned to either Israel or Jordan. The claims of those two countries that they were rightful sovereigns of their parts of Jerusalem, while recognized by some states, have not been recognized by others, including the United States, the United Kingdom, France, and the Soviet Union, all of which continued to maintain embassies in Tel-Aviv and Amman.[43]

During 3000 years of history, control over Jerusalem has been almost invariably acquired by conquest.

B. Protection of and Access to the Holy Places

The historical record shows that Jerusalem has long been regarded as a place of religious significance to the adherents of three world religions all of which seek protection of their interests. Jerusalem has been revered by Jews for 3000 years, by Christians for nearly 2000, and by Moslems for more than 1300 years. Many of the shrines represent a common inheritance of three religions. Even the name of the city in Arabic (*Al-Quds*) means "The Sanctuary."[44] Although it has been said

---

[39] For text see CMD. No. 1785 (1923).

[40] P. DE AZCARATE, MISSION IN PALESTINE 1948-1952, at 182 (1966).

[41] G.A. Res. 181, 2 U.N. GAOR, Resolutions 131, 132 (1947).

[42] *See* 1 M. WHITEMAN, *supra* note 37, at 699, 701, 703.

[43] *Id.* at 594, 595, 699.

[44] P. MOHN, JERUSALEM AND THE UNITED NATIONS 427 (International Conciliation pamphlet no. 464, October 1950).

that "the business of Jerusalem is eternity,"[45] regrettably, through much of history, its spiritual significance as a city of God, of peace and of brotherly love, has been sadly tarnished by bloodshed, political intrigue and bitter rivalry for the privilege of protecting or adminstering the holy places and shrines. Religious emotion or even fanaticism has at times been exploited by temporal rulers who sought exclusive advantages not primarily those of spiritual uplift or human betterment. The diversity of religious interests—Moslem, Catholic, Jewish, Orthodox, Armenian, Coptic, Abyssinian, Syrian, Anglican and other Protestant, and with institutions established by religious bodies in Europe, Asia, Africa, and the Americas—called for some system of order and protection. In 1757 the so-called *Status Quo* was established to this end. Thereafter, Moslem *temporal* power, on the whole, did not interfere with the management of the Holy Places, but there were claims and counter-claims.[46] The system did not change greatly under the British Mandate, which in Article 13 specified that the Mandatory should preserve existing rights in connection with the Holy Places. But at times, such as 1929, there was serious rioting.[47]

C. Proposals for International Régime

When on November 29, 1947 the United Nations General Assembly recommended partition of Palestine into a Jewish state and an Arab state with Economic Union, it was recommended that the city of Jerusalem (including the existing municipality plus the surrounding villages and towns such as Bethlehem) be established as a *corpus separatum*, under a special international régime, to be administered by the Trusteeship Council on behalf of the United Nations. This régime was to include the appointment of a Governor, responsible to the Trusteeship Council, the establishment of a special police force whose members were to be recruited from *outside* of Palestine, the election of a legislative Council, and the demilitarization of the city.[48] "Jerusalem was envisaged as a *model city*, a *spiritual center*, a *seat of learning*, the influence of which could help to overcome the national and religious animosities and prejudices which for so many years have poisoned the atmosphere of the Holy Land."[49] The proposal for a *corpus separatum* seemed sensible since the General Assembly's Plan of 1947 separated Jerusalem from the proposed Jewish state by a strip of intervening Arab territory assigned to the proposed Arab state. Jerusalem under the 1947 Plan would have been a city of approximately equal Arab and Jewish population, with the Moslem Arabs somewhat more numerous than the Christian Arabs.

---

[45] PEROWNE, *supra* note 38, at 13.

[46] REPORT OF THE COMMISSION . . . , *supra* note 38, at 15-22; W. EYTAN, THE FIRST TEN YEARS 66 (1958); MOHN, *supra* note 44, at 433-38.

[47] C. SYKES, CROSSROADS TO ISRAEL 108-11 (1965).

[48] *See* Part III of the Plan, *supra* note 41; EYTAN, *supra* note 46, at 68-69. For map showing the proposed boundaries of Jerusalem, see annex B attached to the Plan.

[49] MOHN, *supra* note 44, at 451. (Emphasis added.)

A statute for Jerusalem had been drafted by the Trusteeship Council in the spring of 1948,[50] but formal adoption was postponed owing to the state of confusion into which the larger question of Palestine had been thrown by the fighting already in progress and uncertainty as to whether the November 29, 1947 Plan could be implemented.[51] The Arab Higher Committee had rejected the Partition Plan in its entirety; the Jewish Agency accepted it under protest. No international authority had been created to take the place of the British Mandatory authority in Jerusalem which had been supported by British troops for twenty-five years. These were about to depart on May 14, 1948 as the British Government had repeatedly affirmed. Yet it had been clear for months that the Partition Plan with Economic Union could not be implemented by agreement, and it could not be implemented by force alone, since it called for economic cooperation. The Plan was clearly unworkable in the light of political realities.

The divergent policies of the Powers blocked agreement in the United Nations, not of a "definition of the International interest" in Jerusalem, but of a concerted will to implement internationally-defined policy against firm resistance. International policy, defined and redefined by the General Assembly resolutions in 1947,[52] 1948[53] and 1949[54] but not consistently supported by necessary action, was brushed aside by the national policy of a few states with clear goals. Christopher Sykes aptly refers to the "melee of conflicting British and American attempts at policy."[55] The draft statutes of an international régime in Jerusalem, although at least in one case directed to be put into effect despite opposition of Israel and Jordan, were not put into effect, and "came to nothing" in the world of action. Jordanian and Israeli armed forces took and retained control of their respective parts of Jerusalem filling a vacuum with national power. A new kind of *status quo* was maintained in Jerusalem, following the Israeli-Jordan Armistice Agreement of 1949,[56] until it was again upset by force in June 1967.

When the United Nations Conciliation Commission for Palestine[57] realized the impossibility of setting up a genuine international régime (based on the idea of a *corpus separatum*) and drafted a modified statute in 1949[58] compatible with the *fait accompli* of the partition of Jerusalem between Israel and Jordan, it remained

---

[50] 3 U.N. TCOR, 2d Sess., pt. 3, Annex, at 4, U.N. Doc. T/118/Rev. 2 (1948).

[51] Proceedings summarized in Annual Report of the Secretary-General on the Work of the Organization, 1 July 1947-30 June 1948, 3 U.N. GAOR, Supp. 1, at 4-5, U.N. Doc. A/565 (1948). *See also* MOHN, *supra* note 44, at 455-56; EYTAN, *supra* note 46, at 70; AZCARATE, *supra* note 40, at 184-85.

[52] G.A. Res. 181, *supra* note 41.

[53] G.A. Res. 194, para. 8, 3 U.N. GAOR, pt. 1, Resolutions 21, 23, U.N. Doc. A/810 (1948).

[54] G.A. Res. 303, 4 *id.*, Resolutions 25, U.N. Doc. A/1251 (1949).

[55] SYKES, *supra* note 47, at 357. *See also* Report of the Trusteeship Council entitled "Question of an International Regime for the Jerusalem Area and the Protection of the Holy Places," 5 U.N. GAOR, Supp. 9, U.N. Doc. A/1286 (1950).

[56] 42 U.N.T.S. 303, no. 656; 4 U.N. SCOR, Spec. Supp. 1, U.N. Doc. S/1302/Rev. 1 (1949).

[57] Established by G.A. Res. 194, *supra* note 53.

[58] 4 U.N. GAOR, Ad Hoc Pol. Comm., Annex., vol. 1, at 10, U.N. Doc. A/973 (1949).

only a "blue-print," although one worthy of study both then and now. The draft sent to the General Assembly September 1, 1949 was "pigeon-holed without even being accorded the honor of a debate," as a result of the pressure of various delegations. Some, sympathetic with the Vatican's point of view, "were not prepared to accept anything less than integral and complete internationalization."[59] All of the Arab states except Jordan also sought a more thorough-going internationalization.

Israel, on the other hand, was antagonistic because the Conciliation Commission's plan involved too much international control. The Israeli government argued that the plan ignored the "physical facts" and "deeper truths of sentiment and allegiance," adding that "For the first time in modern history, political authority in the greater part of Jerusalem rests not on military conquest but on the will and consent of the population of the city."[60] The crux of the matter was that the Conciliation Commission was responding to the General Assembly's Resolution 194(III) of December 11, 1948 wherein the General Assembly had decided that the Jerusalem area should be accorded "special and separate treatment from the rest of Palestine" and that it should be placed "under effective United Nations control." Israel's policy did not support that objective: it favored national control of Jerusalem, its new capital, in a nation re-created after decades of struggle under Zionist leadership, catapulted to birth by the agony produced by the Nazi slaughter of millions of European Jews.

V

REFLECTIONS ON THE PRESENT
INTERNATIONAL SYSTEM AND JERUSALEM'S FUTURE

The future status of Jerusalem is obviously related to the larger question of the fundamental characteristics of the future international system of the Middle East. As for the international system of the past two decades, of which international law is only a part, if we judge it primarily by the *practice* of states rather than by the *proclaimed principles* which states affirm as principles that ought to be applied, we can only conclude that the use of force in pursuit of national policy is not altogether ruled out. Almost invariably when force is used, the claim of the exercise of the right of self-defense is asserted, and sometimes justified. The Arabs of Palestine asserted the right of self-defense in 1948 against the Partition Plan, adopted as a recommendation of the General Assembly. They regarded the Plan as immoral and illegal.[61] The Israeli Government asserted the right of self-defense to maintain

---

[59] AZCARATE, *supra* note 40, at 184. *See also* remarks of the Lebanese Delegation (Malik) to a committee of the General Assembly on May 5, 1949, 3 U.N. GAOR, pt. 2, Ad Hoc Pol. Comm. 219-26.

[60] Memorandum on the Future of Jerusalem, prepared by the Israeli Delegation, Nov. 15, 1949, at 2, U.N. Doc. A/AC.31/L. 34. *See also* remarks by the Israeli Delegation (Eban), 3 U.N. GAOR, pt. 2, Ad Hoc Pol. Comm. 230-37 (1949).

[61] The Arab Higher Commitee contended, at the 2d Special Session of the General Assembly, in April 1949, that the Mandate for Palestine disregarded the right to self-determination, and that the Arabs had no alternative but "to resort to the sacred right of self-defense." The Arabs had done "'what any

national identity threatened by Arab governments in 1948, in 1956, and again in 1967.[62] The United Nations did not clarify the legal situation that existed.

In this existing international system—this system more political than juridical, this system that does not assure the rule of law or international security by collective measures to frustrate a breach of the peace—perhaps the best hope for progress towards peace and security must rest with the policies of states which surely must increasingly understand the unwisdom of continued belligerency and war. While some wars can be deterred by threat of force or reprisal, the basic Middle East problem calls for other approaches. The great imperative is for a changed approach, a new attitude on both sides, which will permit the leaders of both sides to show greater understanding of the fears, the needs, and the legitimate interests of other states. This line of thinking brings us back to the idea that governments as well as leaders of public opinion should respond to the over-riding need for national self-restraint, fairness to others, and for easing tensions between nations, thereby assisting the growth of a new spirit of confidence that men can act more wisely in the future for peace and justice. It is a new vision of the practical advantages that will accrue to those who accept a community of mutual rights and responsibilities that is needed, not a continued devotion to political myths that insist on national or group exclusiveness and enmity. On what other basis can we hope for a solid political foundation on which to develop a more adequate international law?

Surely the present need is for a more realistic understanding by peoples generally of their national and regional interests. Hostility, belligerence, non-recognition of the right of neighboring states to exist, and disregard of the rights of others to territorial integrity are basic causes of insecurity for all. Perhaps it would help in resolving the problem of Jerusalem if the parties most concerned would not overemphasize the importance of political images of Jerusalem formed centuries ago in a very different age. Historic national dreams, perhaps vital in ages past, may need updating if the fundamental interests of the peoples of our time are to be advanced. Imagine the benefits that would flow if nations would discard from national myths that which is provocative and unjust to others, thereby facilitating the growth of the more constructive aspects of nationalism and encouraging healthy international cooperation. The Jerusalem question, if viewed with this spirit, with everyone avoiding malice and vituperation, might gradually be transformed to more optimistic proportions, with reduced likelihood that Jerusalem will be in the future, as it has been all too often in the past, a center for pathetic rivalry and a continuing object of re-conquest, perhaps headed once again for destruction.

---

other Member State would have done" fought in self-defense. The Partition resolution was "ill-advised," "illegal," and "could not be carried out." U.N. GAOR, 2d Spec. Sess., vol. II, Main Committees 93 (1948).

[62] *See* remarks by the Israeli Minister for Foreign Affairs (Eban) to the Security Council, U.N. Doc. S/PV. 1375, Nov. 13, 1967, at 6-36; ISRAEL'S STRUGGLE FOR PEACE, chs. VIII, IX and X (Israel Office of Information, New York, 1960).

This is the time for states generally to support the efforts of the United Nations Special Representative, Dr. Jarring, as he explores with the parties most directly concerned the broader dimensions of peace-making in the Middle East.[63] Will the Arab states and Israel work to establish the foundations for peace in the spirit of that resolution? Or will shortsighted, particularistic interests of states sidetrack progress toward an agreed settlement by inducing them to nullify one or the other of the basic principles adopted unanimously in the Security Council resolution of November 22, 1967?[64] It is acceptance of the entire package which is a valid test of one's interest in peace with justice. At least this seems to have been the view of the Security Council.

One would hope that the world will not experience disappointment similar to that of 1947-1952, when an opportunity for a peaceful resolution of the Arab-Israel problem foundered. Every nation's stake in moving toward peace based on agreement is enormous. This is the prerequisite for strengthening international law in the Middle East, in view of such conflicting definitions of justice as have been spread on the United Nations record for the past twenty years.

If a new appreciation of national self-interest can be developed in the months ahead, based on a wider recognition of the futility of Middle Eastern politics of recent years, presumably some agreements would become possible. It should then become possible to agree on an acceptable formula of "the national and international interest" in Jerusalem, which could then be guaranteed by the principal Powers. The balancing of interests and claims in the Middle East becomes an imperative, in view of the uncertainties of law and the facts of power, if some tolerable stability is to be achieved. The definition of justice in such a politically divided area could hardly be expected to conform to the fullest expression of national aspirations and national morality—either Arab or Israeli. A rational solution calls for a negotiated settlement (sooner rather than later) under the auspices of a third party utilizing any arrangement agreeable to the parties most concerned, and, failing that, under an arrangement determined by the Security Council.

In the interest of long-run cooperation among the peoples and nations of the Middle East, it is believed that the advantages of a *corpus separatum* for the walled City of Jerusalem could be a desirable goal for the overwhelming majority of the members of the United Nations, and would probably serve the higher, long-range interests of Israel and Jordan. To achieve this objective, it might become desirable for the states of the world to recognize West Jerusalem as the capital of the state of Israel. So much of Israeli nationalism is centered on Jerusalem as a focal point in national political life that it would seem practical to accept this reality. However,

---

[63] A recent statement of relevant U.S. policy was made on Dec. 8, 1967, by the Under Secretary of State for Political Affairs, Eugene V. Rostow, 58 DEP'T STATE BULL. 41 (1968).

[64] For text of Resolution 242, see Rosenne, in this symposium, pp. 44, 56.

this line of thinking would reserve the walled city as an International Zone—a *corpus separatum*, but would not necessarily be restricted to it.[65]

These concluding ideas do not constitute a proposal for the future status of Jerusalem. They are suggested only as possible ideas for consideration by those concerned. Both a *national* and an *international* presence would be embraced in a greater Jerusalem. An international statute would once again be drafted, and would constitute a part of the peace settlement hopefully to grow out of Ambassador Jarring's step by step efforts to build a peace on the principles of the Security Council's Resolution 242 of November 22, 1967.

But are these ideas practical? They could become practical, when carefully re-vamped by legal and political experts—if, but only if, the parties most concerned will re-evaluate their national interests in harmony with the greater need for genuine peace. The future of Jerusalem is inevitably entwined with the larger aspects of Arab-Israeli relations. In March 1968 serious violations of the cease-fire which brought renewed consideration by the Security Council confirmed earlier impressions that the prospect for genuine peace and for a rule of law in the Middle East seemed as elusive as ever. In the interest of international peace and security, perhaps the time is near when the Security Council will act to assert its authority under the Charter.[66] If not, the outlook seems one of continued belligerency, bitterness, and danger. The Middle East is faced with important choices in 1968. We can do no other than to hope for a new vision grounded in justice and focusing on a better day.

---

[65] *See* proceedings regarding Jerusalem in the Trusteeship Council 1949-1950, summarized in the special report cited *supra* note 55. *See especially* Private Memorandum from the Archbishop of Canterbury, Oct. 31, 1949, *id.* at 9-11. The Statute for the City of Jerusalem approved by the Council, April 4, 1950, is set forth *id.* at 19. *See also* Darin-Drabkin, *Jerusalem—City of Dissension or Peace?*, NEW OUTLOOK: MIDDLE EAST MONTHLY, Jan. 1968, at 12, for an Israeli interpretation.

[66] On May 21, 1968 the U.N. Security Council adopted Resolution 252 on Jerusalem; for text, see El-Farra, in this symposium, pp. 68, 73.

THE LIMITS OF PERCEPTUAL OBJECTIVITY IN INTERNATIONAL PEACE OBSERVATION*

Thomas M. Franck† AND Kenneth H. Gold‡

I

Introduction

Methods of determining questions of fact have long been of concern to those interested in the legal process. Since the Second World War the use of military or civilian observers, international third-party peace-keepers, stationed along cease-fire lines separating hostile forces has become a major instrument of fact-finding in international disputes; yet no systematic attempt has been made to assess the role of these truce observers nor, indeed, to define scientifically, and perhaps, empirically, the possibilities and limitations of third-party decision-making in international disputes.

Preliminary study of the voluminous reports of cease-fire observation organizations suggests that the issues faced by the observers can be grouped into a number of recurrent typologica. This paper has not attempted such a systematic chronicling, since a few "typical" questions suffice for our purposes.

What kinds of factual issues have these "impartial" observers tried to solve? "The firing incident of 26 May, 1958 on Mount Scopus"[1] provides an excellent illustration of the workings of the observers. The incident began when the Jordanian delegation to the Jordan-Israel Mixed Armistice Commission telephoned the United Nations Truce Supervisory Commission (UNTSO) to claim that Israelis located on Mount Scopus were firing on the Arab village of Issawiya. Within a few minutes, the UNTSO Chief of Staff's representative from Mount Scopus, Lieutenant-Colonel Flint, accompanied by one United Nations Military Observer (UNMO), proceeded to Issawiya while another UNMO observer set out for the Jewish sector of Mount Scopus to arrange a cease-fire and investigate the incident. While arranging for the cease-fire Colonel Flint was killed by a sniper's bullet. So were a number of Israelis.[2]

The Mount Scopus incident presented a number of issues that had to be decided,

* © 1968 by Thomas M. Franck.
† B.A. 1952, LL.B. 1953, University of British Columbia; LL.M. 1954, S.J.D. 1959, Harvard University. Professor of Law and Director of the Center for International Studies, New York University. Author, COMPARATIVE CONSTITUTIONAL PROCESS (Cases and Materials in the Comparative Constitutional Process of Nation Building) (1968); THE STRUCTURE OF IMPARTIALITY (1968); co-author, WHY FEDERATIONS FAIL (1968).
‡ B.S. 1963, Babson Institute; LL.B. 1967, LL.M. 1968, New York University. Research Assistant to Professor Thomas M. Franck and Editorial Associate at the Center for International Studies, New York University. Member of the New York bar.
[1] Report dated 7 June 1958 by the Chief of Staff of the United Nations Truce Supervision Organization in Palestine to the Secretary-General concerning the firing incident of 26 May 1958 on Mount Scopus, 13 U.N. SCOR, Supp. April-June 1958, at 1, U.N. Doc. S/4030 (1958).
[2] Id. at 2.

all of them of a "factual" nature: Who was at fault? Who had fired the first shot? Where did the shot come from that killed Colonel Flint? Was Issawiya being used as a base by Arab troops before and during the incident?

There were other types of issues lurking in the background. Prior to the incident, two maps were in existence, one being relied upon by Israel, the other by Jordan. The maps conflicted as to the location of the demilitarized zone (DMZ). Which of the two maps should be controlling? What kinds of activities may rightfully be carried on in a DMZ? Is it closed to troops of each side? Is it closed to cultivation by civilians of each side? What patrolling responsibilities does the UN have to prevent infiltration through a DMZ? What, if any, preventive actions may be taken by either side if the UN fails to stop infiltration?

These would appear to be questions to which an impartial third-party decision-maker could give answers, employing neutral, reciprocally-applicable principles. Yet these are the very questions the truce-observation organization did not feel itself empowered to answer. Being questions of "law" they were beyond its powers.

Instead, UNTSO investigated and answered the "factual" questions. As it happens, these involve the observers' direct sensory perception of a number of transient events, perceptions of a visual and audial nature.

Why was UNTSO authorized to answer questions of "fact" but not of "law"? It may be that we have to realize that "law-making" is a process involving the preferences of the decision-maker, however impartial, while we still believe that questions of "fact" when examined by an impartial decision-maker, can be objectively determined.

This paper hypothesizes that the distinction, at least so far as it encompasses "facts" based on perceptions of transitory sense-data, is misconceived. A neutral's finding of such a "fact," like a judge's finding of law, is *not* objective. That this is now scientifically provable shatters the myths which have supported impartial fact-finding processes just as, in an earlier part of this century, the insights of legal realists destroyed the myths of judicial objectivity. In both instances, however, the purpose is not to destroy valuable order-creating institutions but to make a more accurate estimate of the limits of their potential—what they can and cannot do—to help the institutions do better those things which are properly within their competence and to find other methods for resolving those types of problems which are not.

II

THE NEURO-CHEMISTRY OF VISUAL PERCEPTION

It is not an easy thing for a lawyer, accustomed to separating sheep of truth from goats of falsehood, to accept that the events we see are not photographs of some reality "out there" but a series of events within our own bodies which have little objective relationship to the "picture" that forms in our heads. In the words of Dr. R. L. Gregory,

There is a temptation, which must be avoided, to say that the eyes produce pictures in the brain. A picture in the brain suggests the need of some kind of internal eye to see it—but this would need a further eye to see *its* picture . . . and so on in an endless regress of eyes and pictures. This is absurd. What the eyes do is to feed the brain with information coded into neural activity—chains of electrical impulses —which by their code and the patterns of brain activity, represent objects. . . . When we look at something, the pattern of neural activity represents the object and to the brain *is* the object. No internal picture is involved.[3]

Thus, for example, *colour* has no objective existence in the sense (or code) in which we "picture" it. "[S]pectral colour, or hue, is light of a different frequency."[4] In the "real" world, "out there," we do not have greens and reds, but only radiations of differing lengths and frequencies. The "picturing" of these radiation bands in terms of colour is something subjective we bring to the objective event. Consciousness, the perception of redness, for example, is defined by a leading British scientist as a "brain state" which in turn is a pattern of electrical impulses, "a certain structure of events in space-time" which, seen from the outside is, of course, not in the least red.[5]

And *none* of us bring this subjectivity to the totality of such events occurring "out there," for none of us, for example, "see" radio waves, infra-red or ultra-violet light which are part of the same set of phenomena but beyond our visual perception. And more surprisingly, approximately one man in fifteen also cannot accurately perceive a difference even between red and green![6] Bronowski notes that colour-blindness does not appear to have come to the notice of science until 1777.[7] Other even less intrusive aspects of visual subjectivism are only now beginning to be explored.

How do we see?

The visual process appears to involve a complex interaction between mechanical, electrical and psychological factors. The eye, which, as we shall see, is "an integral part of the brain"[8] both structurally and functionally, contains two kinds of cells in the retina which receive data-light waves—from "out there." These are called *rods* and *cones*. The cones function in daylight and give colour vision. The rods respond to very low levels of illumination and do not differentiate colours except in shades of grey. The rods are believed to be more primitive (in their lower levels of discrimination) but also more sensitive than the cones which give better detail and colour but only under conditions of more intense stimulation. The rods are thus believed to be closer to the primordial origins of the eye, or to lower rungs of the evolutionary ladder, being highly sensitive—the hawk's visual acuity is four times

---

[3] R. GREGORY, EYE AND BRAIN 7 (1966).
[4] *Id.* at 16.
[5] R. BRAIN, THE NATURE OF EXPERIENCE 64 (1959).
[6] J. BRONOWSKI, THE IDENTITY OF MAN 53 (1965).
[7] *Id.* at 52.
[8] R. GREGORY, *supra* note 3, at 46.

our own—but distinguishing only those things, movement, and shadows in particular, which are essential to animal survival.

It appears that light hitting the cells of the retina causes a bleaching of its pigmentation, a chemical change,[9] which, by an unexplained process, stimulates the optical nerve. Brightness is the basic rudiment of seeing. But even here, as in most aspects of visual perception, what is seen is not merely a carbon copy of an external event.

> Brightness is not just a simple matter of the intensity of light striking the retina. The brightness given by a given intensity depends upon the state of adaptation of the eye, and also upon various complicated conditions determining the contrast of objects or patches of light. In other words, brightness is a function not only of the intensity of light falling on a given region of the retina at a certain time; but also of the intensity of the light that the retina has been subject to in the recent past, and of the intensities of light falling on other regions of the retina.[10]

In part, this is because the chemical bleaching process requires some time to reverse itself, to return to a state of equilibrium in readiness for the next stimulation. The state of disequilibrium can best be seen in its negative implications by the "after-image" we see when we close our eyes or stare at a dark wall.

Similar subjective "fatigue" factors come into operation when we follow or fix moving objects or scenes in which objects are in movement. Some of these are muscular but others are electrical, as when the brain countermands certain electro-chemical impulses to take into account its own knowledge that it is a horse rather than a race-track which is in motion. The dizziness that follows after one has stopped whirling is one evidence of the distortions which may result from data-countermanding continuing beyond the end of the circumstances in which it is needed for correct perception.

We still know very little of the steps which follow the original reception of light by the retinal rods and cones. Sir John Eccles states that there is

> much neurophysiological evidence that a conscious experience arises only when there is some specific cerebral activity. For every experience it is believed that there is a specific spatio-temporal pattern of neuronal activity in the brain. Thus with perception the sequence of events is that some stimulus to the sense organ causes the discharge of impulses along afferent nerve-fibres to the brain, which, after various synaptic relays, eventually evoke specific spatio-temporal patterns of impulses in the neuronal network of the cerebral cortex. The transmission from sense organ to cerebral cortex is by a coded pattern of nerve impulses that is quite unlike the original stimulus to that organ, and the spatio-temporal pattern of neuronal activity that is evoked in the cerebral cortex would be again different. Yet as a consequence of these cerebral patterns of activity, I experience sensations (more properly the complex constructs called percepts) which in my private perceptual world are "projected" to somewhere outside . . . .[11]

---

[9] *Id.* at 49.

[10] *Id.* at 74.

[11] J. Eccles, The Brain and the Unity of Conscious Experience 17-18 (1965).

Eccles warns that the investigation of this sequence "is still at an extremely primitive stage."[12]

The process of visual perception has as its "basic component" the nerve cell or neuron which, as we have seen, generates an electric impulse which may be chemical in origin, as in the case of the bleaching described above.[13] These electrical impulses, which also have chemical aspects, travel along branches of the neurons called axons, which are joined at switches or junctures (*synapses*) to other long, thin branches (*dendrites*) which carry impulses to nerve cells. The messages thus reach the cerebral cortex by a complex "series of relays of neurons which at all levels communicate with adjacent neurons."[14] The relay is not, however, simply a system of communications—like the telephone switchboard to which it is sometimes compared —because, as the coded impulse-message moves along the system it is at each junction subject to a process of selection, rejection, or merger with other impulses.

In the cerebral cortex, there is a point-to-point topographical representation of the retina on its layers. Thus stimulation of one part of the retina activates a specific corresponding area of the visual part of the cortex[15] where a response-circuit or complex is formed which is our perception: what we "see."

"What we see" is therefore a combination of many body-factors which are independent of, but act upon, the data received by the eye from the outside world. Some of these body factors are mechanical, some are neurological, some are psychological, and many are still unknown to us.

Bronowski, for example, tells us that "our senses doctor their messages before they reach the brain . . ."[16] and that

the eye does not send blank and unbiased signals to be interpreted in the brain . . . . [T]he rods and cones in the retina are connected together in complex groups . . . within the eye. The number of cross-links is huge, and their business is to integrate the individual sensations before they leave the eye. . . . And the single fiber is imperious; often, it does not so much inform the brain as instruct it, by sorting its messages in advance; and it does this most effectively by simply withholding information—by judging for itself what is irrelevant, and discarding it, without leave from the brain.[17]

Thus "the eye is not only an optical instrument; it is also an electrical network in which each unit integrates the darks and lights that it sees into messages, and decides which message should alert the attention and which need not."[18] Gregory confirms that the retina

---

[12] *Id.* at 18.

[13] J. VON NEUMANN, THE COMPUTER AND THE BRAIN 40-41 (1958).

[14] G. WYBURN, R. PICKFORD & R. HIRST, HUMAN SENSES AND PERCEPTION 5, 7 (1964).

[15] *Id.* at 77.

[16] J. BRONOWSKI, *supra* note 6, at 30.

[17] *Id.* at 31.

[18] *Id.* at 32.

is a specialised part of the surface of the brain which has budded out and become sensitive to light, while it retains typical brain cells lying between the receptors and the optic nerve . . . which greatly modify the electrical activity from the receptors themselves. Some of the data processing for perception takes place in the eye which is thus an integral part of the brain.[19]

From these discoveries Bronowski concludes that we have put an end "to the belief of philosophers that the brain receives a neutral picture of the world and sits in judgment over it."[20]

Von Neumann states, less romantically but to the same effect, that

pulses (which appear on the axons of a given neuron) are usually stimulated by other pulses that are impinging on the body of the neuron. This stimulation is, as a rule, conditional, i.e. only certain combinations and synchronisms of such primary pulses stimulate the secondary pulse in question—all others will fail to so stimulate. That is, the neuron is an organ which accepts and emits definite physical entities, the pulses. Upon receipt of pulses in certain combinations and synchronisms it will be stimulated to emit a pulse of its own, otherwise it will not emit. The rules which describe to which groups of pulses it will so respond are the rules that govern it as an active organ.[21]

Thus certain neurons will respond only when they receive two simultaneous incoming pulses from two other neurons. Other neurons may require as their minimum input-price for stimulation not only a certain *number* of pulses from other neurons, but also that those pulses arrive in a certain spatial relation to each other.

That is, one may have to face situations in which there are, say, hundreds of synapses on a single nerve cell, and the combinations of stimulations on these that are effective (that generate a response pulse in the last-mentioned neuron) are characterized not only by their number but also by their coverage of certain special regions on that neuron (on its body or on its dendrite system), by the spatial relations of such regions to each other, and by even more complicated quantitative and geometrical relationships that might be relevant.[22]

What we have, therefore, is a complex of nerves reaching from the retina to the cerebral cortex—and each of them a small "brain" unto itself, each with criteria for accepting, rejecting or fusing and restructuring inputs. Indeed, since the decision as to this may in fact be a function of the synapses—the junctures of nerve cells, these even more numerous instrumentalities may be the basic "brains" of the perceptual system, employing a mathematic (rather than logical) system of thinking.[23]

What makes this important is not merely that it shows us the extent to which the transmission of visual data is, even at a physiological level, a process of selectivity

[19] R. GREGORY, *supra* note 3, at 45-46.
[20] J. BRONOWSKI, *supra* note 6, at 32.
[21] J. VON NEUMANN, *supra* note 13, at 43-44.
[22] *Id.* at 54-55.
[23] *Id.* at 79-80.

and of structuring and not merely a game of pass-it-on; it is, particularly, that the criteria employed in selecting and structuring, at every juncture, is a highly personal one and that no two persons have the same system of neural criteria. Thus, it is not only the colour-blind who see differently. Each of us sees differently from all the rest.

What gives each of our perceptive systems its uniqueness is just beginning to be explored. There is evidence that, to some extent, the criteria of the system are products of experience as well as of heredity. Von Neumann accepts that memory, in its physical embodiment, must have something to do with it. Thus the thresholds or stimulation criteria of each nerve cell over a period of time may be changed in response to experience. Frequent use of a nerve cell might have the result of lowering its criteria for the stimulation required to make it "fire." Memory thus becomes, according to this theory, a storing of experience in variable stimulation criteria.[24] He adds that a

> still more drastic embodiment of the same idea would be achieved by assuming that the very connections of the nerve cells, i.e., the distribution of conducting axons, vary with time. This would mean that the following state of things could exist. Conceivably, persistent disuse of an axon might make it ineffective for later use. On the other hand, very frequent (more than normal) use might give the connection that it represents a lower threshold (a facilitated stimulation criterion) over that particular path. In this case, again, certain parts of the nervous system would be variable in time and with previous history and would, thus, in and by themselves represent a memory.[25]

Von Neumann adds to these as-yet unproven hypotheses that "[a]nother form of memory, which is obviously present, is the genetic part of the body: the chromosomes and their constituent genes are clearly memory elements which by their state affect, and to a certain extent determine, the functioning of the entire system."[26]

Since our experiences and our genetic code are unique to each of us, and since these almost certainly have a direct *physiological* impact on the "machinery" through which the body interprets sensed data to arrive at its perceptions of "out there" it seems inevitable that those perceptions should be to a significant degree, unique to the perceiver. In addition, we appear to develop electric circuits in which stimulation of a part stimulates the whole "systems of nerve cells, which stimulate each other in various possible cyclical ways"[27] much like a computer. These circuits, too, would appear to be "memories" built up by experience, although some circuits may also be genetically transmitted. But it is clear that, whatever their origin, they are manifestations of the unique, perceiving self. "[M]y visual perception," Eccles tells us, "is an interpretation of retinal data that in a lifetime of experience I have learned

[24] *Id.* at 64.
[25] *Id.* at 64-65.
[26] *Id.* at 65.
[27] *Id.* at 66.

to accomplish, particularly in association both with sensory information provided by receptors in muscles, joints, skin and the vestibular apparatus, and with the central experience of willed effort."[28]

Another perhaps less physiological way of looking at this is in terms of the learning process, which may or may not be understood in terms of "mutually-stimulating cyclical systems of nerves." In any event, while we know rather little about the internal or physiological nature of memory and learning, we do know rather a lot about its external or behavioural aspects. We know, in particular, "that, as a consequence of active or trial-and-error learning, the brain events evoked by sensory information from the retina are interpreted so that they give a valid picture of the external world that is sensed by touch and movement. . . ."[29] In other words, we tend to see what experience teaches us we ought to expect to see.

For the most part this interaction of experience-data with sense data makes it possible for us to operate in a three-dimensional, populated world, by correcting sense-data which would mislead us in the light of what "we know is there." Yet, since behavioural experience, while to some extent universal, is also to some extent idiosyncratic, it too adds its part to "the uniqueness of the conscious experiences that each of us enjoys."[30] Putting it another way, "[o]bjects are far more than patterns of stimulation: objects have pasts and futures; when we know its past or can guess its future, an object transcends experience and becomes an embodiment of knowledge and expectation"[31]—but of *my* knowledge and my expectation. Thus the "seeing of an object . . . involves knowledge of the object derived from previous experience"— but of *my* experience which becomes embodied in *my* knowledge. Therefore, the object I perceive becomes, to that extent, perceptively-speaking *my* object.

Psychology of visual perception goes so far as to say that "the senses do not give us a picture of the world directly; rather they provide evidence for checking hypotheses about what lies before us. Indeed, we may say that a perceived object *is* a hypothesis, suggested and tested by sensory data."[32] But the hypothesis itself is inevitably and irreducibly a creative act of the individual self.

One way of comprehending this is through an examination of situations of conflicting sense-data. We have all watched one of those rotating spirals, sometimes found on phonograph-record labels, which seems to grow outward or to shrink, and at the same time to remain exactly the same size. Our brains *know* this to be impossible, and yet our eyes continue to send to the brain conflicting sets of data which the brain cannot reconcile. It must therefore choose one over the other, or suspend judgment, or reject both as "illusion." The brain, in this instance, has been

---

[28] J. ECCLES, *supra* note 11, at 11.
[29] *Id.* at 13.
[30] *Id.* at 36.
[31] R. GREGORY, *supra* note 3, at 8.
[32] *Id.* at 11-12.

described as being like a trial judge getting incompatible evidence from two witnesses and, for a time, accepting both.[33]

The work of psychologists in studying perception through the learning process is complemented by art historians. E. H. Gombrich's justly celebrated study, *Art and Illusion*,[34] adopts the "searchlight theory" of perception of K. R. Popper[35] which emphasizes the "activity of the living organism that never ceases probing and testing its environment"[36] and shifts attention away from the approach—Popper calls it the "bucket theory of the mind"[37]—which emphasizes the stimulus rather than the organism's response to it. When I answer such a simple question as: "how did she look?" I am drawing on visual sense data, of course, but also, and perhaps preponderantly on a complex of perceptive (neural) factors inherent in me; acquired attitudes towards persons, towards women, towards her; as well as to her perception of herself as perceived by me (her subjectivity); and finally to factors external both to her and to me (what she was doing, where she was standing, how the light illuminated her, and so on.)

It is appropriate that art history should come to the aid of psychology in the study of perception. For, in no other field is it more clear that what we see is in large part what we bring from the rich storehouse of our experience to the relatively austere visual stimulus of the existential moments that the artist captures for us. A painting is a stylized code for reality which our experience lets us break, thereby making a two-dimensional representation achieved by use of line and colour "come alive" in our mind's eye. Size, distance, depth, dimension—all these we bring to the artist. All the artist brings to us is an ability to call us to draw from our experience the beauty or horror which he knows to be there, even when we ourselves may have forgotten or denied it, and to do so at a command to us written in paint on canvas.

Another simple way to test the impact of what we *know* on what we see is to look at our two hands held in front of us—one at arm's length, the other at half the distance and to the left. The two hands will of course look about the same size, confirming what we know. But move the nearer hand directly in front of the line of vision of the further, and it will look twice as large, which is the way the sense-data registers on the retina. As long as the hands are separate, the mind can correct the sense data's proportions. When the hands are brought to overlap, their comparative size as sense-data can no longer so readily be overruled by a puzzled mind which nevertheless "knows better." To psychologists the mind's corrective process is known as "constancy scaling."[38]

---

[33] *Id.* at 108.
[34] E. GOMBRICH, ART AND ILLUSION (1960).
[35] *Cf.* 2 K. POPPER, THE OPEN SOCIETY AND ITS ENEMIES 260-62, 361 (4th ed. 1963).
[36] E. GOMBRICH, *supra* note 34, at 28.
[37] 2 K. POPPER, THE OPEN SOCIETY AND ITS ENEMIES 214, 260, 361 (4th ed. 1963).
[38] R. GREGORY, *supra* note 3, at 151, 152.

If the mind draws on experience to achieve "constancy scaling" it is not surprising that the eye cells can (and, in their own way, do) perform similar feats.
We know, of course, that the pupils of the eye expand and contract in direct relation
to the amount of light entering. But when one light of X intensity is lit in a dark
room and thereafter an additional, dimmer light of Y intensity is also lit, the pupil's
contraction will be responsive not to the light intensity of $X + Y$ but rather to
$\dfrac{X + Y}{2}$, which is to say, the average between the two intensities!

Finally, the cooperative work of anthropologists has enriched perception-psychol-
ogy by providing us with studies of "primitive" people living in dense forests who
do not have the opportunity to experience distant objects over unbroken vistas. When
such persons were taken out of their forest home to open plains, they saw remote
objects not as *distant* but as small. People like ourselves, who live our lives on the
ground, experience similar failures of the "constancy scaling" mechanism when we
look down at objects from a height. On the other hand, persons who spend much
of their time in high buildings report seeing people below without the sense of their
being toy miniatures.[39] This, too, tells us much about the role of previous experience
and trial-and-error learning in perception.[40] It is, incidentally, worth noting that there
is no evidence that these corrective mechanisms by which we restructure what we
see by what we know exist in any other animals except possibly the monkey.[41] It is
also significant that the one area in which we seem unable to make such a perceptive
readjustment is where there is a conflict in *time* (as opposed to space, where we do
learn to make adjustments) between what we see and what we know.

To the subjective aspects of perception, then, we must add another: what we see is
in part a function of acculturation. Different societies learn to adjust to visual sense-
data in different ways. This need not even be tested by examining forest people or
cliff-dwellers. It is sufficient to leaf through a book on the history of art, such as that
of Professor Gombrich, and see the totally different ways in which different civiliza-
tions learned to code reality. The Chinese, early Egyptian or renaissance art seems
to us as "unreal" today as French impressionism would strike an ancient Mesopo-
tamian—because each society's artists use different artistic codes to represent or
suggest reality and each society, reciprocally, learns to be called to that reality by
that system of representation, to do its "constancy scaling" in accordance with a data-
code particular to itself. Thus most of the members of one society in one age cannot perceive the art of another age as anything but "unreal."[42]

Before leaving this aspect of the subjectivity of visual perception it must be stated
that an increasing number of psychologists are willing to entertain heredity-theories

---

[39] *Id.* at 161-62.
[40] *Id.* at 180.
[41] *Id.* at 216.
[42] More exactly, there is usually a lag between the invention of a new artistic style and the time when
the society learns to "see" it as "real."

to explain a part of the subjective self brought to the interpretation of sense-data, just as neurologists and physiologists are giving greater credence to genetic factors in neural stimulation-criteria. Professor Gregory in his study of the psychology of perception states that

> [t]he visual brain has its own logic and preferences which are not understood cortically. Some objects are beautiful, others ugly; but we have no idea, for all the theories which have been put forward, why this should be so. The answer lies a long way back in the history of the visual part of the brain, and is lost to the new mechanisms which give our intellectual view of the world.[43]

This hypothesis is, of course, still an open and controversial one. But his conclusion is not: non-visual characteristics (of the individual) affect how objects are seen.

III

CONCLUSION

In the truce observer context, those questions of fact which are concerned with sensory perception of transient events or conditions are not appropriate for impartial third-party decision-making. The reason these issues are inappropriate is that they cannot be answered objectively because even the most neutral of observers brings to his sensory-perceptive process a subjectivity which is the greater for being hidden deep in the sensory-perceptive process where reason and conscious argument do not enter. Such perceptions are really like opinions, but the more tenacious and irreversible because they come to our consciousness disguised as objective truth.

There are, however, other ways to achieve order in a dispute such as that of May 26, 1958, which do not involve attempts to ascertain the unascertainable. The objectives of UNTSO were twofold: to prevent recurrence of the incident, and to compensate the victims.

There is no need for findings of "fact" in order to achieve these ends. Recurrence can best be prevented by prospective administrative arrangements. These require the good will of the parties, which is only diminished by attempts to fix "guilt" for prior occurrences. As to compensation, it would be reasonable to anticipate that a certain number of such incidents would occur in the course of any truce, that it would be troublesome and probably impossible to assign fault, and therefore the parties agreeing to the establishment of the truce regime might also agree to establish a joint compensation fund. The role of the truce observer would then be to assess actual damage done, rather than fixing "fault." The fund would then provide compensation while administrative efforts were bent toward preventing the incident's repetition.

---

[43] R. GREGORY, *supra* note 3, at 224.